THE KARMA OF BROWN FOLK

vijay prashad

UNIVERSITY OF MINNESOTA PRESS

MINNEAPOLIS — LONDON

The University of Minnesota Press gratefully acknowledges permission to reprint the following. Chapter 5 contains an excerpt of poetry from *White Elephants,* by Reetika Vazirani (Boston: Beacon Press, 1996); reprinted by permission of Reetika Vazirani. Chapter 6 contains an excerpt of poetry from "Chameleons," from *No More Watno Dur,* by Sadhu Binning (Toronto: TSAR Publications, 1994); reprinted by permission of TSAR Publications. Chapter 7 contains lyrics excerpted from "Desi Like Dat," by the Desi Jersey Mafia; reprinted by permission of Soam Acharya. Chapter 9 contains an excerpt of poetry from "Ghandi Is Fasting," from *The Collected Poems of Langston Hughes,* by Langston Hughes (New York: Alfred A. Knopf, 1994); copyright 1994 by the Estate of Langston Hughes and reprinted by permission of Alfred A. Knopf, Inc.

Every effort was made to obtain permission to reproduce material used in this book. If any proper acknowledgment has not been made, we encourage copyright holders to notify us.

Published by the University of Minnesota Press
111 Third Avenue South, Suite 290
Minneapolis, MN 55401-2520
http://www.upress.umn.edu

Library of Congress Cataloging-in-Publication Data

Prashad, Vijay.
    The karma of Brown folk / Vijay Prashad.
        p.   cm.
    Includes index.
    ISBN 0-8166-3438-6 (hc) — ISBN 0-8166-3439-4 (pbk.)
        1. South Asian Americans—Race identity.   2. South Asian Americans—Social conditions.   3. East Indian Americans—Race identity.   4. East Indian Americans—Social conditions.   5. United States—Race relations.
    6. Racism—United States.   I. Title.
    E184.S69 P73 2000
    305.891´4073—dc21   99-047918

Printed in the United States of America on acid-free paper

The University of Minnesota is an equal-opportunity educator and employer.

11 10 09 08 07 06 05 04 03   10 9 8 7 6 5 4

CONTENTS

KARMA SUTRA: THE FORETHOUGHT

I first stumbled upon W. E. B. Du Bois's *The Souls of Black Folk* (1903) some two decades ago in a cluttered bookstore on Free School Street in Calcutta. Why I selected that book instead of the many tattered novels that I normally purchased, I cannot say. My only recollection is that after I read the book, even so far away, it moved me deeply. Part of the magic was the style, the sheer exuberance of the prose, but the main reason was the way Du Bois so lovingly offered his sharp criticism of the effects of white supremacy. Reading the book over and over again, I cherish the throaty cadences of Ma Rainey mixed in with the stern dialectics of Hegel, the popular traditions that Du Bois sought after and the elite theories that provided him with a framework. The book you hold in your hand is offered as my flawed attempt to draw from Du Bois as I write of my South Asian American brethren whose presence in the United States complicates the narrative Du Bois offered a century ago. "How does it feel to be a problem?" Du Bois begins *Souls*.[1] White supremacy treats black folk as if they are themselves a problem, a history that lingers on as more and more is said about "personal responsibility" and as the U.S.

government divests itself and the economic system of any culpability in the genocide against blacks.[2] As South Asians have entered the United States in the past thirty years, there has been a tendency to compare our destiny with that of black folk. If these brown folk can make it, say people like Thomas Sowell, Dinesh D'Souza, and the neoconservatives, then why can't black folk? A hundred years after *Souls,* Du Bois's question remains.

But there is also another question that needs to be asked, and this book will take it as its central problem: "How does it feel to be a solution?" Addressed to all Asians, but increasingly with special reference to South Asians, this question asks us brown folk how we can live with ourselves as we are pledged and sometimes, in an act of bad faith, pledge ourselves, as a weapon against black folk. What does it mean, this book asks, for us to mollify the wrath of white supremacy by making a claim to a great destiny when we are ourselves only a product of state engineering through immigration controls and of the beneficence of more socialized systems of education in South Asia, or when we are but the children of those who have accumulated a certain amount of cultural capital because of those processes? This book, then, is about the feelings, the consciousness of being South Asian, of being *desi* (those people who claim ancestry of South Asia) in the United States. It is also a set of *sutras* (aphorisms) of the *karma* (fate) of desis, who must now imagine ourselves within the U.S. racial formation and seek to mediate between the dream of America and our own realities.

In 1938, while fascism crept into place in Europe, while imperialism continued to do its dirty deeds in India, and while Jim Crow preened over black folks in the United States, Du Bois bemoaned India's "temptation to stand apart from the darker peoples and seek her affinities among whites. She has long wished to regard herself as 'Aryan,' rather than 'colored' and to think of herself as much nearer physically and spiritually to Germany and England than to Africa, China or the South Seas. And yet, the history of the modern world shows the futility of this thought. European exploitation desires the black slave, the Chinese coolies and the Indian laborer for the same ends and the same purposes, and calls them all 'niggers.' "[3] Du Bois opened his heart to a wide solidarity, an invitation that desis and others need to accept even at this late date. Since we, as desis, are used as a weapon in the war against black America, we must in good faith refuse this role and find other places for ourselves in the moral struggles that grip the United States.

This book emerges from participation in that moral struggle, especially in the time I have spent with my fellow desis in our various political activities. Many of the ideas that follow developed in discussions with activists and students across the country, and some saw the first light of day in our community periodicals. In June 1998 I sat with my computer and my many notes to lay bare some of these ideas and to offer a view on the trials of desis in the United States. There are several good historical overviews on the same topic, and there are also many fine essays that sketch out some of the points that I will simply indicate in the text that follows. Though this book does offer a historical look at U.S. desi life, it attempts to address the dilemmas of desi life in the United States and it suggests passages to transform our current aporias.

There is much in this book that may appear parochial, but if we are to be truly critical multiculturalists, we must be willing to enter domains without safe translations so that we can understand and engage with the complexities that affect the lives of others. There is, in other words, something refreshingly educational about "parochiality." Given other circumstances, I would have much rather addressed this book to an unmarked human subject, one who is like the Subject of so much European philosophy, but such a choice is not available as long as "race" continues to be a searing category through which we are so habitually forced to live.[4] As a social fact, race organizes the way we are viewed in society, how we often produce our own cultural communities, and how we struggle against the supremacist parochialism of many of our institutions (that, for all their openness, continue to support unspoken forms of whiteness).[5] The resilience of race in our lives cannot be easily dismissed in favor of an imputed universalism, since we might want to allow those who fight from standpoints of oppression to come from concrete identities (such as race, but also ethnicity, regions, sexuality, gender, and class) to produce forms of unity that can only be seen in struggle rather than in some abstract theoretical arithmetic. Most notions of identity are not unalloyed, and many celebrate the importance of the politics of identification; we must learn to harness these identifications in the hope of a future rather than denying the right of oppressed peoples to explore their own cultural resources toward the construction of a complex political will.

The ethos of identification requires that we be scrupulous about the different histories of differentiated groups, that we not assume that all people come at identification from the same place. Such an exercise allows us to see the specific cultural locations of groups and provide some avenues toward the creation of a moral solidarity for our present struggles. *The Karma of Brown Folk* begins, therefore, with an assessment of the place of the "Indian" in U.S. thought, first among the intellectuals (such as Henry David Thoreau and Ralph Waldo Emerson) and then in popular culture. My argument is that though desis are seen as nonwhite, they are also seen as bearing an especial spiritual patina, one that is sometimes seen as worthy and other times seen as undesirable. Both intellectual and popular culture approach the desi as something fundamentally different from the "American" (a word that is often used to index whiteness); and both subscribe to the belief that though the latter is practical and worldly, the former is spiritual and ethereal. The distinction of geography (East/West) and of values (practical/spiritual) allows us to see such thought as a specie of "orientalism," and I will show how this U.S. orientalism differs in some measure from that developed in Europe (and, indeed, how the "East" is in many ways constitutive of American culture).[6] When desis come to the United States in large numbers, I argue, they sign a social contract with a racist polity by making a pledge to work hard but to retain a social life at some remove from U.S. society (one that is sanctified as specially spiritual and thus an acceptable, even if lesser, lifeworld).[7] When the desis find that the racist polity simply wants their labor but does not care too much for their lives, the social retreat sanctioned by U.S. orientalism provides a space to develop a life, even if this is a space under constant threat from educational and other institutions. The claim to a higher spirituality (and civilization) allows the desis to be positioned in such a way that they are seen as superior to blacks, a social location not unattractive to a migrant in search of some accommodation in a racist polity. The tragedy of this social compact is that it perpetuates and reproduces antiblack racism. This book unravels and argues against the logic of this racist contract and it offers some traces toward a renegotiation of it.

ACKNOWLEDGMENTS

Without the vibrancy of the U.S. left, this book would not have been written. Reds and Greens of all shades provided me with the solidarity for struggle and for reflection—people such as Libero Della Piana, Alisa Gallo, Mark Toney, Shannah Kurland, Brian Steinberg, and especially Elisabeth Armstrong (as well as the Hartford YCL). Their consistent activism never allowed me to stray from the course. Work at Direct Action for Rights and Equality in Providence, Rhode Island, allowed my Ph.D. in Indian history to become a tool in the fight for social justice in the United States. This location brought me into connection with the South Asian students at Brown University who shared the fight against desi intolerance (regards to Pooja Sarin, Raj Dave, Sangeeta Rao, and Kanishka Ratnayakar, among others).

From Providence I went to Ithaca, New York, where Gary Okihiro gave me the opportunity to teach "South Asian Diaspora" for two years at Cornell University. My students challenged many of the formulations in this book, and some of them provided me with useful leads to follow (regards to Vinod Mathew, Gladys Sundaram, Uttam Tambar, Priya Chandrasekharan, Anjana

Samant, Monami Maulik, Sanam Majid, Nirej Sekhon, Rina Agarwala, and Catherine Oh, among others). Some of the accounts I produced at Cornell emerged in books edited by two extraordinary people, Rajini Srikanth and Sunaina Maira; they began the process that led to this book.

Along the way, Russell Leong *(Amerasia)*, Bob Wing and Jeff Chang *(RaceFile* and *ColorLines)*, Nurjehan Aziz *(The Toronto Review)*, Kanak Dixit and Deepak Thapa *(Himal South Asia)*, N. Ram *(Frontline)*, S. Shankar and Anannya Bhattacharjee *(SAMAR)*, and Achal Mehra *(Little India)* graciously opened their periodicals to my rants. My friends at *Monthly Review* (especially Kira Brunner and Chris Phelps) gave this book more grace than I could muster.

I gave many of these formulations as talks at Desh Pardesh (thanks to Steve Pereira); at South Asian Students Association (SASA) 1996, 1998, and 1999 (thanks to Kanishka, Sima Patel, Amy Paul, Palak Shah, and Sonya Laroia); at Michigan's ISA (thanks to Ankim Shah, Sonia Mathew, and Supendeep Dosanjh); and at numerous other schools and community gatherings.

In the midst of this, conversations with friends and comrades helped me push some of these ideas from rage to analysis. Many of these people continue to build the Forum of Indian Leftists (FOIL), our U.S. base of struggle (whose website at www.foil.org is ably managed by Rahul De and Sharmila Chakravarty). Several of them are active in the collectives of the Youth Solidarity Summer (Ananya Mukherjee, Biju Mathew, Mir Ali Raza, Mona Ahmed Ali, Raju Rajan, Rupal Oza, Sangeeta Kamat, Sharmila Desai, Sunaina Maira, Surabhi Kukke, Svati Shah, and V. Balaji) and the South Asian Solidarity Summer for Youth (particularly Aparna Sindhoor, Jayanta Dey, and Raju Sivasankaran). Amitava Kumar (whose *Passport Photos* pioneers a South Asian American cultural studies), Gautam Premnath, John Hutnyk, Maya Yagnik, Mir Ali Hussain, Kasturi Ray, Phiroze Vasunia, Sudhir Venkatesh, and Vivek Renjan Bald make the struggle worthwhile. Kartar Dhillon and Ved Prakash Vatuk remind us consistently that we are not the progenitors of struggle, but only the most recent participants in an enduring tradition: thanks.

Best love to all the Prashads, the Armstrongs, Rosy Samuel, the Delhi clan (especially Brinda Karat, Radhika Roy, Prakash Karat, and Prannoy Roy), and to those in Los Angeles (Boses, Pains, and Bose-Paynes) who are beloved all.

And now, at Trinity College, a most congenial place for reflection and for action, thanks to Raymond Baker, Maurice Wade, Ellison Findly, Dario Euraque, Luis Figueroa, Janet Bauer, and Johnny Williams for support and encouragement and to my students (especially Anhoni Patel, Toufiq Haddad, and Maria Sulit) for spirit. The weight of these people hangs heavily on this small axe.

Many colleagues helped me put these ideas into shape, among them Gary Okihiro, George Lipsitz, Kamala Visweswaran, Lewis Gordon, and Robin D. G. Kelley. These five exponents of ethnic studies are notable for their exertions and for their critical insight. I cannot hope for more compassionate and engaged readers for any book. Carrie Mullen is a stupendous editor who cannot be thanked enough for her confidence in the book and for the speed with which she has allowed it to see the light of day. Many salaams to Kathy Delfosse, whose copyediting is exemplary.

Two people made this book possible. Elisabeth Armstrong, who teaches us the imperative of organization and of everyday solidarity, and Biju Mathew, who guides us to victory. Tender comrades, both.

OF INDIA

India as a *Land of Desire* forms an essential element in General History. From the most ancient time downwards, all nations have directed their wishes and longings to gaining access to the treasures of this land of marvels, the most costly which the Earth presents; treasures of Nature—pearls, diamonds, perfumes, rose-essences, elephants, lions, etc.—as also treasures of wisdom.

—G. W. F. Hegel, *The Philosophy of History*

India came to America by mistake. A Genovese navigator landed in the Bahamas in search of India. He saw and slaughtered the Bahamians (and rescued for world history one Bahamian word, "hammock"). Those whom he found he named "Indians," and the land he called "India." Aided by his maps of the world *(mappemondes)* and his medieval library, Columbus could have called the land China (for he thought he was somewhere in the vicinity of Cathay). He had read the diaries of Marco Polo and was in search of landmarks noted by the Venetian. To Columbus, the Caribbean appeared at times much like the familiar descriptions

1

of China and at other times like the popular textual accounts of India by the fictitious Sir John Mandeville. Constrained by his charge to seek out Prester John in order to open a second front against the "sect of Mahomet," Columbus was happy to think he was in India, the supposed home of this other Christian king. Till the end of his life, he was convinced that America was but India.[1]

India emerged in the Americas as a fantasy of redemption for the trials of this world. Columbus's journal begins with a summary of the political economy of contemporary Spain: The union of Castile and Aragon enabled the defeat of the Moors, the expulsion of Jews from the Iberian peninsula, the start of the Inquisition, and finally, the continuance of the crusades against Islam. For all this, the military might of the Spaniards required treasure and allies, both of which it hoped to gain from India by way of a sea route toward the west. Even though India did not appear in the west, the western lands provided ample silver and gold to prop up a withered monarchy. Not six years after Columbus reached the Americas, Vasco da Gama found the original India by sailing around Africa, but the record was not set straight. We now had two Indies, one in the east and one in the west. India did not vanish from the western lands, now called the Americas. As an idea it was to reappear numerous times, but mostly to chastise the opulent flamboyance of the Americas. It continues to appear in our own day, in the body of people such as Deepak Chopra, those sly *baba*s (Godmen) who peddle opiates that comfort our decrepitude rather than challenge us to change what produces our distress in the first place.

India is present today in the body of the Indians and others from the South Asian subcontinent, who now number 1.4 million in the United States.[2] But these people are not all "Indians." Many are from Pakistan, Bangladesh, India, Sri Lanka, Bhutan, the Maldives, Africa, England, Canada, Fiji, or the Caribbean, and many are born and bred within the United States. The stain of ancestry and the hegemony of the word "India" remains with us as we seek to make our own way through the morass of the contemporary world. We are "Indians," not of India necessarily, but certainly seen as spiritual beings who are pliant and cooperative—those willing allies sought by Columbus, allies now not only against Islam but against those who are deemed by the power elite to be the current foes of U.S. civilization, black Americans. For it is here that we can make sense of that gallant ideologue of the Right, Dinesh D'Souza, who reveals a hidden transcript that needs to be confronted rather than denied. Far more South Asian Americans than I wish to admit find merit in many of his arguments, notably his pompous claim that immigrants of the right sort are a special breed (since, we are told, they demonstrate the finest qualities of hard work and an impatience to succeed). This is why Phil Gramm was feted by many South Asian Americans during his run for president in 1996. When asked about immigration policy, he pointedly noted that "people who work in America often talk with distinct foreign accents. Do you know why? Because we have a welfare system that rewards our own citizens for not working. I do not think it is fair to say because people come to America and they are willing to work, when some Americans are not, that they are taking jobs away." The way to fix the problem, he noted, is not to end immigration policies but to end the welfare system.[3] The immigrants are good; the blacks are bad. Punish the latter. And many South Asian Americans applaud. Though there is some consensus in South Asian America that D'Souza has a point, there is also a sense of embarrassment over his open and aggressive posture. When he draws attention to the comparison between blacks and the "right sort" of immigrants, he exposes the sorts of arguments that many South Asian Americans would prefer to see acted out in social policy rather than in political debate. South Asian Americans prefer to detach themselves from the minutiae of democracy and to attach themselves solely to the task of capital accumulation. All the while, there is a sentiment that we will be praised by white supremacy and left alone to do our own work at society's margins. Ed Koch, former mayor of New York City and now talk-show host, summarized our position in the United States: "They give us their culture and their taxes—and their wonderful restaurants."[4] And we are happy to oblige.

When Dinesh D'Souza published *The End of Racism* in 1995, most commentators found it excessive and racist. Glenn Loury, otherwise in step with D'Souza, noted that he "violated the canons of civility and commonality."[5] D'Souza, a migrant from Goa in western India, argued that the oppressive conditions of life among black Americans is more a result of their civilizational collapse than of the persistence of racist structures. The crisis of black America, he claimed, is made more acute by "the embarrassing fact of Asian American success which has become evident to most people in recent decades." D'Souza's racism is premised upon a faulty analysis of Asian success in the United States. Those attainments are *not* caused by natural or cultural selection; rather, they are the result of *state* selection whereby the U.S. state, through the special-skills provisions in the 1965 Immigration Act, fundamentally reconfigured the demography of South Asian America. This skewed demography is only now being corrected as nonprofessionals migrate to join families, as economic and/or political refugees; as workers in the transportation, lodging, and other trades; and as small businessmen (running shops, motels, and so on). Ignoring these facts of South Asian America, D'Souza asks, "why can't an African American be more like an Asian?" It is not an unusual question. "Where did you learn to speak such good English?" "Your people work hard." "We like your people." These are the inevitable chatter of a benevolent racism. On *The Jerry Seinfeld Show* when Elaine chides Jerry for being partial toward Chinese women, he responds, "It is not racist if I like your race."[6] Many folks feel, it seems, that to make positive statements about what they consider to be a race is just fine; racism in this light becomes the use of negative statements about a people. In my mind, the very conceptualization of a people as having discrete qualities is an act of racist thought, whether the resulting statements be charitable or not. "Why is it that all Indians are so smart and well-behaved?" Piyush Jindal, confronted with this question by his elementary school teacher, paused and then, "being a smart-aleck, told her it was the food."[7] These are not only statements of admiration. Apart from being condescending, such gestures remind me that I am to be the perpetual solution to what is

India Day parade, New York City (1998). Courtesy of Sunaina Maira.

seen as the crisis of black America. I am to be a weapon in the war against black America. Meanwhile, white America can take its seat, comfortable in its liberal principles, surrounded by state-selected Asians, certain that the culpability for black poverty and oppression must be laid at the door of black America. How does it feel to be a solution?

Obviously, it is easier to be seen as a solution than as a problem. We don't suffer genocidal poverty and incarceration rates in the United States, nor do we walk in fear and a fog of invisibility. To be both visible (as a threat) and invisible (as a person) is a strain disproportionately borne by black America. This is not to say that we don't feel the edge of racism (both as prejudice and as structural violence), but we do so in a far less stark sense than do those who are seen as the detritus of U.S. civilization. Nevertheless, to be a solution has its problems too. When one is typecast as a success, one's abilities cease to be the measure of one's capacity. A young Asian child now, like a pet animal, performs his or her brilliance. Those Asians not gifted in technical arts see themselves as failures and suffer the consequences of not being able to rise to the levels expected of their genes. Jazz musicians! Poets! Carpenters! Taxi drivers! Homeless! Many Indian American parents worry that their children will not inherit the values they themselves embody. When Michigan State University published a study in 1994 showing that second-generation Asian children have lower GPAs than new immigrants, it was reported as the "'Americanization' of Immigrant Children."[8] The study showed that the average U.S. GPA is 2.0, whereas immigrant children earn an average GPA of 2.58. The average GPA for second-generation children is 2.44, a fraction lower than that of immigrants. Confronted with such studies, we tend to forget the Immigration and Naturalization Services' rigorous filtering out of those who are not already furnished with the cultural capital for success. We tend to assume that the high averages have something to do with the immigrant's genetics or culture (in the sense of a noun, as static) rather than something to do with the process of selection adopted by the U.S. state.

But this is not the only thing that counts. We are not simply a solution for black America but, most pointedly, a *weapon* deployed against it. The struggles of blacks are met with the derisive remark that Asians don't complain; they work hard—as if to say that blacks don't work hard. The implication is that blacks complain and ask for handouts. After the historic Civil Rights Act and in the context of the Watts uprising of 1965, *US News & World Report* ran a story on Chinese Americans, who believe, we are told, in "the old idea that people should depend on their own efforts—not a welfare check—in order to reach America's 'promised land.'"[9] This autonomous effort, the magazine argued, came at "a time when it is being proposed that hundreds of billions of dollars be spent to uplift Negroes and other minorities." As if to say protest is un-American, the myth of the model minority emerged in the wake of the Civil Rights movement to show up rebellious blacks for their attempts to redress power relations. The state provided the sop of welfare instead of genuine redistribution of power and resources, and even that was only given as reluctant charity. And whatever good social change emerged from the social struggles of the 1960s came as a result not of benevolence but of the unyielding passion of the oppressed, who fought to keep this racist polity even an iota honest.[10] Look at the Asians, the black intelligentsia was told, they work hard without complaint. True, to some extent, but they don't seem to get very far either. Or else the yearly reports of the glass ceiling must be concocted by those who complain too much and don't themselves work hard enough; or else the unrealized sentiment among South Asian Americans that they must retire in the homeland, away from a racist society, must be a collective hallucination. A heart that beats to justice must murmur in this state.

Jesse Helms addressed the Indian American Forum of Political Education in early September 1997. "Indian Americans represent the best and the brightest the United States has to offer," said the senator from North Carolina. "You go to the finest hospital, you can go to the universities, you can go into business and there they are, people from India." His praise was boundless.

7

"We are the bangla niggers," New York City (1997). Courtesy of Amitava Kumar.

"You understand the free enterprise system far better than a lot of people who were born and raised in this country."[11] The language is a code.[12] I am being told that I am good not according to my own terms but according to terms devised by the values upheld by Helms. My being good is easily used to denigrate those who not only do not do well but who also deride the values upheld by Helms ("free enterprise" is, after all, not so much an economic system as an ideological value system). The foes of this civilization, in Helms's view, are those in poverty (in the main, the black and Latino working class). Both liberals and conservatives have entered a dreary theoretical and moral desert in which it is impossible to see the persistence of structural barriers to equality (the speaker could just as well have been Daniel Moynihan or Bill Clinton). That some people of color achieve appreciable levels of success, for whatever reason, is used as evidence that racism poses no barrier to success. We obsess on these stories of success not to praise the few that make it (some despite tremendous odds) but to argue that the rest fail of their own accord. In the midst of all this, the South Asian Americans provide a role model for success, and too many of us uncritically adopt that role without conscious reflection on the political and racial project to which it is hitched. In loving detail I will try to offer the karma that has befallen my people as we wend our way in the United States, unaware of how we are used as a weapon by those whom we ourselves fear and yet emulate. This is our dilemma.

OF THE MYSTERIOUS EAST

> The Orientals behave well, but who cannot behave well who
> has nothing else to do? The poor Yankees who are doing the
> work are all wrinkled and vexed.
>
> —Ralph Waldo Emerson, journal entry of 12 March 1844

The senior Henry James once called Ralph Waldo Emerson an
American John the Baptist. John the Baptist offered tidings of a
future kingdom; Emerson sketched the lines for much that is
now commonplace in U.S. thought. Even so his vision of India.
As a young man, Emerson stood with his confreres who saw
India as a repulsive place that nevertheless showed occasional
glimpses of genius (particularly when, in July 1805, the *Monthly
Anthology* published Act 1 of Sir William Jones's translation of
Shakuntala, the first Indian work published in the United States).
Emerson's view was to change as he read deeply in the trans-
lated corpus of Asian texts made available by the labors of the
European orientalists. In 1820 Emerson wrote in his journal of
his belief in the Eastern birth of humanity: "All tends to the mysterious East," he copied from a contemporary book of his day.[1]

The young Emerson simply repeated what was commonplace for his time, the assumption that the "East" was the cradle of civilization and that its ancient past was, therefore, rather wise. "We find that Materialists and Immaterialists existed in India and that they accused each other of Athiesm, before Berkly or Preistley, or Dupuis, or Plato, or Pythagoras were born," wrote John Adams to Thomas Jefferson in 1817. "Indeed, Newton himself, appears to have discovered nothing that was not known to the Antient Indians. He has only furnished more ample demonstrations of the doctrines they taught."[2] Adams trod the same ground as Hegel, who argued in his ruminations on world history delivered in the winter of 1830/31 that history began in this "East" (since light comes from the east, a play on *ex orient lux*). None of these accounts privilege the knowledge of the "East," since these are, in Hegel's version, "unreflected consciousness."[3] The ancient Indian past is full of insights, but these are not rationally elaborated in the manner of Isaac Newton's *ratio*.

Like European orientalism, U.S. orientalism too divides the world into two halves, with the border being the Levantine coast. Everything east of that coast is the "East" (the Orient), notably India and China. All that is west of it is the "West" (the Occident), which was assumed to have inherited and continued the civilization of the Greeks, some of whose elements the American republicans wished to see in their newly conquered land. "Orient" and "Occident" did not simply refer to geography, for their principal use was in reference to the values that U.S. orientalism imputed to the two zones. The bulk of the U.S. intellectuals saw the Orient as poor and unfree, with an especial endowment of ahistoricalness. From the young Emerson we hear of the "squalid and desperate ignorance of untold millions who breathe the breath of misery in Asia, Africa, yea, in the great globe. Why is this?"[4] Two decades later, he argued that this poverty was caused by a reticence to act, a reticence due to the ideology of fate, the "dread reality."[5] This overwhelming sense of fate prevents the Asian from dynamic action and places Asia under the rule of Europe. "It is race, is it not," Emerson asked in *English Traits*, "that puts the hundred millions of India under the dominion of a remote island in the north of Europe."[6] The British ruled India, that is, because the Indians lived in a universe of static impracticality that led them to poverty and famine. Imperialism, then, was a worthy effort to keep the Indians alive.[7] This was the essence of the East. Whereas Asian people were held in a static history by "a deaf, implorable, immense fate," Emerson wrote in his essay on Plato, "the genius of Europe is active and creative . . . it is a land of arts, invention, trade, freedom."[8] The "West," particularly, for Emerson, England and the United States, was the active conquistador, rich and free but above all dynamic. Even Thoreau, otherwise so critical of U.S. civilization, thanked God that "no Hindoo tyranny prevailed at the framing of the world, but we are freemen of the universe, and not sentenced to any caste."[9] "Behold the difference between the Oriental and the Occidental," Thoreau wrote in 1849. "The former has nothing to do in this world; the latter is full of activity. The one looks in the sun till his eyes are put out; the other follows him prone in his westward course."[10] There is an "East" (static and unfree), and there is a "West" (dynamic and free). The European orientalists felt that the twain (of East and West) would never meet; the U.S. orientalists, on the other hand, hoped for some transfer of values to benefit their new republic and prevent its decline into the morass of materialism.

Being different in essence, the "East" remained mysterious to the New Englanders. It was mysterious, however, not because Emerson and his peers knew little of it. After all, the United States had only recently been part of an English Empire that included India. After Gen. Charles Cornwallis lost at Yorktown in 1781, he made his way to India, where he defeated the formidable Tipu Sultan in 1792 to consolidate British rule in the southern part of the subcontinent. Also, New England was well acquainted with Indian goods, since the eighteenth-century Yankee clippers plied their trade from the many India Point dockyards to the Indies. Products of that trade, such as fine textiles and jewels, can still be seen at the Peabody Essex Museum at Salem, and Salem's town seal reads "*Divitis Indiae usqua ad ultimum sinum* [To the farthest

East India Marine Hall sign, Salem, Massachusetts. Courtesy of Peabody Essex Museum, Salem, Massachusetts.

gulf for the wealth of India]." One consequence of this trade was that some Indians settled in Salem; they married black American women and disappeared from the historical record.[11] The Yankee traders, one of whom enjoyed the services of "a tall, black-bearded Sikh who stalked around town in the turban and white woolen coat and red sash of his sect," were reputed to enjoy vast wealth. In 1804 the traders organized an East India Marine Society parade in which marched "a person dressed as a Chinaman, but wearing a mask, then four husky Negroes dressed as East Indians and bearing the famous palanquin still to be seen in the museum, and then the brethren, two by two, each carrying some East Indian curiosity."[12] There was no secret about these events in Boston or in the interior of Massachusetts, where Emerson was to make his home after leaving Harvard. Apart from the traders, New England also saw many missionaries, those men of the cloth who not only trumpeted the Gospels in Asia but also brought home with them Asian texts for study (and sometimes ridicule). One early aficionado of Asian texts was the Protestant theologian Cotton Mather, who read deeply of Islam. Mather was also aware of India, for it was he who convinced Elihu Yale (who was born in New England and became a prosperous governor of Madras) to donate the money that founded Yale University.[13] In 1842 Boston's Brahmins started the American Oriental Society for the "cultivation of learning in the

Asiatic, African and Polynesian languages." The society's journal was published from 1843 to 1900, and its twenty volumes carried over a hundred articles on India (mostly on ancient literature and philology). Emerson knew the journal, and he knew many of the ancient books. "In the sleep of the great heats there was nothing for me but to read the Vedas, the bible of the tropics, which I find I come back upon every three or four years," he wrote in 1840. "It is sublime as heat and night and a breathless ocean. It contains every religious sentiment, all the grand ethics which visit in turn each noble and poetic mind."[14] He knew India, yet it was mysterious.

The "mystery" of India resides in the other, somewhat archaic, meaning of the word: a revealed religious truth. The East is mysterious in that the texts of its ancient past hold within them something akin to the Holy Grail. Emerson followed a well-worn European tradition in this, for the philosophes had already deployed the "East" to offer stern criticisms of their "West." The East has its genius too, for it is especially endowed with an impractical fascination with the transcendental. Thus Emerson and Henry David Thoreau edited several volumes of *The Dial*, a journal of Transcendental philosophy, in which their "Ethical Scriptures" included selections from Indian and Chinese texts. This East is seen as impractical in a gendered way, for it is claimed that the region is both romantic and overly emotional.[15] Emerson referred to his wife in person and in letters as "Mine Asia," his own beloved but inferior continent. Not only was the East gendered in terms of the social constructs of the day, but it was also gendered in the sense that it was seen as inscrutable, as not fully knowable. Despite all these caveats, the East was not seen as fundamentally lesser (as it was by Thomas Macaulay, a member of Britain's Supreme Council of India, and in official British policy); rather, it was seen to bear within it some lessons for social life in the West, at least in the United States.

Whereas the East had some lessons for the West, the latter could offer nothing to the former. Certainly, the West had accomplished some useful technological developments, but as Thoreau and Emerson emphasized, the people of the East did not require any improvement of their means of life, for their wants were deemed to be less. "In looking at Menu and Saadi and Bhagavat," ancient texts all, "life seems in the East a simple affair, only a tent, a little rice, and ass's milk; and not, as with us, what commerce has made it, a feast whose dishes come from the equator and both poles."[16] No doubt Thoreau too knew of the wealth of Asia being brought to New England by the Yankee traders. Their ships entered Salem harbor laden with ceramics, enamels, furniture, lacquerware, silverware, jewelry, textiles, and all manner of spices and beverages. These goods showed that life in India was not as simple as it seemed. Nevertheless, Thoreau wrote in 1855 that the texts of the ancients were the real wealth of that part of the world: "If here is not the wealth of the Indies, of what stuff then is it made? They may keep their rupees this and the like of this is what the great company traded and fought for, to convey the light of the East to the West, this their true glory and success."[17] The British did not go to India for very complex reasons; as one English East India Company official put it in 1767, "It is commercial interest we look for."[18] For Thoreau, far from the values of the English East India Company, the real India was the spirit. This spirit, or *Geist*, was its true gift for the West, whose own sad destiny in Thoreau's eyes was to be wrapped up in the factories of alienation.

But the destiny of the West could be shifted if it was complemented by careful, Christian doses of the spiritual wealth of the East. Voltaire was disinclined to be balanced in his assessment of Asian faiths. He condemned his fellow Christians for their religious failure and congratulated the Indians for a constant religiosity. "The ancient religion of India, and that of literary men of China," he wrote, "are the only ones wherein men have not been barbarous."[19] The men of Concord, Massachusetts, did not believe that their faith was inadequate, but they felt that the development of practical wisdom required a portion of the transcendental wisdom developed in ancient India. Occidentals may be practical, they thought, but they are also politically and socially conservative. "There is such a thing as caste, even in the West," Thoreau wrote, "but it is comparatively faint; it is conservatism here. It says, forsake not your calling, outrage no institution, use no violence, rend no bonds; the State is thy parent."[20] At the opening of *Walden*, Thoreau describes the tests of the flesh of the "Bramins" in detail and then notes that "even these forms of conscious penance are hardly more incredible and astonishing than the scenes which I daily witness."[21] Thoreau meant the everyday penance of his hardworking neighbors. They toiled without any sense of the spiritual, whereas the Brahmins tortured themselves without any sense of the practical. Both are incomplete, although Thoreau (like Emerson) evinced strong admiration for the life of the transcendental.

Let us remain with *Walden*. It was written during the period of the Great Potato Famine in Ireland (1845–49) and the California Gold Rush (1849), one an emblem of agrarian distress and the other of the avarice of industrial modernity. In *Walden* Thoreau bemoaned the gradual industrialization of New England. As proto-industrialism impinged upon agrarian life, "the laboring man has not leisure for a true integrity day by day; he cannot afford to sustain the manliest relations to men; his labor would be depreciated in the market. He has not time to be anything but a machine." And later, Thoreau found echoes in Massachusetts of the Manchester described by Friedrich Engels in 1844: "I cannot believe that our factory system is the best mode by which men may get clothing. The condition of the operatives is becoming every day more like that of the English; and it cannot be wondered at, since, as far as I have heard or observed, the principal object is, not that mankind may be well and honestly clad, but, unquestionably that the corporations may be enriched."[22] Thoreau recognized that the trials of industrialism produced both material and spiritual hardships for working people. Dissatisfied with industrialism, Thoreau, like many of his generation, hid themselves away from its ills (in beautiful, bucolic Walden) and offered a nostalgic romanticism in its place. Thoreau attributed the ills of his day to the entire "factory system" rather than to the social relations that organized technology to alienate workers. If he had gone in the latter direction, Thoreau (like Marx and Engels) may have recognized the contradictions within the modern rather than retreating into an imagined past from which to excoriate the contradictory present.

For Thoreau, as for much of U.S. orientalism (and here again distinct from European orientalism), the East was not a genetic inheritance unavailable to the West. That is, the cultural wealth of India could transform the alienated American into a spiritual and yet material being. The solution to modern alienation, for Thoreau, lay in the East. This East, however, was not just the geographical east; it was also a metaphor that represented the spiritual in general, whereas the West represented the material. "There is a struggle between the Oriental and Occidental in every nation," Thoreau wrote.[23] Given this metaphorical use of India, Thoreau could opine, "to some extent, and at rare intervals, even I am a yogin."[24] But the East (and "India") for U.S. orientalism was not just an artifice that faciliated the criticism of a conservative industrial society. In some places it emerged as a romantic fantasy of India itself. Mark Twain, in his late-nineteenth-century journey to India, was happy to find the combination of "splendor and rags," for "this was as it should be, also, for nothing is quite satisfyingly Oriental that lacks the somber and impressive qualities of mystery and antiquity."[25] In the next section, "Of the Oriental Menagerie," I will spend some time assessing the popularization of what had hitherto been an intellectualized form of orientalism. When the East entered popular culture, it did so partly as a metaphor of spirituality in excelsis, but mainly as a set of exotic, spiritual specimens that at times were reviled but at other times provided perverse forms of entertainment.

Emerson and Thoreau felt that the East provided a troubled West with a small emolument; Walt Whitman, by contrast, relegated the East to a past that cleaves to the present, this to the dismay of the champions of a one-dimensional modernity. Whitman's "Passage to India" (1871) begins with the completion in 1869 of the Suez Canal and the trans-U.S. railroad network. He celebrates these feats in an urgent voice that mimics the limitlessness envisioned by the technocrats. Whitman was no ordinary romantic, but, as C. L. R. James rightly noted, he was an "individualistic Romantic" and he "could find neither feudalism nor oppressive capital nor any striking combination of both to revolt against." Since the United States at midcentury was "traditionally and actually a land of equality and heroic individual achievement" for white males, "Whitman accepted it. Individualism, Romanticism *in the United States*. That is Whitman."[26] Whitman's romanticism, however, did not call for the preservation of nature. He was romantic about capitalism's capacity and technology's need to tame nature and make it subservient to humanity. Romantics influenced by the English did, of course, *tame* nature by their picturesque and pastoral rendition of a world without nature's threats and without the inconvenient Amerindians. Whitman, like Teddy Roosevelt, on the other hand, admired technology's will to dominate and frame the natural world for humanity's pleasure.

The West, well served by capitalism, was amply celebrated by Whitman in his *Leaves of Grass*. In the complete opus, "India" serves as a metaphor for the soul itself, for that sublime spirit that was lost in the throes of a capitalism that Whitman admired:

> Passage O soul to India!
> Eclaircise the myths Asiatic, the primitive fables.
> Not you alone proud truths of the world,
> Nor you alone ye facts of modern science,
> But myths and fables of eld, Asia's, Africa's fables . . .
>
> (Lines 16–20)

Some of the proponents of the modern wanted to damn the past to itself, but Whitman was inclined to disagree. He detected the sound of the past rising up to remind the present of its persistence. What is this "past"? It is none other than the spiritual that urges the poet to conduct that passage to India, that "Passage indeed O soul to primal thought" (line 165). The United States, in this worldview, is pure materialism, as pure want and hard realities; this is the land of those Emersonian Yankees "wrinkled and vexed" by their work. India, on the other hand, comes as a site of pure spiritualism, as pure fantasy. The fantasy of India reminded

Whitman of such things as the soul, a human attribute lost in the triumphant capitalism he otherwise celebrated. That "soul" needs to be cultivated, and there is no better place to do this, for Whitman, than through an engagement with this thing called "India." The multitudinous realities of India are irrelevant to those, like Whitman, who find in it elements for the salvation of the United States. Further, the present of India does not intrude in this elevated reverie on the ancient past of the subcontinent. That the essence of India is seen as Hindu is a problem that I will take up later, for it bears directly upon the kinds of religious politics at play within the United States today. In Whitman's work, the East appears as the depository of ethical and spiritual values, those values lost by the United States (the West), according to Whitman, because of the alienation of industrial capitalism.

The elevated thoughts of Emerson, Thoreau, and Whitman emerged in the first films on "India," just as they do in the world of popular orientalism. The first motion picture on India was called *Hindoo Faqir* (Thomas A. Edison, 1902). It was followed by a host of films that portrayed the subcontinent as the home of fatalistic spirituality and sensuality; *Oriental Mystic* (Vitagraph, 1909), *Soul of Buddha* (Fox, 1918), *The Green Goddess* (Distinctive, 1923), *Mystic India* (20th Century Fox, 1944), *Mysterious Ceylon* (Warner Bros., 1949), among others.[27] In the undisciplined world of U.S. orientalism, we already see those of the subcontinent represented as fundamentally different from those of the Occident and, in essence, overly spiritual and sensual. This image will be further developed in the popular den of orientalism that we shall now enter.

OF THE ORIENTAL MENAGERIE

The most common impression that prevails of the great east, its philosophy and mysticism, is akin in character and color to the impression that was received from the reading of the "Arabian Knights" [sic]. Perhaps in the whole of literature, excepting the Bible, there is no book that has left so marked an impression as these thousand fairy tales. They are entrancing in themselves and were read and are read by every boy and girl in the land when the mind and imagination were so susceptible to such influences that the impressions are indelible. The popular mind in a hazy sort of way realizes India as a land of ghastly and beautiful mysteries.

—*Detroit Journal*, 14 February 1894

The Greatest Show on Earth is back. The 126th edition of the Ringling Brothers and Barnum & Bailey Circus went on the road in 1998 to entice children away from video games and cartoons and toward the magic of the Big Top, trapeze artists, exotic animals, and human cannonballs. As part of the treat, the circus includes such unusual humans as Michu, who stands thirty-three inches tall, or Khan, who towers at eight feet. Khan, who hails from Pakistan, came to the United States in 1981 to make his fortune. He drove a taxi, sat in a security booth, worked as a cashier, and tried to survive as a bouncer. Now he stands outside the Big Top, dressed like an oriental prince, to answer questions about his physique (he wears size 20 shoes) and to re-create the mystery of the circus in an age when the outlandish is made rather normal.[1] Khan is not the first Asian to be Barnum's colossus. About a hundred years ago, Chang Yu Sing stood where Khan stands now, as "the Chinese Giant, the Tallest Man in the World." In those days, the circus was a primary form of entertainment as well as the main artery for the dissimulation of information about an exotic world. When India appeared in the popular imagination, it did so through the agency of Barnum, of the Christian missionaries, and of such traveling Indian lecturers as Swami Vivekananda. These agents of orientalism created and circulated images of India among the bulk of U.S. residents, people who cherished a menagerie of things oriental. India does not emerge, in this discourse, as simply romantic and beautiful; it also comes across as hideous and barbaric. As the *Detroit Journal* noted, India is seen as "a land of ghastly and beautiful mysteries," a contradiction that creates the framework through which India is rendered alien and simultaneously desirable and undesirable.[2]

The excesses of a popularized orientalism became apparent to a reviewer in *The Nation,* who wrote in 1865 that "in the strength of our superior civilization and the arrogance prompted by our consciousness of its possession, we are in danger of doing less than justice to Orientals." Though he challenged the population's cultivated ignorance toward Asia, he did not question India's lowly place in an established hierarchy of civilization. He simply worried that "our general public need to be made to realize much more fully than at present that the Oriental is our brother in intellect as in destiny; that his soul will cry out as loudly to its Maker under injustice and oppression as would the European." This fellowship was undermined by such movements as evangelical imperialism ("the kingdom of heaven may be the appointed inheritance of the poor in spirit; but the good things of the earth are for those who can win and keep them") and tendencies of proto–social Darwinism ("Why should not the lower race give way to the higher, that the sum of human happiness may be increased?"). The scholarly reviewer revealed the depths of the public's illiteracy, for that he himself was aware of some of the materials that earned the Asians a right to be treated as human (just as he noted that "to win for the African the rights to which, as a human being among human beings, he is entitled, we have to prove him by his gifts a full man, to show that he is in many respects equal, in some, perhaps, superior, to ourselves; that he can think, feel, plan, act, fight even, like a real man, made in the image of God"). His was a view not commonly found among his fellows, whose own view of India was rendered in technicolor by Barnum and the missionaries.[3]

Despite the general idea of the inferiority of certain races, missionaries heeded the Biblical charge to "go ye into all the world, and preach the gospel to every creature" (Mark 16.15). So too did Cotton Mather; in 1721 he wrote a manual to help missionaries convert people in India *(India Christiana),* and he carried on a long correspondence with a German missionary in Madras who sent a New Testament in Tamil to Mather in Boston. After Mather, a series of Protestant missionaries traveled to far-off India in order to "save souls." These men and women of the Gospel returned to the United States periodically to raise money for their ceaseless efforts. The campaign to raise money required publicity, so many of them wrote books and went on lecture tours from church to church, dipping into the collection plates. If India could be shown to be a den of heathens steeped in the worst forms of idolatry, then there was a better chance of raising funds to save the Indians' misbegotten souls. This song from the mid-1800s was published in a popular U.S. missionary tract:

> See that heathen mother stand
> Where the sacred current flows:
> With her own maternal hand
> Mid the waves her babe she throws.

Hark! I hear the piteous scream;
Frightful monsters seize their prey,
Or the dark and bloody stream
Bears the struggling child away.

Fainter now, and fainter still,
Breaks the cry upon the ear;
But the mother's heart is steel
She unmoved that cry can hear.

Send, oh send the Bible there,
Let its precepts reach the heart;
She may then her children spare—
Act the tender mother's part.[4]

Only the Bible, we are told, had the capacity to save the innocent children from the hideousness of their parents. The Bible was further needed to properly feminize the women, now made unfeminine by idolatry. This was staple fare in church circles, and it continues to be the mode used by missions to raise funds on television to this day.

During the 1857 uprising in India against the British, the missionaries told stories of the rebellion to demonstrate what they saw as the brutality of the non-Christian Indians. "The Indians are a people so filled with hate," wrote Rev. Isador Lowenthal, "that it is surprising their essentially depraved natures had not been displayed in acts of violence even more numerous and appalling." There was no savior for India "until the spirit of the Gospel fused the hearts of the people in a common mould."[5] There was little concern in these texts for the natives, barbarized by the British for almost a hundred years. Such accounts presented India as the "ghastly mystery," filled with hook-swinging men, thugs, oppressed and secluded women, and the strangeness of esoteric religious practices. The missionary texts read much like those of other U.S. travelers, such as one R. S. Minturn, who landed in Calcutta and was surrounded by naked "niggers, members of a race for whom one cannot help feeling contempt since they are all such miserable, fawning, cringing, slavish cowards, especially when flogged for they don't resist but shriek frightfully for mercy."[6] These books sold very well; for example Caleb Wright's *Historic Incidents and Life in India* was published in five editions, and the 1862 edition alone sold over 38,000 copies.[7] The missionary texts exaggerated certain features of Indian life to emphasize the need for Christianity. Despite their long tenure in the subcontinent, the missionaries did not mention the social reform movement whose roots may be found in the early 1800s among the intelligentsia of Bengal. Raja Ram Mohan Roy and the Brahmo Samaj are given some space, but only to claim that Brahmoism was a Bengali form of Christianity.[8]

The missionaries used the "plight of women" as a weapon against the totality of Indian society. There was little concern, again, with the efforts of Raja Ram Mohan Roy or Isvar Chandra Vidyasagar on behalf of women[9] or with the struggles of Jotibhai Phule and Savitribai Phule, who started schools for girls in the 1840s. The contradictory tissue of struggle was reduced to a caricature, even if the person making the statement tried to be more nuanced. Such was the case of Pandita Ramabai, a remarkable nineteenth-century woman who traveled to the United States in 1886 and in 1898. She came to attend the graduation of her kinswoman, Anandibai Joshi, herself an extraordinary character. Joshi, a Brahmin woman from Poona, came to the Women's Medical College of Philadelphia to study medicine in 1883. Three years later, she received her MD degree and returned to India, but she died tragically within a few months. Joshi had planned to conduct extensive reform in her native town, a dream shared by her relative, Ramabai. Unlike Joshi, Ramabai converted to Christianity and wished to work within the framework of the Gospels. The work was essentially identical to that envisaged by Joshi, but with an emphasis on education rather than medicine and hygiene. While in the United States, Ramabai gave a few lectures to raise money for her endeavor. In her wake, several supporters set up the American Ramabai Association, whose Ramabai Circles (led by Rev. Lyman Abbott) raised money for her reform organization (Sharada Sadan) from several colleges—

including Smith, Bryn Mawr, Mills, Wellesley, and Cornell—and numerous churches and civic bodies. Ramabai's *The High Caste Hindu Woman* (1888) was the primer of the circles, and despite its own balanced approach to the oppression of women, it fed the exaggerated notions of the bondage of pitiful Indian women at the hands of brutish Indian men.[10] When Vivekananda toured the United States in 1893–94, he was consistently attacked by these circles, whose strident Christian supremacy was intensified by the currents of Christian revival of the time.

There is little sense of shared humanity in the texts of the missions, nor is there any notion of the problems common to people in the United States and in British India. There was oppression on the subcontinent, but there was also certainly oppression in the United States, both against blacks and Amerindians and also against women. The missionaries did not make these connections, but radicals in India did. Jotibhai Phule dedicated his 1873 tract *Gulamgiri* (Slavery) to the "good people of the United States. As a token of admiration for their sublime disinterested and self-sacrificing devotion. In the course of Negro slavery; and with an earnest desire, that my countrymen may take their noble example as their guide in the emancipation of their Sudra [oppressed caste] Brethren from the trammels of Brahmin thralldom."[11] The missionaries wrote in the manner of Katherine Mayo, a member of the Society of Mayflower Descendants, whose 1927 *Mother India* was filled with spectacular exaggerations at the service of British imperialism.[12] The existence of home-grown oppression was not to interfere with a denunciation of what the orientalists deemed to be things Indian. Joguth Chunder Gangooly, known as Philip, toured the United States on behalf of the Unitarian Mission in 1860. Gangooly was stunned by the questions from Sunday school children about the hideousness of his native land. "I never heard such stories even from the lips of my grandmother," the distressed Unitarian wrote, "I admit, however, other facts as the burning of shotees [sati] and hook swinging, etc."[13] The fact that hook-swinging and *sati* (immolation of women; the word means literally "to become pure") were marginal activities was of little consequence, since such things began to define "India" on the terrain of popular orientalism. There was little awareness that the deep interest in *sati* and hook-swinging was a means toward the primitivization and barbarization of "India."[14] The texts that concentrated on such spectacles produced a vision of India that legitimized the power of those who both wrote those texts and attempted to write the future of Indian history through their rule. All this was irrelevant to the missionaries and to those who drew upon such accounts to create a vision of India as a ghastly mystery.

Most Americans came in contact with the hideous mystery of India in the confines of their churches, but many would have also experienced the "beautiful mystery" of India in the circus and the vaudeville houses. In those domains, India was presented in the context of a generalized Orient, one that included images of an opulent and effeminate sultan surrounded by oversexed women, animals, jewelry, and the scent of the unknown. This is the generic Orient of those old warhorses used in the circus, such as "The Cataract of the Ganges," "Timour the Tartar" and "The Forty Thieves." P. T. Barnum's dream palace in Bridgeport, Connecticut, called Iranisthan, was a metaphor for the exotic mystery of popular orientalism. Designed in the manner of the Brighton Pavilion in England, Iranisthan was a medley of domes and minarets (an early expression of a style later represented by Walt Disney's Magic Kingdom); it "rose in more than Oriental splendor above the placid New England landscape."[15] The main template for this form of popular orientalism was *The Arabian Nights*, a text well known among the population, in illustrated editions both for adults and for children (for "family readings").[16] The reach and influence of the text was such that *The Nation* bemoaned the fact that "it will be a long while, we suspect, before our first impressions of the East cease to be derived from the 'Arabian Nights.'"[17] Beside this great text of orientalia sat Thomas Moore's fantasy, *Lalla Rookh*, subtitled "an oriental romance" and first published in the United States in 1817.[18] This text was made into a pantomime and a pageant that was displayed across the United States during the nineteenth century. In one such pageant in Baltimore in

1895, 500 extras "clad in Oriental robes" processed through a stage set of Delhi, "home of the Fire-worshippers." Ballet dancers "danced, pranced and whirled before a blazing background of pyro-technics," and Venetian gondolas reposed upon an artificial lake.[19] The pageant was so famous that an elephant in Van Amburgh's Circus was named Lalla Rookh.

This brings us to elephants. The first Asian elephant to enter the United States came on board Capt. Jacob Crowinshield's Yankee clipper in 1796. This unnamed elephant did not make the kind of impact that Barnum's stream of pachyderms did, both in the Great Asiatic Caravan, Museum, and Menagerie (1849) and in the 1851 parade of twelve elephants down the avenues of New York City. Barnum's mahouts (elephant trainers) wore the costume of orientalia, that is, splendid clothing from anywhere east of the Suez Canal. The silver screen closely linked India to elephants through the movies of Sabu, who was discovered in the maharajah of Mysore's stables by Alexander Korda's cameraman and who starred to acclaim in *The Elephant Boy* (Korda-UA, 1937).[20] Sabu's film career was tied to those animals and forests that denoted India, such as the tiger (*A Tiger Walks,* Disney, 1964), and to the jungle (*Drums,* London Films, 1938; *Jungle Book,* Korda-UA, 1942; *Jungle Hell,* 1955). To be indisputably "oriental" and "Indian," Sabu also starred in *The Thief of Baghdad* (1940) and *Arabian Nights* (1942), films that conjured up the generic Orient of which India was to be a major part. These "jungle thrillers" were set in lush forests filled with wild animals and adventures such as the Big Hunt. George Dorsey indulged in the imperial hunt while he shot his six-reel documentary *India* (United Photo Plays, 1916), the precursor of Louis Malle's 1969 *L'Inde fantôme.* "I had the honor of being the guest of His Highness the Nizam of Hyderabad, on a cheetah hunt planned in honor of His Highness the Aga Khan," Dorsey wrote in *Motion Picture News.* "His Highness was also kind enough to let us photograph his menagerie. This is his hobby—the collecting of strange animals and birds. He has a number of white elephants. I expect to finish with India in about forty days more. While here we will join

Sabu in *Jungle Book* (1942). Photograph courtesy of Malcolm Willits, Collectors Book Store, Hollywood, California.

a tiger hunt and an elephant hunt."[21] India, like Africa, required animals in any representation for its essence (in U.S. eyes) to be truly realized.

animals?

In the gaze of U.S. popular culture, Sabu and the elephant appeared as specimens of India. In 1847 Charles Huffnagle, one-time U.S. consul at Calcutta, opened a private museum at his home, called Springdale, in New Hope, Pennsylvania, to house his collection of humped Brahmani bulls (one named Maha Rajah), safari trophies, books, and household idols. Visitors from the Atlantic coast viewed the museum on Tuesdays and stopped to "eat crystallized Calcutta sugar and to sip Mocha coffee and rare Assam teas."[22] Such museums complemented the spectacles organized by Barnum, notably, the Congress of Nations (1874) and the Ethnological Congress (1884). In these congresses, Barnum paraded people from the wide world before a U.S. audience. Whereas the 1874 congress displayed *representatives* of the various parts of the world, the 1884 congress portrayed *specimens* of different (and lower) races. That is, the former congress emphasized the idea of a universal royalty (a portrayal that appears as early as the seventeenth century, in Aphra Behn's novel *Oroonoko*) and the latter congress marched out those deemed lower to be looked upon and jeered at. As Bluford Adams noted, "the reconceptualization of the Oriental as the savage 'specimen' rather than the potent, civilized monarch reveals the sharper, institutionally policed racial lines that characterized Barnum circuses after 1880."[23] The pageant of Ota Benga in 1906 was no different from the fate of the Indian circus midgets, brought to be gaped at and to represent the essential strangeness of their land.[24] Popular orientalism paraded out both the ghastly and beautiful mysteries of India as racial specimens that represented the multiplicity of Indian society, entertained U.S. residents, and validated the U.S. way of life in opposition to that deemed to be general in the East.

But this validation was not as simple as it seems. In the legitimation of U.S. style, the panoply of desire was also transferred onto the demeaned East, not as something good but as excess. For example, veiled "oriental women" sat in various stages of undress or in the garb of belly dancers and fawned upon "oriental men" in the pageants and tableaux of popular orientalism (often played by white men and women in brown-face).[25] Even elephants came surrounded, in the words of a *New York Herald* reporter, "by the beautiful houris."[26] These brown women appeared as seductive houris, but they, just like those other brown women depicted as overworked laborers or secluded wives, were seen as having no

Indian circus midgets at Ellis Island (1908). Courtesy of National Park Service, Ellis Island Museum.

sense of agency and certainly as fundamentally oppressed by brown men. Further, since it was known that these were actually white women, the tableaux provided a sense of anxiety over the protection of the chastity of the white woman (a U.S. cultural feature that emerged with a vengeance in the riot of lynchings of

weak

black men).[27] The men being fawned upon came dressed in the robes of monarchy, a social institution delegated to the past and seen as generally abhorrent in the United States. Barnum's 1851 parade of elephants was led by a mahout who, Barnum's publicists claimed, was a chief of a "Ceylonese tribe." As a degraded chief (at work now as an elephant trainer), he must have allowed the U.S. audience to celebrate their own emancipation from the decadent aristocracy and to enjoy seeing the oriental aristocrat in a position of servility. That the orangutan at the Bronx Zoo in the 1920s was named Rajah (King) was not coincidental. The dethroned oriental despot was a popular theme in the circus, and it was even more popular in the vaudeville acts. Bluford Adams argued that the "circuses exploited the non-Westerner not simply as the decadent Other of their images of potent white manhood, but also as a vehicle of an implicit critique of Western rationality, science and capitalism."[28]

Certainly, the cult of masculinity in the late nineteenth century called more for athletics and militarism than for bureaucratic repose. The presence of the "primitive" as physical body (however sexualized) was a counterpoint to the reduction of the bourgeois body to its mind (and those appendages useful for mechanical activity). However, popular orientalism did tend to display the "primitive" from the "East" as a being blind to the discipline of industrial labor and thus as a sloth comparable to those heathens who faced God's wrath at Sodom and Gomorrah. Since the "East," and in particular "India," was reduced so fundamentally to the *corporeal* (as opposed to the mental), a U.S. consul in India in 1888 refused to see the value of mechanization of Indian agriculture. "A threshing machine in the hands of an Indian farmer," he wrote, "would be like an elephant in the hands of an American."[29] The parallel with the elephant was perhaps no coincidence.

The ghastly and beautiful mystery of India was married in the presence of Swami Vivekananda on his 1893–95 U.S. tour. This disciple of the Bengali sage Ramakrishna left India to attend the World Parliament of Religions, a conference organized by liberal clergy to complement the historic 1893 Columbian Exposition held in Chicago. Four hundred years after Columbus's landing in the West Indies, the plutocrats in the United States felt the need to thank him as a distant ancestor of the contemporary white people in the Americas. Of course, many of these "Anglo-Saxons" kept their distance from the Italian immigrants of their day. The Italians, who numbered in the millions by the early twentieth century, earned the pejorative title "guinea," a word long used to refer to African slaves (many of whom hailed from the northwest coast of Africa, renowned as the Guinea or Gold Coast for its fabled wealth).[30] But Columbus was no ordinary Italian, for he was the legendary Alexander of the New World, the *white* man who found America for industry and prosperity.

To celebrate Columbus, the elite of Chicago financed the construction of a *White* City to display the merchandise of industrial civilization. Down the street, at the Midway Plaisance (in front of the University of Chicago), the city burghers exhibited the wares of the racial specimens from around the globe. The multitude flooded in, many financed by commercial enterprises (for example, the tea bureau underwrote the Ceylon pavilion), "to huckster goods and gull Americans on the very soil where Barnumism flourished."[31] Jackson Park, the home of the White City, was transformed into "a fairy scene of inexpressible splendor reminding one of the gorgeous descriptions in the Arabian Nights when Haraun al Raschid was Caliph."[32] Twenty-one million viewers came to see the "coochee coochee" sideshow (featuring the belly dancer Little Egypt), Harry Houdini and his escape tricks, Indian jugglers, mosques and pagodas, and George Washington Ferris's first steel wheel. These same people saw the unveiling of Whitcomb Judson's zipper and sampled the new Crackerjacks and Aunt Jemima Pancakes. (Nancy Green, a domestic worker, was hired to play the part of the Mammy; this was one of the few representations of black Americans in the exposition, a fact not lost on Ida B. Wells and other black leaders.)[33] Not to forget patriotism, the White City also inaugurated the first rendition of the Pledge of Allegiance. "A wurruld's fair is no rollin'-mills," we hear from the fictional Mr. Dooley. "If it was, ye'd be paid f'r goin' there. 'Tis a big circus with manny rings an' that's what it ought to be."[34] In other words, it was an exotic pageantry for the tired workers in this puritan land.

The exposition was itself filled with the emblems of a "primitive" spirituality, the type of complex brew doled out by the Theosophist and spiritualist Madame Helena Blavatsky, but here it was represented by those deemed to be close to the soil in terms of labor and consciousness. The generic Orient was coupled with the Indians of the Americas, cousins, it seems, in their purported link with the soil to which a Lockean imperialism denied them title. "Close to the soil" implies a relationship to an unsullied nature, a relationship with some ability to transfer knowledge about the spiritual realm even if in a primitive form. Those urbanites of the West, it was claimed, were liberated from the soil and could only appreciate the spiritual realm textually, not viscerally. Hence, in some way, we can locate the fascination with the "primitive" (and later, "indigenous peoples"). Less than three years after the slaughter at Wounded Knee, the exposition acknowledged the spirituality of the Amerindians, who were now hailed and courted for their culture at various pavilions and by the large totem pole erected for the occasion (it now stands outside the Field Museum).

In addition to Amerindians, the White City and the Parliament of Religion were crowded by people from the East, including India. Of the Eastern peoples, the hits of the parliament included Vivekananda and the Ceylonese Buddhist leader Anagarika Dharmapala. The Monk of Bengal arrived in the United States a few months before the Chicago event, so he went on a lecture tour to raise funds and to find his feet in this new land. The publicists who managed his tour took to "beating his drum as if he were a circus turn."[35] He was advertised routinely as the "Indian Rajah" or the "Hindoo Rajah," and his prospective audience was promised that "the Rajah will wear his native costume." He did indeed dress in his marvelous saffron robes and his turban, a sight that was unusual in the parochial United States. At his lectures, the audience felt emboldened to satisfy their curiosity, one crafted over the decades by pulp fiction and the tabloid press. What about levitation? The Indian rope trick? The bed of nails? Communication by telepathy (a feat attested to by the Theosophists)? Vivekananda was nonplussed. "We do not believe in miracles at all," he told one crowd, "but that apparently strange things may be accomplished under the operation of natural laws." Those who levitate, for instance, "starve themselves, and become so thin that if one presses his finger upon their stomachs he can actually feel the spine."[36] Vivekananda's nuance was lost on the local reporter, who nevertheless proceeded to paint a portrait of the mysteries of the East. The swami, despite his loose statements about levitation, was very cautious about his reception. Of the parliament he noted in a letter that it "was intended for a 'heathen show' before the world," a display, Barnum-style, of the religious types with emphasis on the exotic.[37] This was not acceptable to the swami, but one man's hesitation could not hold back the juggernaut of popular orientalism.

Though Vivekananda did recognize his emplotment into the orientalist framework, he himself was in tune with the kinds of sociological statements made by the gentlemen of Concord, notably Thoreau. "You of the West are practical in business, practical in great inventions," he told an audience in Minnesota in 1893, "but we of the East are practical in religion. You make commerce your business; we make religion our business."[38] First, the swami created a divide between East and West, with India in the former and the United States in the latter. Second, he offered each of these geographical zones a cultural value, with the East being the upholder of the spiritual, the religious, and the transcendental. The West, Vivekananda conceded, was to be seen as superior in the arts of the practical and the mundane, not just because in the realm of the mundane, India was a British colony, but also because of the sheer visible wealth of U.S. cities. "You Americans worship what? The dollar. In the mad rush for gold, you forget the spiritual until you have become a nation of materialists. Even your preachers and churches are tainted with the all-pervading desire."[39] The West, that is, had overdone the practical and eschewed a real interrogation of the transcendental (this was the verdict of Thoreau, Blavatsky, and Col. Henry Olcott, a student of Blavatsky and the first president of the Theosophical Society, as well). "I think that the Hindoo faith developed the spiritual in its devotees at the expense of the material, and I think that in the Western world the contrary is true. By uniting the materialism of the West with the spiritualism of the East I believe much can be accomplished."[40] Entire traditions of Indian science and U.S. theology were dropped by the wayside in this overgeneralized and orientalist statement. That did not seem to matter to Vivekananda (as it did not to the gentlemen of Concord). In late 1893, the swami wrote to his followers in India to explain that "we will teach [Americans] our spirituality, and assimilate what is best in their society."[41] "I must touch the brain of *America*," he said in 1894, "and stir it up if I can."[42] Vivekananda is not unusual among Indians in the construction of this split. When Swami Paramhansa Yogananda decided to come to the United States in the mid-1920s to bring Americans the teachings of his Babaji (Guru), he was told by his teacher that "although high in intellectual attainments, many Westerners are wedded to rank materialism. India has much to learn from the West in material development; in return, India can teach the universal methods by which the West will be able to base its religious beliefs on the unshakable foundations of yogic science."[43]

The presentation of "yogic science" as a panacea for alienation opened the door to numerous Godmen and lecturers, such as Super-Akasha Yogi Wassan, a Punjabi who offered techniques for life (in anticipation of Deepak Chopra). In 1901, a man named Ottoman Zar-Adusht Hannish began to claim that he was the emissary of the Dalai Lama, and he preached a version of Tibetan Buddhism with much fanfare. After Dr. Bhagat Singh Thind was refused citizenship on racial grounds in a landmark 1923 case (the United States declared that Thind was a "nonwhite Caucasian"), he lectured in the late 1920s on such topics as "Jazz Mania: Its Cause and Cure and the Psychology of Relaxation," "The Sacred Hum of the Universe," and "Can We Talk with the 'Dead' and How?"[44] Not to be outdone, a number of white Americans joined the Circus of the Transcendental. Peter Bernard of New York City taught hatha yoga and tantrism under the name of Oom the Omni-

Swami Vivekananda statue, Chicago. Photograph by L. Mikelle Standbridge.

potent, and Yogi Ramacharaka started his own cult. Prince Ram Maharaj, another white man, claimed to have learned his craft in Tibet, home also to those "great masters" of the Theosophical Society who, the prince hoped, would some day visit Los Angeles.[45] Har Dayal, in exile in the United States for his anticolonial revolutionary activities, was horrified by this use of India. Though most Indians worked as farm laborers, some earned their living as bogus palmists or Hindu teachers. Those charlatans duped "credulous middle-aged ladies out of their dollars," wrote Har Dayal. He was happy that these bogus sadhus (Godmen or ascetics) "have been able to teach even a few of these overfed self-complacent Americans the value of restraint and self-mortification as practiced by earnest Hindus." In many cases, however, the Hinduism imparted

37

in the United States was deeply conservative, since it taught those interested to "desire *mukti* [liberation] but hug their chains," that is, to want spiritual peace, but not social justice.[46]

These examples are mainly from the world of white America. Black Americans did not linger far behind in the fetishization of India as a spiritual place, although the strategic deployment of India was far more nuanced, particularly because it was used as a means to undercut racist authority. In New York's Harlem, a black man from the U.S. South adopted the name Sufi, passed as "a man of the East" and "organized a party, picketed shops, and helped to force employers to give one-third of their jobs to Negroes."[47] Sufi used India to further the antiracist struggle; others used India to survive the indignities of everyday racism. Dizzy Gillespie, for instance, tells a number of stories of black musicians who either converted to Islam or who acted as if they had converted so that they might be allowed to pass as white in restaurants. "Man, if you join the Muslim faith," his friends would tell him, "you ain't colored no more, you'll be white. You get a new name and you don't have to be a nigger no more." Since the U.S. state was paralyzed in its decision over the "race" of West Asians (many of whom submit to Allah), the black musicians took advantage of the space to renegotiate the identities they claimed on such things as police cards. Oliver Mesheux entered a restaurant in Delaware and was told that he could not be served because he did not appear white to the waiter. "I don't blame you," he replied. "But I don't have to go under the rules of colored because my name is Mustafa Dalil." Dizzy Gillespie said that he sometimes wore a turban and folks would think he was "an Arab or a Hindu"; since he would pretend not to speak English, they would leave him alone.[48] After Babs Gonzalez (Lee Brown) saw a Sabu movie in Newark, he decided that "although my skin was brown if I could speak a language or fool 'whitey' I had a chance [not to feel the rough edge of racism]." He began to wear a turban. "My friends just laughed, but I noticed that white people who didn't know me, showed me respect." When Babs Gonzalez moved to Los Angeles, he took the name Ram Singh, worked as Errol Flynn's chauffeur, and enjoyed it when southern whites bowed to him "because they thought I was an Indian."[49]

These black men (and I have no examples of women, but this is perhaps from want of information) used India with virtuoso grace as a device against racism. There is also evidence of one black man who donned the yogic posture to sell the snake oil of mysticism before a largely white audience. Joe Downing, "of coal black visage," adopted the name Joveddah de Raja and toured Benjamin Franklin Keith's vaudeville circuit. Joveddah and his wife (Princess Olga, posing as central Asian) did mind readings for a startled audience. In the mid-1920s, Joveddah sold his "words of Oriental comfort and wisdom" on New York radio.[50]

But even among Joveddah, Dizzy Gillespie, and Babs Gonzalez, there is no contempt for things Indian. In one of Jessie Fauset's Harlem Renaissance novels, the protagonist Angela passes as white and bears no special love for blackness. When she goes to hear a black speaker talk on race, she sees an East Indian in him and is filled with pride. "He sat with a curious immobility, gazing straight before him like a statue of an East Indian idol. And indeed there was about him some strange quality which made one think of the East; a completeness, a superb lack of self-consciousness, an odd, arresting beauty wrought by the perfection of his fine, straight nose and his broad scholarly forehead."[51] The black man is perfect and complete when he is seen as an Indian, a vision born partly from U.S. orientalism but also partly from the strong wave of solidarity for the anticolonial struggles in India that swept parts of black America. The year after Fauset's novel was published, W. E. B. Du Bois sent a letter to the newspaper *People* (10 January 1929) in Lahore to underscore that "the people of India, like the American Negroes, are demanding today things, not in the least revolutionary, but things which every civilized white man has so long taken for granted, that he wishes to refuse to believe that there are people who are denied these rights."[52] The stamp of radical India was made popular in the black press, and I will visit such periodicals later in the book.[53]

Like Du Bois and much of the black media, some whites refused to condemn India to an essential spirituality and found fellowship in the anticolonial struggles of the nationalist movement. Agnes Smedley spent much of her early life alongside Indian revolutionaries in the United States and in Germany, fighting for the freedom of India. Drawn by the vision of Indian nationalist Lala Lajpat Rai during his New York sojourn, Smedley helped Indian revolutionaries create a base in New York, a service for which she served time in the Tombs (New York's prison) in 1918 along with Sailendranath Ghosh, the Indian American radical. While there, they met Roger Baldwin (a founder of the American Civil Liberties Union), and in 1920 the three of them, along with Upton Sinclair, Taraknath Das, Jabez Thomas Sunderland, Franz Boas, Du Bois, and others, formed the Friends of Freedom for India.[54] Such people forced themselves on Congresswoman Jeanette Rankin after she offered her resolution on behalf of Irish independence in 1918. Her sympathy for the cause of Irish independence drew her to India, to which she traveled over two decades, not to search for the mystical East but to elaborate her own pacifist philosophy by learning from Gandhi and his ilk.[55] This minority tradition is worthy of resurrection, since it was the major force to promote the radical tendencies of the people of the East. The bulk of the population did not find such a representation as palatable as that of India as the land of ghastly and beautiful mysteries.

The Godmen of the fin-de-siècle who came from India to the United States did subscribe to the view that the former (the East) was essentially spiritual and the latter (the West) essentially practical. This divide also facilitated their own attempts to gain supporters among those in the United States who gravitated to the essentially spiritual from which to imbibe wisdom. Beyond that there was little that linked the Godmen to the sorts of assumptions made by popular orientalism when it entered social policy. The U.S. government, for instance, concurred (for wholly different reasons) in the British imperial policy of neglecting the physical plant of the subcontinent, since it was assumed that India's economy was based on the expenditure of manual labor. There was no need to mechanize agriculture, proponents of this official U.S. view argued, for the Indian peasants could not decipher the devices. "Cities seem to be more advanced and take up with improvements more readily than the country," noted one U.S. consul in 1899, "though the entire people of India are exceedingly conservative."[56] Indian agriculture, therefore, was to produce raw materials by the toil of what was seen as a multitudinous and hidebound population. Labor was not controlled with the economic discipline of unemployment or the political discipline of militarization; rather, the Indian peasant was assumed to be controlled by the spiritual discipline of karma and other such attributes of predestination.[57]

Such views of India rankled Vivekananda and several others of the Godmen. The tendency to view India as solely spiritual obscured the devastation wrought on the subcontinent by capitalism and colonialism. In Brooklyn, New York, Vivekananda attacked imperialism's contempt for the people of his land. "The world waded in [Indian] children's life blood," he said, "it reduced India to poverty and her sons and daughters to slavery."[58] The United States, itself once an English colony, should have been generally sympathetic to these words. However, by century's end, the United States was getting ready to take up the "white man's burden" in the Caribbean and in East Asia; besides, James Monroe had already liberated the United States from any inhibitions about exercising its "manifest" legacy over the Americas.[59] At the World Parliament of Religions, Vivekananda was furious with the United States for its belief that religion was its sole export to the subcontinent. "You erect churches throughout India," he said, "but the crying evil in the East is not religion—they have religion enough—but it is bread that the suffering millions of burning India cry out for with parched throats. They ask us for bread, but we give them stones. It is an insult to a starving people to offer them religion."[60]

Vivekananda's frustration with U.S. orientalism came partly from his own sense of the material problems of his native land. "The only hope of India is from the masses," he wrote. "The upper classes are physically and morally dead."[61] Anger at British imperialism

41

and at the logic of capitalism led Vivekananda to declare his allegiance to social justice in this world. "I am a socialist," he declaimed, "not because I think it is a perfect system, but half a loaf is better than no bread."[62] Vivekananda's unequivocal socialism was not to be imported into the United States by his adherents. In 1910 Swami Trigunatita, who ran the Vedanta Society of America in California, offered a speech to the San Francisco branch of the Socialist Party entitled "Every Man and Woman Is Born a Socialist."[63] There certainly was no aversion to the idea of socialism, and in fact the swamis did not avoid such mundane topics. However, the U.S. branch of Vivekananda's movement did not derive the full import of the founder's socialism. Swami Prakashananda, Trigunatita's assistant, argued that Vedanta (that is, the summation of Vedic thought in which humans are seen as divine beings who must strive to realize their divinity) "includes socialism also, which principally aims at material and social upliftment and perfection. Thus [socialism] can be called a phase of Vedanta." However, Prakashananda warned that if socialism meant absolute equality "it is not only dangerous, but impossible. So-called equality means death and degeneration."[64] This dialogue with socialism makes little sense if we see India as a spiritual place whose essence is located in an ahistorical Hindu religious lineage (with a one-dimensional transcendentalism). For this reason, perhaps, few care to reflect on this heritage of Vedanta, preferring to remain at the level of the more theological accounts (such as Swami Nikhilananda's translation of the Bhagavad Gita or Vivekananda's books on the various yogas). An analysis of the totality of the thoughts of Vivekananda or Trigunatita shows that the framework of theology can enable a fruitful engagement with the contradictions between the celestial and the mundane.

U.S. orientalism constructs India as the domain of spirituality, albeit a spirituality that many saw as inferior to the real sacrament, Christianity. When confronted by real, living Indians, however, the California Bureau of Labor Statistics was so bold as to state that "the Hindu has no morals."[65] We are told, further, that the Indian "is the most undesirable immigrant in the state. His lack of personal cleanliness, his low morals and his blind adherence to theories and teachings, so entirely repugnant to American principles, make him unfit for association with American people."[66] Before this confuses us too much, the writer makes it very clear that "these references apply to the low caste Hindu or Sikhs." In other words, the Brahmins, those men of lofty thoughts, are acceptable (at least as fellows, if not as neighbors), but those who migrate (non-Brahmins) are certainly unacceptable. So much for a society without status! In 1908 Teddy Roosevelt was cavalier about the fact that the western United States was to be a white man's land. "Gentlemen," he told four Canadian members of Parliament, "we have got to protect our workingmen. We have got to build up our western country with our white civilization, and we must retain the power to say who shall or shall not come to our country."[67] Roosevelt spoke to receptive ears. MacKenzie King, the Canadian deputy federal minister of labor, had the previous year told the British leaders that "the native of India is not suited to this country," and he devised several clever means to ensure that they did not enter the country and to deport those in the country to India or to British Honduras (strong resistance from the Indians prevented the latter).[68] Canada joined the United States in an unofficial gentlemen's agreement to restrict migration to their western territories, a policy that earned the favor of the vaudeville halls:

> For white man's land we fight.
> To Oriental grasp and greed
> We'll surrender, no, never.
> Our watchword be "God Save the King,"
> White Canada Forever.[69]

As Vivekananda marched across the prairies in the late 1890s, the United States was already in league with Britain and Canada to stop the immigration of Asians into the Americas and to deport anti-imperialist radicals. Pung Kwang Yu, a Chinese consular official in Washington, D.C., urged the World Parliament of Religions to treat "all my countrymen just as they have treated me."

As the diplomat left the stage, an organizer noted that the parliament would stand against the "obnoxious Geary law" (the current version of the 1882 Chinese Exclusion Act banning Chinese immigration). A Japanese Buddhist, Kinzai R. M. Hirai, told the parliament about the heinousness of whites who barred Japanese residents from schools and from public places. It was hard to think of Christian morality "when there are men who go in procession hoisting lanterns marked 'Japs must go'. If such be Christian ethics," he noted, "we are perfectly satisfied to be heathen."[70] Vivekananda, who had little contact with the West Coast, made no direct statements about anti-Indian activity, but it would not have been outside his range to have done so had he known of Canadians there. On social justice, Vivekananda was very consistent. Other Indians did contribute to the fight against this racism, people such as Baba Gurdit Singh, who hired the S.S. *Komagata Maru* to carry 376 South Asians to challenge the 1908 Canadian Continuous Journey Provision (which required people migrating to Canada to come directly from their homelands; this was not easy for Indians, since ships had to dock en route and few ships sold direct tickets from India to Canada). The Canadian government detained the ship and held the passengers on board. The Indians already in British Columbia, organized in the Khalsa Diwan Society, formed a shore committee and raised funds for the stranded migrants. Hussain Rahim (publisher of the newspaper *Hindustanee*) and Bhag Singh led the quixotic fight on shore, but eventually the ship was escorted out of the harbor by the Canadian navy (one official wrote to the prime minister that "by a strange irony, this nucleus of the Canadian Navy was first used to prevent British subjects from landing on British soil").[71] The radicalism of Hussein, Bhag Singh, and Vivekananda did not seem intelligible to those who only saw India as spiritual. Few cared for the living Indians in their midst or for the systematic poverty produced and maintained in India by imperialism. Only the British and Americans—people such as Katherine Mayo, for example— had license to comment on contemporary India.[72] Indians themselves could only speak of India's ancient heritage as a cog in the general tableaux of humanity.

Without a doubt, the trials of capitalism significantly damaged the concern of social individuals for their fellows. Har Dayal was right in thinking that most people in the United States and Canada searched "for some great spiritual force, which should rescue us from the slough of despondence and sensuality in which civilization seems to be perishing. And civilization knows it."[73] One approach to the alienation of the masses was to rearrange the socioeconomic system of value extraction, but there was also a demand for some sort of spiritual response to this alienation. Rather than a turn to *spiritus sanctus,* to submission to a transcendental divine (or the sublime dollar), Har Dayal and others called for the formation of an esprit de corps, an ethos of comradeship. The spiritualism of the East was fundamentally associated with the first, with transcendental piety (and by the time Deepak Chopra arrived in the United States, his form of devotion dovetailed with the veneration of the market economy, another form of spiritualism). The creation of the integrated personality, one of the tasks of the Left, is not addressed at all by this type of East, but it will be addressed toward the end of this book when I consider the role of solidarity in the creation of a beloved community.

OF SLY *BABA*S AND OTHER GURUS

I am the Messiah America has been waiting for.

—Bhagwan Shree Rajneesh

And it is a matter of Karma and reincarnation, when will I ever learn? All the saints like Shivananda handing me rupees & books of yoga and I'm no good. My hair getting long, wearing a huge thin silk shirt, useless to perfect my conscience. A smoking habit my worst Karma to overcome.

—Allen Ginsberg, *Indian Journals, March 1962–May 1963*

On 21 April 1997 mythical India appeared again, this time on *Politically Incorrect with Bill Maher*. Sitting beside the comedian Carrot Top, the best-selling author Deepak Chopra offered the U.S. public a vision of the guru with his pithy and banal lines ("Sex is not the path of happiness" and "Surveys silence the voice of individuals"). At the same time, he offered once more to save the United States from its crises by a dose of eastern thinking. "We are waiting for America to grow out of its adolescence," he said, "and truly embrace freedom." Unable to dominate the space as he does

47

in his solo performances, he leaned forward to make his point, and Bill Maher asked, "Are you trying to hypnotize me?" The guru was reduced to a joke.

But Chopra laughs along with the United States, as he dons the robes of the East to peddle a form of escapism that not only trivializes the conundrums of people in the United States but it also mocks the real crises of people in South Asia. He offers exotic statements as a way to cover over what amounts to a Dale Carnegie ideology. Do not struggle, he says; work hard and be as self-interested, self-indulgent, and selfish as possible. If there are problems in the United States, he tells us, they are to be located within the deep structures of an essentialized human personality and not in the institutions and social structures of our world. He uses "Eastern knowledge" to answer the burning questions of our time, but all he seems to provide is a banal exoticism. "We are divinity in disguise," he wrote, "and the gods and goddesses in embryo contained within us seek to be fully materialized. I will release this list of my desires and surrender to the womb of creation."[1] Chopra's style is as much "Indian" as it is "American," in that it melds together the spiritual and the scientific to create a Ten-Step program for life. Wendell Thomas wrote that Paramahansa Yogananda's cult of the 1920s "abounds in such terms as electricity, vibration and evolution; will, concentration and meditation; consciousness, subconsciousness and superconsciousness; immanence, divinity and revelation. He is American in both the terseness of his style and the exuberance of his claims."[2] We may say the same of Chopra, a Punjabi doctor who is the Vivekananda of the New Age. Chopra fails even to mention the structural poverty of his homeland, nor does he offer any type of criticism of capitalism as Vivekananda did. He is now the complete stereotype willed upon India by U.S. orientalism, for he delivers just what is expected of a seer from the East. Chopra offers a way to be a better consumer and person within the system; his words resemble those of so many other charlatans whose snake oil only leads people toward further self-despair rather than solidarity.

In Vivekananda's wake, a host of Godmen came to the United

Swami Trigunatita, one of the Godmen, at a yoga class, California (1910). Courtesy of Vedanta Society of Northern California.

States. In 1902 Baba Bharati, by profession a journalist, migrated with a form of Vaishnavism that he taught from his Krishna temple in Los Angeles. Soon obscure Godmen encircled Hollywood, eager to heal the entertainers (who, in turn, sought to entertain an alienated population). Rishi Singh Gherwal taught yoga, and Sant Ram Mandal offered correspondence courses on the yogic sciences through his Universal Brotherhood Temple and School of Eastern Philosophy. Kedarnath Dasgupta attempted to unite the sundered East (spiritual) and West (practical) in his Threefold Movement based in his International School of Vedic and Allied Research. All this came to a head in the famous Self-Realization Fellowship and the Yogada-Sat-Sangh of Paramahansa Yogananda, who came to Los Angeles in 1925. These movements, like the Vedanta Society of America, remained small, and they cultivated devoted followings. The caesura in Asian migration did not stop the trickle of gurus from importing their version of the East into the heartland of alienation.

The proto–New Age found its market among the slowly

growing Beat generation. In New York City, the Japanese Zen master D. T. Suzuki lectured on Zen Buddhism to young Beats, themselves frustrated by the bureaucratically organized system of social life, by the shallowness of their social development, and by the overabundance of consumer goods produced to seduce them (like bread and circuses) into becoming consensual participants in the system.[3] Some of these disaffected young white people joined the ongoing Civil Rights and Free Speech movements; others adopted the cultural garb of the Beats and enjoyed a flirtation with the mysterious East. In 1952 Meher Baba's Hinduism began to address these Beats, but many got their first real dose of the "East" after 1959 when Maharishi Mahesh Yogi, a physics teacher, imported his transcendental meditation (TM) system to Hawaii and then to the mainland. Buddhism took root with the first Tibetan Buddhist monastery in the United States at Freewood Acres, New Jersey, in 1955, home to Robert Thurman, leading Buddhologist (and father of actress Uma Thurman).[4] Following TM, Swami Satchinananda founded the International Yoga Institute in the 1960s and preached hatha yoga. A. C. Bhaktivedanta, who once worked for a chemical company, created the International Society of Krishna Consciousness (ISKCON), the home of the Hare Krishnas, in New York City in 1965. In 1970 Swami Muktananda introduced siddha yoga, and a year later Maharaj Ji set up his Divine Light Mission.

The United States welcomed these gurus as a tonic against the disaffection produced first by abundance (during the boom cycle from 1945–67) and then by economic instability (after the start of stagflation from 1967 onward). The social discontent with economic surfeit was triggered by the long-term crisis generated by a collapse of the demand side (rising oil prices) and of the supply side (deterioration of productivity rates and labor unrest). "The economic malaise," noted *Fortune* magazine, "has manifested itself in two exceedingly distressing symptoms: rampant inflation and stagnating productivity."[5] The military-industrial U.S. state opted to address its crisis by making significant structural alterations, notably, ending its meager commitment to social welfare

policies, intensifying military Keynesianism, waging a tough battle
to reduce wages and labor benefits, and finally, offering incentives
to firms to move their shops overseas to states whose sovereignty
had already been compromised by U.S. military interventions
(Indonesia, Dominican Republic, Philippines). By the early 1970s
a considerable percentage of the assets of U.S. firms was located
outside its borders, including three-quarters of the electrical industry, half of the oil industry, and two-fifths of the consumer industry.[6] Finally, the uncertainty of the economy led to a brutalization
of the production process wherein capital attempted to increase
productivity without care for the increased alienation of the workforce on the shop floor.[7] The crisis is lingering as the United States
continues to attempt to stabilize the economy by cannibalizing its
resources, increasing the exploitation of overseas labor, and bor-
rowing from those foreign powers for whom it has become a mer-
cenary force (such as the oil sheikhs). I will return to the effects of
this stagflation on medicine in the United States. For now, it is
enough to see this as the context in which the hippies adopted
India to energize the proto–New Age.

The hippies turned to India as spirituality to seek an individual rather than collective experience, just as they conceptualized
their opposition to the system through sartorial and other effects.
Whereas the Beats turned to the artifacts of black culture in the
1950s, the hippies turned to the Amerindians and the Indians,
mainly, as Stuart Hall remarked, because of the militancy of black
liberation and the imputed perception of passivity among the
segregated Amerindians and the distant Indians.[8] Furthermore,
Harvey Cox shows the connection between the "turn on" of the
1960s (when Timothy Leary and Richard Alpert, or Baba Ram
Dass, began to experiment with psychedelic drugs) and the "turn
East" of the 1970s. "Both are a scream of longing for what a consumer culture cannot provide—a community of love and the capacity to experience things intensely. Both may supply temporary,
short-term relief," he noted, "but neither has the answer we need
so badly ourselves."[9] The hippie worldview saw the United States
as the industrial-consumer society par excellence and thereby as

the antithesis of spirituality (the nullity of the spiritual). India, on the other hand, was seen as the answer to the crisis of stagflation and social discontent, not in its economic policies but in its supposed spiritual social relations (a spirituality, by the way, that is conceptualized without any sense of India's colonial past). The young hippies, this "lumpen bourgeoisie," led a revolt "underpinned by privilege." Their "singular blend of eco and ego, of technologically minded worldliness and etherealism, of overripe self-consciousness and opulent complacency" enabled them to walk away from their system, a solution not available to those trapped within it.[10] The white, middle-class youth turned to various alternative traditions for sustenance, such as EST, Scientology, primal scream, and the Jesus revival. These youth, this me-Left, conducted an "apolitical withdrawal" into "organic food gardens and a life of sex, music and drugs," as well as India.[11] Leary and Baba Ram Dass, for example, reduced the complexity of Tibetan Buddhism and its Book of the Dead into a manual for enhanced hallucinogenic experiences.[12] Gita Mehta called this spiritualism karma cola, and John Lennon called it instant karma: instant gratification through oils, drugs, and other indulgences.[13] Two decades later Deepak Chopra arrived on the U.S. scene as the heir to this tradition, which ignores the complexity of social problems and offers banal solutions clothed in exotic garb. The Maharishi Mahesh Yogi taught the white youth to drop out, Bhagwan Shree Rajneesh turned them on, and Deepak Chopra came to heal their middle-aged bodies and their guilty minds.

India within black America, on the other hand, was engaged as a place from which to share ideas on social protest and the project of social justice.[14] The hippie turn to the East was not met with much enthusiasm by those who struggled for liberation, except insofar as black figures drew strength from Mao Tse-tung, Ho Chi Minh, and Jawaharlal Nehru. Revolutionaries like George Jackson found that the hippie rebellion opposed bourgeois mores but not white supremacy. There may have been many black people who participated in various ways with the exoticization of India (notably through the persistence of the dream books, an aid in the numbers business), but such participation was not the whole of the complex relationship with India produced by the Civil Rights movement. Certainly, Jimi Hendrix used Hindu calendar art iconography for the cover of his album *Axis: Bold as Love* (October 1967), but this seems to have been influenced primarily by his long stay in London, from 1965 until his death (England's own relationship with India was far different).

Of all the black musicians who turned frequently to India, John Coltrane was the most complex. Coltrane enjoyed a long friendship with the Indian sitarist Ravi Shankar (he named his son after him), and he adopted the raga key of G (one of the traditional Indian melodic patterns) for many of his tracks.[15] During a time of musical seclusion, Coltrane read deeply in the corpus of such people as Krishnamurti (the philosopher whose lectures filled auditoriums in the United States) and Paramahansa Yogananda (whose *Autobiography* Coltrane read in the mid-1960s). Alice Macleod (who played with Coltrane and later married him) was a devotee of Swami Satchinananda; she took the name Turiyasangitananda, founded a Vedanta center in California in 1975, and now spends much of her time in India. Coltrane's complex spirituality did not abandon the urges of liberation, a fact that led Ravi Shankar to leave one session in dismay, since "I was very much disturbed by his music. Here was a creative person who had become a vegetarian, who was studying yoga and reading the Bhagavad-Gita, yet in whose music I still heard much turmoil. I could not understand it."[16] Coltrane, despite his schooling in the arts of India, remained grounded in the class cultures of the United States, and he continued to express his link to the antiracist struggle in his soulful but turbulent passages.[17]

Less rich is the terrain upon which the hippies and New Age orientalism flourished. Rather than conduct a complete diagnosis of New Age orientalism (and its hip precursor), I shall offer a detailed analysis of the figure of Deepak Chopra in the 1990s, a study that must be located in terms of the crisis in allopathic medicine and the U.S. health care system. Chopra is not alone on the terrain of New Age orientalism. Much that I will say about him can fit such luminaries as Andrew Weil, the author of *Eight Weeks to Optimum Health,* who declared that "the book I most wish I'd written is *The Autobiography of a Yogi* by Paramahansa Yogananda, because then I would have had all of the fabulous experiences he described growing up in India in the early part of this century. Who would not want to have known genuine gurus and living saints?"[18] Like Chopra, Weil studied and worked in the finest allopathic medical institutes (Harvard and the National Institute of Mental Health) before deserting them to work within the subset of New Age orientalism known as "alternative Medicine." My analysis of Chopra would fit people such as Weil accurately, although there is something of interest in Chopra's South Asian background. It is hard to argue that Chopra is simply misinformed about the reality of India (as some do in defense of orientalism). Rather, I will show that the flaw in Chopra's philosophy lies not in any lack of information but in the very enterprise produced by New Age orientalism.

Allopathic medicine is based on two Cartesian binaries: the first, between mind and body (so that the body is treated in isolation from its social and psychosocial settings), and the second, between the subject and the object (so that the doctor, the knowing subject, can study the body, the object, without any fundamental interaction with the patient). These principles came under attack from the homeopaths, notably their founder, Samuel Hahnemann. He believed that disease is a matter of spirit, not of the physics of the body. Hahnemann created a clinical practice based on the law of similars (hence, "homeopathy") in which the patients are given minute doses of exactly what ails them in order to tackle a suppressed itch, or "psore." Homeopathy demanded a close patient-doctor relationship, and it opposed the pharmacological excesses that had already begun to mark allopathy in the nineteenth century. Allopathy (cure by opposites) relies on fighting symptoms with strong medicines that withstand clinical trials to show their efficacy. The allopaths took over the American Medical Association (AMA), expelled the homeopaths, and began a long march toward our current medical crisis.[19]

Without a doubt, treating symptoms with heavy doses of medication does succeed in its objective (that is, to alleviate the symptoms), but it fails to vanquish the causes of illness. Chopra's writings hinge on this critique of allopathy. An endocrinologist trained at the prestigious All-India Institute of Medical Science in New Delhi, Chopra taught allopathic medicine at Tufts University, Boston University School of Medicine, and was chief of staff at New England Memorial Hospital. He described allopathic treatment thus: "If you can't sleep at night, there's a sleeping pill. It will cure insomnia. You're feeling anxious? There's a tranquilizer. It will give you tranquility. You have an infection? Take an antibiotic. It will cure the problem of infection. You have cancer? There's chemotherapy, radiation, surgery. If you have chest pain, you can pop some nitroglycerin. Better still, have a bypass operation." This approach, he argued, "relieves symptoms or at best masks symptoms while the underlying process remains unchanged. Sometimes they interfere with mechanisms of disease. And mostly scientific research today is basically elucidating mechanisms of disease."[20]

Chopra follows a romantic tradition that includes Mahatma Gandhi, whose 1908 critique of modern civilization extended to allopathic medicine. "I have indulged in vice. I contract a disease, a doctor cures me, the odds are that I shall repeat the vice. Had the doctor not intervened, nature would have done its work, and I would have acquired mastery over myself, would have been freed from vice and would have been happy."[21] Gandhi assumed that all disease and illness is a result of individual initiative. He did not believe that industrial wastes and other such agents were mainly responsible for the rot in our bodies. Certain things cannot be controlled by powerless individuals who must negotiate powerful and malevolent forces. Chopra and Gandhi unraveled allopathy at its most vulnerable point. Nevertheless, treating symptoms is neither easy nor is it always successful. Many illnesses cannot be cured by allopathy, but the science can help those afflicted live with their trials or at the very most, contain the illness. Just a century ago, many of the problems that clinical and surgical skills and technologies now tackle with ease could not be solved. Instrumental science and medicine divided medical problems into discrete entities to study them in detail. These studies form the bedrock of contemporary medicine, and it is their collective wisdom that enables us to solve dramatic problems. Instrumental success, however, does not negate the problems that persist within the framework of allopathy, problems that render the science open to vital epistemological criticism.

New Age orientalists, like Chopra, make one such criticism: that the science fails to deal with the psychosocial context of a patient's life. This is important, although Chopra makes the monist error of locating illness and treatment in the domain of the individual patient alone rather than in the entire social milieu. I must make one additional criticism of the medical industry before I move on to an analysis of Chopra's New Age orientalism. This has to do both with the uneven delivery of medical technology and with the elitist manner in which disproportionate amounts of medical research is aimed at finding solutions to diseases that affect a relatively small number of the rich (for example, Lyme disease) while disproportionately small amounts are devoted to those that affect huge numbers of the poor (for example, malaria). The notion of "health problem" was reframed in the United States to encompass and stress chronic illnesses (such as cancer, heart disease, obesity, and neurosis) and to minimize infectious diseases (no longer thought to be dangers). The American Medical Association recently reported that 90 million people (about 40 percent of the U.S. population) suffer from some chronic disease.[22] With funding moving toward remediation of chronic ailments, basic health needs are avoided (thereby exacerbating chronic illness) by the medical industry, itself an enormous business in the United States. Since the 1940s the U.S. health infrastructure has expanded dramatically. In 1941 the state spent $18 million on health care, but in one decade its outlay for health care increased to $181 million. From the mid-1960s to 1975, the health industry achieved major results. Death rates dropped by 14 percent, heart disease by 23 percent, infant mortality by 38 percent, and maternal mortality by 71 percent. Among the bourgeoisie, basic life-threatening infectious diseases have disappeared. Among the working class, such basic health problems as influenza, pneumonia, asthma, cerebral palsy, diphtheria, and pertussis continued, largely because of the neglect of the poor by the medical-industrial complex.[23]

In 1968 Martin Luther King Jr., noted that "medical care is virtually out of the reach of millions of black and white poor. They are aware of the great advances of medical sciences—heart transplants, miracle drugs—but their children still die of preventable diseases, and even suffer brain damage due to protein deficiency."[24] As a profit machine, the ensemble of profit (Hospital Corporation of America, Humana) and nonprofit (Kaiser Foundation, Sisters of Mercy) hospitals attempt to keep balanced books and thereby to discourage preventive treatment, which is expensive in the short term (though cost effective in the long run).

> Privately insured patients can be charged what the market will bear. When a hospital has empty beds, Medicare and Medicaid patients are better than cold sheets, and Humana charges off every penny of overhead on them the government will allow. But if it isn't trying to fill a lot of empty beds, Humana treats as few of those patients as possible. Humana prefers to own facilities in suburbs where young working families are having lots of babies. Though young people use hospitals less than the elderly, they are more likely to be privately insured and in need of surgery, which makes the most money. The babies provide a second generation of customers.[25]

Given this structural analysis, the medical-industrial complex cannot hope to be an agent of healing. It obscures its own structural logic behind sappy brochures, but it also obscures social-structural problems (such as poverty produced by capitalism) and reduces them to medical problems, for which it can bill the government and the burgeoning insurance sector.[26] The failure of medicine to deal with the effects of a crisis in the economy meant that the science was both charged with an impossible task and then blamed for its inevitable failure.

Paul Starr, who has studied the history of U.S. medicine in detail, argues that since the 1970s, when "antibiotics were providing effective therapeutic means for treating infectious diseases, chronic illness [has] reengaged medicine intimately in questions of social behavior and moral choice."[27] Certainly, abstinence from cigarettes will reduce the risk of lung cancer, but those who suffer from chronic asthma or pneumonia require better housing and better urban environments, not a powerless charter for self-healing. The poor cannot simply walk away from their social conditions. They require the means to liberate themselves from disease, and these cannot be reduced to social behavior and individual choice. As I will show, New Age orientalists join with the allopaths in demanding that the poor take responsibility for their health, rather than arguing that the poor already bear that responsibility, but without any power. A nineteenth-century tradition in the United States called therapeutic nihilism argued that the cure of disease was best left to nature and to Providence. This approach returned in the 1970s, but with a twist: Disease should be left not only to nature and Providence but also to the care of the isolated self.

The core of Deepak Chopra's ideas stem from this premise, that the individual must not attempt to overcome trials but, rather, must envelop him- or herself in them. "Don't struggle against the infinite scheme of things," he wrote in 1993; "instead, be at one with it."[28] The individual must ignore social connectedness and revel in interiority. Interior knowledge (consciousness) is the source of reality for Chopra; therefore, it is in this realm that change must be effected. "The source of all creation is pure consciousness," he wrote, not labor or nature. To find paradise, then, the seeker must look within. "When you discover your essential nature and know who you really are," Chopra wrote, "in that knowing itself is the ability to fulfill any dream you have, because you are the eternal possibility, the immeasurable potential of all that was, is, and will be."[29] The social world is trivial, since "you alone are the judge of your worth: and your goal is to discover infinite worth in yourself, no matter what anyone else thinks."[30] The fundamental interconnectedness between individuals is irrelevant here, since they are treated as means toward the realization of an atomized individual existence. The irony of this position is that the turn to New Age orientalist thought is intended to respond to the crisis of atomization and of the alienation of the psyche from social existence.[31] The world and its problems must be shunned. Our racist world divides us into various "races" or "ethnicities" to differentiate fundamentally between peoples. Chopra walks away from such real social divisions and offers us a set of neutral divisions called "essences" that tell us about something inherent in our beings. These "essences" facilitate easy marketing, since we are urged to buy products related to our inherent slot (this resembles the idea of skin tones in the cosmetics industry). Chopra preaches a freedom that says good riddance to the real world and offers an imaginary freedom of the spirit. The conditions and circumstances that fetter real, living, embodied individuals are cast aside, and our imaginary, bourgeois selves are asked to be indulgent, pleasant, and nonconfrontational. Freedom, for Chopra, is the freedom to forget and to ignore. This, as we will see, is an inadequate approach to our social turmoil.

Not only does Chopra ask us to shun the world and its problems, but he also encourages us to ignore all philosophies and explanations of the world. "Pay attention to your inner life so that you can be guided by intuition rather than by externally imposed interpretations of what is or isn't good for you."[32] Since the isolated individual is the world, then, he holds, the only theory necessary to change the world is an internal theory, and the only struggle takes place in what Chopra calls the "mirror of relationships."[33] After an attack on theory as such, Chopra makes the typical contradictory move toward an abandonment of engagement. Do not bother to argue and to convince others, he himself argues, for "judgment imposes right and wrong on situations that just are."[34] "I will feel no need to convince or persuade others to accept my point of view," he preaches.[35] The state of pure interiority that he advocates allows the isolated individual to forget the historical production of inequality and of suffering and, tragically, to take complete responsibility for the detritus of history. "Live in the present, for that is the only moment you have"; and further, "healthy people live neither in the past nor in the future. They live in the present, in the now, which gives the now a flavor of eternity because no shadow falls across it."[36] Avoid fear, Chopra admonishes, because it is the "product of memory, which dwells in the past."[37] Fear and history lead to anger and other emotions integral for social protest, but this is contrary to the mind-body thought of Chopra, whose characterization of these human emotions is stunning: "When you find yourself reacting with anger or opposition to any person or circumstance, realize that you are only struggling with yourself."[38] But there is no way to express one's distress at the world without anger. Therefore, if one feels in any way unhappy, there is no need to seek its causes outside, for they are probably lodged deep in the unhappy consciousness of the discrete individual. Chopra counsels us to take resonsibility, echoing the neoconservatives who suggest that social problems can be solved not by the state or by social engineering but by "personal responsibility" and by the production of virtue. "I know that taking responsibility," he wrote, "means not blaming anyone or anything for my situation (and this includes myself)."[39] These words are cheap. The poor and the working class are both responsible and virtuous, but they have no means to liberate themselves from the circumstances and conditions that chain them to the struggle for survival.[40] Chopra, like Francis Fukuyama and Dinesh D'Souza, is merely condescending to those who recognize clearly that they must be their own liberation, but who realize they must do so not only by remaking themselves but by organizing and uniting to confront an antagonistic state and economy.

Liberalism, for all its failings, encourages a sense of guilt toward the poor and a call to act charitably. Chopra's guru, Maharishi Mahesh Yogi, took a very different position toward the poor and the working classes. In 1967, during the Summer of Love, Maharishi Mahesh Yogi gave a revealing press conference in New York City. "The hungry of India, China, anywhere," he noted, "are lazy because of their lack of self-knowledge. We will teach them to derive from within, and then they will find food."[41] Four months before the World Food Conference in Rome in November 1974, the CIA noted that because of grain shortages induced by the shifting cultivation patterns due to the uneven terms of trade "Washington would acquire life and death power over the fate of the multitudes of the needy."[42] These details did not enter the worldview of the guru, who was content with the imaginary freedom for sale to the disenchanted bourgeois. Some reporters found the Maharishi's statement to be unacceptable, and one asked, "Do we have to ignore the poor to achieve inner peace?" The Yogi answered, "Like a tree in the middle of a garden, should we be liberal and allow the water to flow to other trees, or should we drink ourselves and be green?" "But isn't this selfish?" "Be absolutely selfish. That is the only way to bring peace, to be selfish, and if one does not have peace, how is one to help others attain it?"[43] Chopra is not very different. One might expect his Law of Giving to contain a call for charity, but his notion of a gift is once more indulgent. "Wherever I go, and whoever I encounter, I will bring them a gift. The gift may be a compliment, a flower, or a prayer." These neither feed nor clothe anyone. Further, "I will make a commitment to keep wealth circulating in my life by giving and receiving life's most precious gifts: the gifts of caring, affection, appreciation and love." He will give important emotional gifts, but he will be ready to accept "all the gifts that life has to offer me."[44] Of obligations, a classic liberal trope, we hear nothing. Of the poor, we get an idealized picture that rivals Mother Teresa for condescension.[45] "On his many travels to India, [his son] Gautama has witnessed the harsh reality of the street children who have no belongings other than their beautiful souls. In India, even amidst the immense poverty and destitute conditions, one finds in the children no trace of violence, no hostility, no rage, no anger. There is a simple, sweet innocence even among the extremely impoverished."[46] The poor cease to be human with the capacity to struggle and to aspire; they appear as contented people willing to sacrifice their material well-being for the spiritual happiness the bourgeois tourist wants them to enjoy. If the poor are unhappy, it ruins the tour as well as the image of the spiritual East.[47]

If the Maharishi and Chopra only preached a form of individualist asceticism grounded in a moral ethos, then we might be less concerned. However, they are not themselves otherworldly. These gurus of the green have formed various empires through which they flog the idea that the unfortunate are lazy people whose salvation can only come from personal responsibility; all the while, the gurus themselves are making much money and helping corporations staff their offices with a pliable and healthy workforce.[48] Rajneesh stated clearly that the "materially poor can never become spiritual," a reversal of Christian asceticism and of the earlier orientalist position held by the Transcendentalists. But he goes further, for he not only holds that "socialism is impotent," but that "capitalism is not an ideology, it is not imposed on the society, it is a natural growth." Capitalism, for Rajneesh, "simply gives you the freedom to be yourself, that's why I support it."[49] Capitalism and New Age orientalism embrace each other. In 1971 the Maharishi founded the Maharishi International University, but on 27 July 1995 he renamed it the Maharishi University of Management (MUM). The name change is significant, its president, Bevan Morris, explained, because MUM would "apply knowledge to practicalities" and to "practical, professional values. This name [MUM] will also be inspiring throughout the world, as everywhere there is a demand for the knowledge of management—management of business, management of government, management of information, management of health, management of education, management of environment, management of scientific innovation and new technologies, and management of consciousness and creativity and the whole quality of life on earth." A kindred movement, the Rajneesh/Osho group, runs what amounts to a "Club Meditation" on its 126-square-mile ranch in Oregon.[50] Its leader, Swami Prem Jayesh (a Canadian real estate tycoon who was once Michael William O'Byrne) holds management courses on the premises for laid-off executives so that they can "release *that tourism isn't only an escape from place like local to the exotic) but also time (Modern world to ahistorical history ?)*

anger from their systems." The Osho "results seminars" net between $15 million and $45 million per year from clients such as BMW. IBM executives are by now familiar with the New Age, for some senior officers joined AT&T and General Motors managers in New Mexico in July 1986 to discuss the value of metaphysics, the occult, and Hindu mysticism to "aid businessmen in an increasingly competitive marketplace."[51] The motto of such management retraining camps might well be "Don't worry, be happy," the syrupy lyric from Bobby McFerrin's 1988 album *Simple Pleasures,* released at a time of grave economic insecurity in the United States.

One must keep in mind that these developments have occurred alongside the Men's Movement and the general antifeminist backlash that misrecognizes the monopolization of corporate power as a decline of man's power in the home. Ronald Inden argued that the Chopra-type approach attempts to produce a "new Western man" who has benefited from the spiritual East and the material West. This man "can, by signing up with the Jungians or other gurus of the New Age movement, come to know and, as a result, fine-tune his psyche. Not only can the harassed corporate executive adjust to the stress he suffers, he can cultivate a part of his self that stands outside the modern world, expressing itself in those exotic anti-commodities, the vacation to the Orient or the Tibetan sculpture on the coffee table."[52] Inden, of course, is being wry. Just as managers are being retrained, so too are workers being urged to work without protest. "My work is my worship, my meditation," said one Rajneeshi.[53] Beyond the economic discipline of unemployment and the political discipline of incarceration sits the spiritual discipline of worship. We must work without anger, without reproach.[54]

Apart from making disgruntled managers and workers at peace with the system, the Chopra philosophy also aims to develop a savvy and healthy consumer who is neither an ascetic nor an environmentalist (who would have to feel anger). Chopra critiques consumption patterns in the United States but not bourgeois consumerism itself. He warns his followers against toxins, a key word in the New Age movement. "Don't contaminate your body with toxins, either food, drink or toxic emotions. Your body is more than a life-support system. It is the vehicle that will carry you on the journey of your evolution."[55] Eat and drink with care, but do not shun material success and gluttony. In March 1996 Chopra's *Seven Spiritual Laws of Success* reached the *New York Times* best-seller list; by May it headed the list. Chopra wrote that "material abundance, in all its expressions, happens to be one of those things that makes the journey more enjoyable. But success also includes good health, energy and enthusiasm for life, fulfilling relationships, creative freedom, emotional and psychological stability, a sense of well-being and peace of mind." Further, "success is the ability to fulfill your desires with effortless ease."[56] Chopra is a successful man with a host of successful Hollywood friends. Recently, he brought his friends together to produce a two-volume compact disc inspired by the poems of Rumi. (One of Chopra's friends, stunningly, is Rosa Parks).[57] Chopra's friends are the 1990s equivalent of the Maharishi's 1960s friends the Beach Boys, the Beatles, Donovan, Mia Farrow, and her sister Prudence (for whom John Lennon wrote "Dear Prudence" in Rishikesh in 1968).

In the midst of these friends, Chopra wrote a book entitled *Creating Affluence* (1993) in which he shows us how to enlarge our "wealth consciousness." You may ask what this "consciousness" is to be. Chopra's book tells us that "affluence, unboundedness and abundance are our natural state. We just need to restore the memory of what we already know."[58] "I live in an abundant universe," cried Rajneesh, "I always have everything I need."[59] To posit a natural state has been a well-established rhetorical strategy since Aristotle, but to claim that abundance is the state of a primordial nature is to go against every historiographical tradition. What kind of abundance? Was it equitable? There is little evidence of any of this. Chopra has no interest in the intricacies of these questions and explains that wealth consciousness "implies absence of money worries. Truly wealthy people never worry about losing their money because they know that wherever money comes from there is an inexhaustible supply of it."[60] Obviously Chopra knows nothing of the shenanigans of people such as Bunker Hunt, Donald Trump, and Charles Keating, who not only live up to F. Scott Fitzgerald's comment that the "rich are not like us," but also work very hard to preserve their enormous wealth.[61] Chopra conducts his form of Indian healing for these renegade cowboy capitalists. For working people, Chopra also has some advice. He asks them to squander their own dreams and work hard so that the bourgeoisie may realize their dreams (hardly novel in our own times). "Helping others make money and helping other people to fulfill their desires is a sure way to ensure you'll make money for yourself as well as more easily fulfill your own dreams."[62] Despite his lack of any training in economics, Chopra neatly enunciates the supply-side, trickle-down doctrines made famous in the 1980s.[63] Freedom, for Chopra, is the freedom to buy and sell and to choose from an abundant marketplace without consideration for the poverty of the masses, for whom consumption and choice are a mockery. His is not a freedom from the bondage of necessity, a freedom to dream and to struggle to control one's destiny.

Chopra bases his medical practice on the wisdom of *ayurveda* (the science of life), whose principle text is Agnivesa's eighth-century B.C.E. manuscript, revised by Caraka some centuries later. Chopra met this medical tradition through Maharishi Mahesh Yogi, the exponent of Maharishi Vedic medicine, which is practiced at his College of Maharishi Vedic Medicine at MUM as "Maharishi Ayurveda." In 1992 Chopra founded the American Association of Ayurvedic Medicine, he was appointed to the National Institutes of Health's Ad Hoc Panel on Alternative Medicine, he became the executive director of the Sharp Institute for Human Potential and Mind-Body Medicine, he took on the role of chief consultant to the Center for Mind-Body Medicine, and he became involved with the Ayurveda and Indic Traditions of Healthcare working group of the Dharam Hinduja Indic Research Center at Columbia University.[64] Chopra has written a manifesto on Maharishi Ayurveda in which he lays out the mind-body theory at length.[65] In this tradition, the mind and body are integral to one another; to treat one, the doctor must treat the other. This is an important but abstract proposition. Rather than delve into its intricacies,[66] it might be more useful here to assess the way Chopra ignores the social dimension that is heralded by Agnivesa's text.

Agnivesa, unlike Chopra, offered a social analysis that demonstrated his own limitations. Like the protagonist of the *Kama-Sutra* of Vatsyayana, Agnivesa's patient is the *nagaraka* (citizen) who is a rich and cultured man.[67] After an extended description of the apparatus needed to heal patients, the text notes that "by this method, the King, the Kingly and those having immense wealth can be treated with evacuatives."[68] The text does not avoid the poor, for even they require medication and the doctor must facilitate them with whatever means can be applied. "The poor too in case of a disorder requiring evacuation may take the drug even without collecting the rare equipments. . . . Because all men do not have all the requisite means . . . Hence one should take, in case of affliction, the treatment and also the cloths and diets according to his means." Further, the text recognizes that all people do not get the same diseases, since these are themselves class-marked: "The severe diseases do not attack the poor ones," it says.[69] Of course, the poor get severe diseases, but these are not under the text's purview. For Agnivesa's text, the social world must not be neglected in favor of the individual embodied psyche. Rather, while studying the cause of an illness, the text recommends that the doctor collect "knowledge about the patient (these things are considered) such as—in what type of land the patient is born, grown or diseased."[70] This knowledge recognizes that the social is a component of disease and ailment.

Chopra's method, on the contrary, takes the mind-body complex and reduces the "body" to the physical parts of the individual rather than seeing it as the social totality. By reducing the body to the individual body, Chopra can ignore irrefutable social factors that produce social problems, and he can locate the etiology of the problems in the mind-body complex (the individual), which is all that then needs to be treated. Chopra draws from a vast corpus of ancient wisdom on healing, but he makes of the corpus marketable indulgences that are sold to a harassed elite

indulgence
indigue
inwilte
or
vacaho~

and middle-class who want to relax but not to change what makes them tense. He has written books on how to lose weight—a topic alien to the world of Agnivesa—on insomnia, and on digestive problems.[71] Chopra offers a melange of treatments, many of which draw from the types of indulgences made common during the me-decade of the 1970s: aromatherapy, music therapy, bliss technique, diets, pulse diagnosis, primordial sound, panchakarma (laxative use, enema use, and massage), hatha yoga, and transcendental meditation (my information does not show that he teaches the Sidhi program of yogic flying, but we know that at MUM students take these classes to "produce maximum coherence in brain functioning" and "moral reasoning").[72]

Another problem with the Chopra method is that it borrows uncritically from a text that clearly belonged to a socioeconomic order that saw society as an ensemble of status groups, whether *jatis, varnas,* or *gotras* (all ancient forms of social organization). One must be careful of translating its doctrine into a world whose leading ideas are democracy and equity (even though these are often toothless slogans).[73] Further, Agnivesa's text is fundamentally misogynist, for the women depicted therein are dangerous and require control; the text notes that the reader "should not have too much faith in them."[74] Not only does Chopra not engage in productive criticism of the book (and draw out a mind-body theory that is not sexist), but he also ignores those values of noblesse oblige enunciated by Agnivesa that made the hierarchy livable. "One should take up those means of livelihood which are not contradictory to dharma (social and religious) ethics. Likewise, he should pursue a life of peace and study. Thus he enjoys happiness," says Agnivesa. "Life is said to be beneficial if the person is a well-wisher of all the creatures, abstaining from taking other's possessions, is truth-speaking, calm, takes steps after examining the situation, free from carelessness."[75] Without even these noble statements, the doctrines of Chopra and the other New Age orientalists appear to want the mechanics of ancient wisdom but not their ethical basis. This might, to some extent, explain the undemocratic nature of many of these organizations that rely upon enforced subjugation to a charismatic guru rather than upon democratic principles. Certainly, the undemocratic nature explains the corruption at the heart of such cults as ISKCON's New Vrindaban Community in Virginia (called the Palace of Gold) from which Srila Bhaktipada (Keith Ham) ran a criminal empire. Recent revelations of child abuse at ISKCON schools offer further indications of the authoritarian "culture and structure" of the organization.[76]

New Age orientalism is no less a circus than was the pageantry of Barnum. Maharishi Mahesh Yogi planned to build Maharishi Veda Land near Niagara Falls, Ontario, with such rides as the Magic Flying Chariot and the Corridor of Time. The complex was to have "the world's only levitating building," but thus far nothing has emerged (the mayor of the city wonders "if the Veda Land folks are working on a different time frame than the rest of us").[77] In both, India is exotic and spiritual. Within the framework of New Age orientalism, the Indian is seen as intensely spiritual and apolitical, as noble but silent, as knowledgeable but not cosmopolitan. The Indian is a passive character absorbed in the pursuit of pleasure and success without a developed social consciousness, one who embodies the script of U.S. orientalism from its dawn to its yawn. This is a narrow vision of a human being that does not say much of the lives of the real, living Indians, of whom there are now more than a million healthy and sick bodies in the United States. To them let us turn, to see what those lives are able to produce in the vise of orientalism.

OF THE ORIGIN OF DESIS AND SOME

PRINCIPLES OF STATE SELECTION

Culture shock is not your reflex upon leaving the dock;
it is when you have been a law-abiding citizen
for more than ten years: when someone asks your name
and the name of your religion and your first thought is
I don't know, or you can't remember what you said last time;
you think there is something you forgot to sign:
your oath, for one; and you are positive
that those green-shirted workmen in the room right now
want to take you in for questioning.

—Reetika Vazirani, "Ras Mohan"

On 24 July 1997, Susan Au Allen, of the U.S. Pan Asian American Chamber of Commerce, told the House Committee on Small Business (Subcommittee on Empowerment) that "one of our [Asian American] enduring beliefs is that hard work brings rewards. That is why so many of us pursue higher education. We also place great value in individual responsibility and entrepreneurship." Allen offered, in precis, the values associated with the model minority concept, values fashioned three decades ago by the U.S. media. A few years ago, Representative Richard Gephardt noted that Indian Americans are both "highly talented" and "very successful."[1] Or even more egregiously, Bill Gates of Microsoft visited India (where he received a *royal* reception) on 3–4 March 1997. During his trip, he intoned that South Indians are the second-smartest people on the planet (for those who are guessing, he rated the Chinese as the smartest; those who continue to guess should note that white people, like Gates, do not get classified, since it is the white gaze, in this incarnation, that is transcendental and able to do the classifying!). The generic assumption in these statements is that Asians (in general) and South Asians (in particular) are especially endowed with an ability to be technically astute hard workers. The implication is that the high proportion of Asians in the technical fields says something about Asians' nature rather than about their recent cultural history. No explanation is offered for the poverty in the subcontinent, poverty that cannot be overcome despite the inhabitants' "genetic brilliance." As a tonic against the racial determinists and their cognates, the "cultural" determinists (who tend to slide uneasily into the same conclusions as the former), I will consider a version of the cultural history of desis in the United States.

The gestures of Allen, Gephardt, Gates, and their ilk will be further explained through an analysis of the complex immigration policy of advanced capitalist countries, a policy that attempts to manage a contradiction between extant domestic unemployment and continued immigration. Why continue to allow migrants into the country if the unemployment rate has reached double digits in most states?[2] Capital relishes immigrant workers from zones of exploitation, since many of them work for lower wages and their immigrant status renders them less able to be critical than enfranchised workers. The migrant workers can be controlled by the discipline of tenuousness: If you are feisty you are fired, and not just into the labor market to seek alternative employment but out of the country. Import of workers classically allows firms to increase their profits, since these workers are paid lower wages. These workers are also cheaper than enfranchised workers because the education of the former is financed elsewhere, as is their retirement and unemployment compensation (this follows from the expectation that the immigrant worker will return home after several productive years at work).[3] The U.S. state adopted the policy of using foreign workers in its Contract Labor Law (1864), which legalized an earlier arrangement by which contractors went to Europe and Asia to recruit workers on what were virtually indenture contracts. In the 1860s there was even a suggestion made to flood the U.S. South with South and East Asian workers to shift the blacks from the land and to undermine their power as newly freed peoples.[4] Throughout U.S. history, immigrant workers have been used as docile and cheap technical workers (the bulk of South Asian migration since 1965 falls in this category) and manual laborers (as in the influx of migrants from the exploited Third World in recent decades).[5] Both of these reasons share one underlying theme, that the United States wants these workers for their labor, but certainly not for the lives they must import as well. Our exploration of the arrival of South Asians in the United States will be keen to this problematic.

The first desis came to North America in the late 1700s not as migrants but as workers on the Yankee clipper ships that traded between New England and India. A few lascars (sailors) jumped ship, married black women, and disappeared from the historical record. Attempts to find their descendants in the Salem region have yielded nothing. Decades later, more desis arrived in the Americas, but this time in the West Indies as indentured laborers. Of the 5 million who left the subcontinent to work on the plantations of the British Empire, about half a million came to the Caribbean and South America to join the recently freed African slaves in a "new system of slavery."[6] Other desis migrated to southern and eastern Africa as dukawallas (Swahili for shopkeeper), using their extensive contacts in the Indian Ocean trade to insert themselves into the interstices of the colonial economy. Commercial niches abandoned by the colonial state and by imperial capital, such as shopkeeping in the interior, trading in petty commodities, and processing cotton for export, became the preserve of the Indian merchant.[7]

In the wake of the indenture migration came a "tide of turbans" to the western coast of North America. More than six thousand Punjabis (mostly men) entered the United States and Canada from the late 1800s to 1920. They went to work on the farms of California and in the timber industry of the northwest. Run out of Bellingham, Washington, in September 1907, reviled by Samuel Gompers's American Federation of Labor, and denounced by the Asiatic Exclusion League, the Punjabis married Mexicans, formed the revolutionary Ghadar Party (in May 1913), and challenged white supremacy at every opportunity.[8] Attempts to become small farmers ended with the enactment of the 1913 Alien Land Law, and attempts to become citizens crashed with an unfavorable verdict in the 1923 *United States v. Bhagat Singh Thind* (this case claimed that "white person," as far as eligibility for citizenship went, meant immigrants from northwestern Europe).[9] The next year, the National Origins Act effectively shut the door to further migration from the subcontinent to the United States. In 1946 the United States enacted minuscule quotas that allowed a small number of desis to immigrate, but only a few came. For its low-wage agricultural workers, the United States now relied upon indentured workers from Mexico and the Caribbean brought in through the Bracero Program (in which the United States brought in 4 million farmworkers to work on short-term contracts in 1942–64, but also in its variant from 1917–22). For its industrial expansion, business enterprises and urban municipalities relied upon the migration from country to town (especially the trek north by black workers). There was no reason for the state to allow Asians into the country, since sufficient cheap labor was now available. When Dilip Singh Saund (D–Calif.) entered Congress in 1956 (the first Asian American to do so), the desi population was small and invisible. This was all about to change in 1965.

The story actually began in 1957. The USSR launched *Sputnik I* and *II* into orbit and began a panic in the United States.

Indian immigrants, Vancouver, British Columbia (early 1900s). Courtesy of Vancouver Public Library, Vancouver, British Columbia, Canada.

The rockets, it was said, launched "a challenge to our nation's existence," this time from "barbarism armed with Sputniks."[10] John Gunther remarked that "for a generation it had been part of the American folklore that Russians were hardly capable of operating a tractor." Now it seemed the USSR might launch an intercontinental ballistic missile (ICBM) into the heartland. The U.S. state entered a moral panic that would not subside until the moon landing in July 1969.[11] The USSR appeared to be more technologically advanced than the United States. The state and its emissaries tried to rouse the U.S. population from its consumerism to train for technical and military combat against the Soviets. This was a tall order, since in many ways the 1950s was a decade of indulgence. For white boys, the "nerd" was a figure of ridicule and the "rebel" (à la James Dean and Marlon Brando) an icon of a disenchanted youth. "In our society," Paul Goodman wrote in a landmark book of the times, "bright lively children, with the potentiality for knowledge, noble ideals and honest effort, and some kind of worthwhile achievement, are transformed into useless and cynical bipeds, or decent young men trapped or early resigned, whether in or out of the organized system."[12] After *Sputnik,* the U.S. government tried to promote the study of science and technology through an enhanced National Science Foundation and by such local projects as the "math bees." U.S. science, however, relied upon immigrants from the 1940s, refugees such as Albert Einstein and Enrico Fermi (in 1957, two Chinese American physicists won the Nobel Prize), but also Nazis like Wernher von Braun.

When the cosmonaut Yury Gagarin orbited the earth in 1961, the urgency to expand its own space and weapons industry encouraged the U.S. state to consider the immediate importation of technical labor. On 23 July 1963 President John F. Kennedy informed the legislature that he wanted to see the immigration system overhauled so that "highly trained or skilled persons may obtain a preference without requiring that they secure employment here before emigrating." This, he felt, would attract "talented people who would be helpful to our economy and our culture." A year later, Representative Emmanuel Celler (D.–N.Y.) submitted a new immigration bill to the House so that the United States might attract "highly skilled aliens whose services were urgently needed."[13] There was an additional political reason to amend the immigration policy: to end the prevailing belief that the United States was a racist nation. Discrimination based on national origins, Representative Spark Masayugi Matsunaga (D.–Hawaii) told the House Judiciary Committee on 30 June 1964, provided the basis for "Communist propaganda and creates a suspicion among our Asian friends about the motives of the United States."[14] In 1958 Kennedy, at least, forthrightly condemned the racist immigration policy. In a caricature of the Emma Lazarus poem inscribed on the pedestal of the Statue of Liberty, Kennedy wrote that "as long as they come from Northern Europe, are not too tired or poor or slightly ill, never stole a loaf of bread, never joined any questionable organization, and can document their activities for the past two years," let them enter. The "indefensible racial preference," he said, had to end.[15] In 1965 Congress passed the Immigration and Nationality Act that reunited families (mainly of southern Europe), allowed epileptic patients to immigrate, and encouraged skilled labor to enter the United States to fill the U.S. need for more technical manpower.[16] By 1965 the United States was looking not just for scientists but also for medical personnel to fill an increased demand for doctors to staff the Medicare and Medicaid programs recently legislated by Congress.

Between 1966 and 1977, of the Indian Americans who migrated to the United States, 83 percent entered under the occupational category of professional and technical workers (roughly 20,000 scientists with Ph.D.'s, 40,000 engineers, and 25,000 doctors).[17] These early migrations of technical workers came mainly from India, which is why I will spend some time on that country. The sheer number of technical workers startles most people, and many assume that Indians are genetically predisposed to the scientific and medical professions. This is not so. The historiography on science in the subcontinent validates the perspective offered by Joseph Needham of the differential traditions of science developed in separate but related cultural zones for various institutional, material, and cultural reasons. There are scientific traditions in every human society, although these traditions develop from various epistemological standpoints.[18] The work of Debiprasad Chattopadhyaya illustrates the cultivation of specific abstract sciences in the subcontinent's ancient past, heritages that were continued by scholars influenced by the Arabic traditions. During British rule this scientific legacy was devalued and neglected, to be replaced by a scientific tradition (built on many of the insights of the Indo-Arabic tradition) that was wedded to the gains, in some measure, of imperialism.[19] In 1947, months before he became prime minister of independent India, Jawaharlal Nehru noted that the "new India" was to be closely linked to the world of science, not for individual truth but to alleviate the misery of the masses. He told the Indian Science Congress that "a free and self-reliant India" had to be built, an India that would go beyond its gains in theoretical physics and move toward technology for the masses. "If we could tap, say, even five percent of the latent talent in India for scientific purposes," he noted, "we could have a host of scientists in India."[20]

The nascent state worked through the All India Council of Technical Education (1946) and the Scientific Manpower Committee (1947) to extend the number of technical institutions and to create a culture of science in the country. In 1947, 38 scientific and technical institutions trained 2,940 students; by 1961, 102 institutions trained 13,820 students. This rate of growth continues to the present day.[21] There is a prejudice in India toward science, so that most students (male and female) both respect those who study science and appreciate national and personal gains in scientific achievement. In recent years there has been a valorization of the business arts, but this seems to be a development in certain elite schools rather than an overall shift in the interests of college-age students.

For a variety of reasons, technical workers, trained by the good graces of the socialistic Indian state, decided to travel overseas for work. The migration out of South Asia after the creation of independent states appears to be of a different piece from the indentured migrations of earlier years. The post–World War II migration sees itself as a movement of population and not as a migration of labor, even though this is not a tenable distinction. The U.S. state, for instance, tries to fashion immigration laws to draw in migrants for their labor and not for their lives. The bracero program and the H-2 (temporary agricultural workers) visa policy are good examples of how the state allows agribusinesses and large farmers to use seasonal labor to their advantage. In 1998, the U.S. state was considering the Temporary Agricultural Worker Act, a guest-farmworker initiative that "privatizes immigration policy, giving agribusiness what it's always wanted, a free hand."[22] In Europe, where the guest worker policy is well integrated into the economies, states aim to draw in labor (from Turkey and Algeria, for example), not residential populations.[23] The oil-rich Persian Gulf states, unlike the Europeans, hired desi technical workers in large numbers to Europeanize the emirates.[24] The governments in the emirates rotated the immigration workers on short contracts to prevent any hope of long-term residence, and they constructed workers' housing and recreation centers to avoid creating the illusion that this was a concentration camp for contracted workers and not even a tarnished paradise. People came for the money, not for the life. For some countries, such as the United Arab Emirates, visas are hard to come by, but there is no visa needed to enter industrial complexes in Dubai.[25] The tenor of the 1965 Immigration and Nationality Act is not dissimilar to this, since there was no expectation that the migrants who entered under the technical worker category would later use their citizenship to bring in their families (hence the roots of resentment that are only now being fully realized). In the short term, however, few Indian technical workers cared about the intricacies of the act or its implications.

The 1965 law eased entry restrictions just as Britain tightened its immigration provisions. After 1945 the British economy suffered from a deficiency in its working class. The arrival of Caribbean and Asian (mostly Indian and Pakistani) laborers into the transport and textiles trades expanded the reserve population and enabled British capital to stabilize wages.[26] By the mid-1950s immigration from the subcontinent had slowed down for many complex reasons, but the Right's racialism turned on what we might call "forever immigrants" and called for "racial preservation." In August 1958 Oswald Mosley's Union Movement (the heir of the British Union of Fascists) and the White Defence League went on a "nigger-hunting" trip in Nottingham and Notting Hill (in London), only to be met with resistance from the West Indian and South Asian blacks. "The stage was set," A. Sivanandan wrote "for immigration control."[27] In 1962 Britain began to restrict immigration from the subcontinent by demanding that migrants either have bona fide job offers prior to entry or possess scarce skills. Just as the migrants began to put down roots, the white supremacists and the state reminded them of their status as forever immigrants (J. Enoch Powell, a conservative MP, reminded them in 1968 that they would be asked to repatriate some day). Those who would once have gone to Britain now came to the United States.

By 1976, however, the U.S. state had tightened the semi-permissive legislation of 1965. The Immigration and Nationality Act Amendments of 1976 (pushed through by Senator Joshua

Eilberg, D.–Pa.) required that migrants have firm job offers, and the Health Professions Educational Assistance Act of 1976 demanded that health workers also show proof of employment before immigrating to the United States. These restrictions slowed down the entry of technical and professional migrants from South Asia, but they did not stop the entrance of earlier immigrants' family members, who entered through the family reunification program. The 1965 act added the family reunification provision to unite southern Europeans, and the framers did not conduct serious discussions about the value or need of this provision for those who entered the country as technical workers. Would not these workers like to bring over their parents or siblings, especially if they enjoyed such cultural practices as the extended family (or at the very least, if retirement meant putting oneself into the hands of one's children)?[28] Since the 1980s, the percentage of technical workers among South Asian migrants has steadily decreased, and the percentage of family members who come to make their lives in the United States has grown. India and Pakistan continue to be the largest exporters of population, but Bangladesh has slowly edged into the picture (in 1996, 8,221 Bangladeshis came to the United States; 3,678 came on the family reunification scheme, and only 711 by employer preference, that is, as the result of having been recruited by employers). By 1994 employer preference (attracting technical and professional workers) is almost negligible, partly because of the stringent demands placed on employers by the labor certification process in the Immigration Act of 1990.

The shift in immigrants' motives from employer to family preference over the past three decades to some extent explains the change in the kinds of occupations of South Asian Americans. Increasing numbers of South Asians have joined the ranks of the U.S. working class and petty bourgeoisie. The technical workers in the United States sent for relatives in the homelands, but they also sent for those who were already living in other countries host to the South Asian diaspora. And there are those cousins and siblings whose broken lives were rescued by relatives in the United States, especially those families expelled from Uganda and Kenya in the

Table 1. Migrants from India and Pakistan in two categories

	Family Preference	Employer Preference	Total Immigration[a]
India			
1996	34,291	9,910	44,859
1995	26,864	7,164	34,748
1994	26,045	281	34,873
Pakistan			
1996	9,122	1,694	12,519
1995	7,575	725	9,774
1994	7,496	10	8,648

Source: Immigration and Naturalization Service, Annual Statistical Reports.

[a]In addition to family preference and employment preference, total immigration also includes the categories diversity programs, refugee and asylee adjustments, and those under the Immigration and Control Act (IRCA) of 1986 to "deter illegal immigration."

early 1970s who came to the United States via England and Canada. Significant numbers of these migrants invested in land along the highways where they opened cheap motels (many of these are operated by the women while the men hold jobs in industry to earn a stable wage).[29] Those who came as "sponsored relatives" to work in family businesses typically experienced terrible exploitation (since few had recourse to legal redress, given that many came on short-term renewable visas and worked in a structural manner similar to those who now come as domestic servants).[30] Additionally, families displaced by the Green Revolution in Punjab moved to California in the 1970s to work on its farms (either employed by the earlier wave of Punjabis, who might be relatives, or else to work in agribusiness, notably the canneries that hired large numbers of Punjabi women).[31] After the Gulf War (1991) made employment in that region less secure, migrants (especially from Pakistan) tried to make their way to the United States and to Europe.

Many single men come to make their fortune as sojourners

but find that they do not make enough money to return home and enjoy the fruits of their labor. Taxi workers, for example, come from lower-middle-class families who are gradually being impoverished in South Asia. Their working-class jobs in the United States sends their families a small modicum of foreign exchange that enables them to retain their class standing. Given the burden of holding up family status and the harsh conditions of their lives, few drivers return home. They continue to work in order to preserve the fragile family economy their dollars enable.[32] Statistics released by the U.S. Census Bureau in 1993 showed that the average age of migrants from India between 1987–1990 was almost twenty-eight. Of these migrants, 80 percent have completed high school, more than 9 percent are unemployed, 20 percent live below the poverty line, and the average income for the migrant is $22,231.[33] The techno-migrants slowly cease to dominate the demography of South Asian America.

The anti-immigrant sentiment at the end of the 1990s came at a time when the increase in family preference migration reminded South Asian Americans that we are only wanted here for our labor and not to create our lives. As our community is being recomposed, we are told that there are too many of us here, or that our families should not be united. Representative Lamar Smith (R.–Texas) proposed that the U.S. state only admit professional and skilled workers, a coded way of saying that our families must remain divided as corporations make the most of our skills.[34] As the laws are changed, there is little anger at the continuing U.S. policy allowing wealthy investors to get a green card simply by demonstrating that they have the funds to create jobs ($1 million to $2 million). The discussion over the H-1B (temporary, high-skilled worker) visa sharply illustrates the government's anxiety over long-term migration. Transnational corporations import highly skilled technicians, on H-1B visas, to work for three years, with their current skills, and then ship them home as their value begins to deteriorate (especially since, given the rapid depreciation of knowledge in this age of technological transformation, their skills quickly become outdated). A San Jose, California, paper reported that "tapping foreign talent is a tradition in Silicon Valley—part of the formula that made the area an industrial hothouse."[35] Consider the case of Hewlett Packard (HP) and the mental laborers from China, India, and Russia who come to the United States on H-1B visas to write computer programs. These workers, "the high-tech incarnations of the braceros of old," do not have access to basic benefits, such as health care or social security; they earn very modest weekly pocket money, room and board, and a monthly salary of around $250, which is remitted directly to their home countries. For this HP has been accused of "high-tech indentured servitude." Joining HP are a series of major supermarkets, department stores, and utility firms, who exploit foreign software programmers for a few years to hold down their long-term costs (such as health care and unemployment benefits).[36] Despite pressure to slow down immigration, the U.S. legislature remains in the thrall of the software firms who continue to reap the benefits of the H-1B program; the 1998 American Competitiveness Act increases the quota for this immigration to enable these transnational companies to "remain competitive in global markets," according to Senator Spencer Abraham (R.–Mich.).[37] Forty-four percent of H-1B migrants come from India, and 2 percent come from Pakistan (China follows India, with 9 percent). Six of the top seven "job shops" that import the "techno-bracero" workers are owned and operated by Indians or Indian migrants to the United States. India, then, remains at the center of the debate on high-tech immigration. Highly skilled guest workers are now a structural necessity of the U.S. state, and it is a blatant example of the slogan, "We want your labor, we don't want your lives." The U.S. Department of Labor responds to this situation by putting more pressure on the immigrant workers. In two reports, the U.S. state charges immigrants with using their programs to satisfy immigrant needs, "the attainment of the green card—rather than to provide employers access to foreign labor where sufficient US workers are not available." The Department of Labor evinced trepidation that the labor certification program "has become a stepping stone to obtain permanent resident status not only for the 'best and the brightest' specialists but also for students, relatives and friends."[38] How horrible: People may want to construct their families and societies as they see fit, and not just be used by monopoly capital and a state that operates at its behest!

The middle passage for desis is comfortable and even profitable, but it is a transit into indenture nonetheless. Regardless of our commitment to reside in the United States, we will be seen as forever immigrants. But we are seen as good immigrants, not like those bad immigrants who travel illegally across the Rio Grande, despite the fact that only about 41 percent of "illegal" immigration comes across the U.S.-Mexican border. Only 8.5 percent of the U.S. population are first-generation immigrants. Of these, 85 percent entered legally (75 percent via family reunification or employment preference and 10 percent as refugees). Only about 15 percent come "illegally," yet their presence defines the debate on immigration. Now stories emerge of Indians being smuggled into the United States as purported musicians or other entertainers in the mode of U.S. orientalism.[39] In late November 1998, the Immigration and Naturalization Service (INS) arrested thirty-one people (most of them Indian Americans) for smuggling workers into the United States to work as livery drivers, newspaper vendors, waiters, gas station attendants, and in similar occupations with a night shift and with low pay.[40] The stereotype of the Indian American as techno-migrant is blurring.

But we are good immigrants. We have advanced degrees. Sotto voce, our desi brethren on the Upper East Side of Manhattan bemoan the fact that almost 50 percent of the taxi workers are now from South Asia. These cabbies, noted one such professional, are "lowering the tone." They are "spoiling things for us," even "ruining our image" in the United States. "In just five years they've undone all the good work. These uncouth chaps, straight out of Punjab, can't even speak proper English—can't even drive. I don't know how they got here. Must be through Mexico or something. I don't know why they let them in."[41] This act of differentiation among the self-appointed cream of the desi community is a screen against the racism that I will document in the next section. There is a hesitancy even in these offensive comments, an uneasiness with our position here. The new working-class migration is turning *us* into Mexicans! That means we know that we are, after all, just about the same as Mexicans in the eyes of white supremacy.

Thumbu Sammy, Indian immigrant after his middle passage, at Ellis Island
(1911). Courtesy of National Park Service, Ellis Island Museum.

OF A *GIRMIT* CONSCIOUSNESS

So look at me, Jack, I'm comina name of Black
But you label me immigrant, ban my family
Let fools run around beating brothers like Ali
That's what it's like when you're livin' on the front
Front, front, front, frontline . . .

— Fun'Da'Mental, "No More Fear," *Seize the Time*

These days white supremacy does not necessarily come cloaked in white sheets. In 1991 Klu Klux Klan (KKK) leader David Duke removed those garments to run for governor of Louisiana; 55 percent of whites voted for him in his failed bid. Pat Buchanan took the pulpit at the Republican National Convention that year to tell his troops that "our culture is superior to other cultures, superior because our religion is Christianity." As Loretta Ross of the Center for Democratic Renewal put it, these figures champion "white rights" and give a large swath of disaffected people "permission to practice a kinder, gentler white supremacy."[1] White militancy in the present adopts the language of rights and argues that privileges accorded to nonwhite people need to be recovered for whites. In this book I use "white supremacy" to index not just those who are virulent and overt racists (the militias and the Klan) but also those who are passive participants in a culture that reviles black people (if not in word, then certainly in deed).[2] In addition to demanding "white rights," white militancy harbors the sentiment that nonwhite people do not deserve equality with white people. Certain nonwhites, such as Asians and Latinos, appear in this discourse as fundamentally "immigrant" despite their generations-long presence in the United States. As immigrants, it is claimed, Asians and Latinos cannot assimilate into U.S. society, so they should be sent home. How many times have we desis been asked when we are going to return home? How much frustration have we felt saying that this is our home or that we don't know any other home, having been born and raised here? And yet we are the forever immigrants. In an essay published in 1969, Martin Luther King Jr. wrote that "white America is still poisoned by racism, which is as native to our soil as pine trees, sagebrush and buffalo grass."[3] At the turn of the millennium, one might write very much the same thing.

Or at any rate, many South Asian Americans wrote just this in 1995. That was the year of the Republican Revolution, when the impatient followers of Newt Gingrich sent a torrent of intolerant legislation to the Congress both to end compensatory discrimination toward historically oppressed minorities and to dismantle the threadbare safety net. Sandwiched between the anti-immigrant Proposition 187 (the so-called California Voter Information initiative of 1994) and the antiminority Proposition 209 (the so-called California Civil Rights initiative of 1996), the Republican congressional legislation attempted to reconfigure the shaky social compact forged in the 1960s between the disenfranchised and the power elite. To reinforce the idea that immigrants are only wanted for their labor and not for their lives, Senator Alan Simpson (R.–Wyo.) and Representative Lamar Smith (R.–Tex.) submitted the Immigration Reform Act of 1995 that aimed to slow down legal immigration, curb family reunification, and toughen the hiring of foreign graduate students when they received their degrees. Simpson's bill emphasized the allocation of visas to "the brightest and the best," who might be hired by transnational firms, and to those workers "who are truly needed by American employers." The axe was to fall on family reunification.[4] Family reunification survived, but the next year the Illegal Immigration Reform and Immigrant Responsibility Act passed Congress and was signed into law on 30 September 1996. It is a draconian measure that carries over many of the provisions from the Simpson-Smith bill, with some amendments to mollify "legal" immigrants.[5] In 1996 Congress also passed the Welfare Reform Bill, which virtually eliminated legal immigrants' right to gain access to food stamps and to supplemental security income (SSI). "I never thought the Republican Party would do this," complained Inder Singh, a longtime GOP member.[6] Buffeted by these new laws, Shahid Siddiqi, a Pakistani migrant, formed the Asian American Republican Club National Committee to counter "the weakness of Asian-American political participation."[7] The level of penalization and stigmatization of immigrants intensified, but the structural message was unchanged: We want your labor, we don't want your lives.

Immigrants can work, but if they choose to enact their cultural resources they may face anti-immigrant wrath. Since 1994 the National Asian Pacific American Legal Consortium's annual audit of violence has shown a gradual increase in the number of racist assaults. Many of these are gory (such as the homicidal immolation of Srinivas Chirukuri, a graduate student at University of Nevada, on 22 July 1993), but most of them have attained the status of the banal (such as the experience of the desi woman in Queens, N.Y., whose neighbors yelled, "You Hindu bitches, why did you have to move in here?"). Though desis have faced the tyranny of white supremacy since the nineteenth century (keep in mind the Bellingham, Washington, riot of 1907 and the Live Oak, California, riot of 1908), the incident of the "Dotbusters" reminded us of the threat to our existence. In her useful study of Indians in New York City, Maxine Fisher noted that "nothing about Indian women seems to arouse more curiosity in Americans than the typically red circle of powder or dye which they wear in the center of

Indian grocer, New York City (1997). Courtesy of Amitava Kumar.

the forehead."[8] Some white youths in New Jersey fastened upon that "dot" (the *bindi* or *putu*), dubbed themselves "Dotbusters," and issued a manifesto to the local press: "We will go to any extreme to get Indians to move out of Jersey City," they wrote. "If I'm walking down the street and I see a Hindu and the setting is right, I will hit him or her." The word "Hindu" referred to all desis, just as the idea of the exponential "Patels" referred to all brown folk: "We use the phonebooks and look up the name Patel. Have you seen how many of them there are? You will hear of at least 3 Patel attacks as we call them during the night."[9] Not much later, white supremacists beat to death Navroze Mody, a thirty-year-old banker, and grievously injured Kaushal Sharan, a physician, in two separate incidents. A few weeks later, in a taped interview, one white supremacist youth stated that "we're just jealous because they have more money than we do. Why should they have more money than we do? They don't want to do nothing. They wanna just live in their houses and they don't want to kill any thing. And that's ruining our neighborhoods. Now our neighborhoods look like, you know, we have rats running through the streets. It's disgusting." Another demanded that "they should live the way everybody else lives—normal. Dress normal. Eat normal. Smell normal."[10]

After Mody's death, two unaffiliated fourteen-year-old boys from New Jersey told the press that "it's white people against the Hindus" and "I just don't like them, I can't stand them."[11] In 1992 the Dotbusters seemed to return, as B. Patel was assaulted and his family harassed with slogans like "Hindu, go home." In 1996 at the University of Illinois at Urbana-Champaign, a white male yelled at a South Asian woman, "You fucking Hindu, fucking Hindu, go back to your fucking country, where's your fucking Dot."[12] The words "Red Dot Special" were spray-painted on a desi student's car in Queens. The stain of the dot remains. In New Jersey a famous Bengali film director began a new life as the manager of a pizza parlor. Soon he owned his own pizza place in a white area of the state. The local paper did a story on him to highlight his success. He began to get nasty phone calls. Kids said mean things, the business dwindled. He remembers one caller who said, "When I eat your pizza and I think of your face, it makes me sick."[13] In Artesia, California, home of one of the many "Little Indias," five desis felt the sting of an acid spray from a passing car whose occupants yelled, "Go back to India. You don't belong here." It did not matter that some of the men came from Pakistan. "This is not an isolated incident," said Hamid Khan of South Asia Network.[14] In South Ozone Park in Queens, Rishi Maharaj, a twenty-year-old U.S.-born Indo-Trinidadian, was beaten senseless by three young men. "This is never going to be a neighborhood," they yelled, "until you leave."[15] In mid-October 1998 two Indian workers at a Dunkin Donuts shop in Camp Springs, Maryland, were killed and the store was set on fire in mimicry of a funeral pyre. In Jackson, Mississippi, Charanjit S. Aujla was killed by the local police on 4 December 1998 in a mysterious altercation while working at a convenience store. Nag Nagarajan, a biochemist from Indianapolis who wanted to run for Congress, lost a primary race to Bob Kern, a felon who was convicted of theft, forgery, and resisting arrest in 1994 but who was acquitted of solicitation of prostitution.[16] Nag made them sick in Indiana as well, I guess. We don't want your lives.

We want your labor. But, we are told, professional-technical desis are wanted only in technocratic jobs, not in the high-remuneration managerial positions. In 1995 the Glass Ceiling Commission reported that despite their high qualifications, Asians did not rise within their firms or institutions. The commission noted that since the 1960s Asians have benefited from the stereotype that they are intelligent and diligent workers. In time, however, "these stereotypes do turn negative."[17] At the annual American Association of Physicians from India meeting, Representative Robert Andrews (D.–N.J.) noted that "the best people are not always running a hospital because they are limited as to how high they can go because of ethnic prejudice and religious or cultural discrimination."[18] This is not a new phenomenon. In the 1970s Maxine Fisher found that most Indians did not find work commensurate with their qualifications.[19] In the context of downsizing, however, the pressure to be quiet about the glass ceiling is very high. Many technocrats feel that those who complain will be the first to be fired when the firm inevitably decides to "trim the fat." Given the preponderance of technical workers in the post-1965 wave of migrants, one might assume that there are a large number of Asians teaching science (both as faculty and as administrators). The numbers of faculty are reasonable, but the milieu is not entirely hospitable. One useful study documents the low regard given Asian scholars by their peers and by deans, who in one example condescended to the worker with the "harmless" statement "We will give him two bowls of rice instead of one" if he did the job well. However, according to data from the 1990 census, Asians occupy a meager 1.9 percent of administrative jobs, a figure that fuels much anger. "If one person comes out, like the chancellor of Berkeley, a Chinese person, it's news to the whole world," noted

Ravi Sinha, who teaches geology in North Carolina. "It should not be this way."[20]

The Mody, Sharan, and Chirukuri incidents are spectacular cases of violence against the professional-technical workers. Most anti-Asian violence, however, occurs in conjunction with anti-worker violence, as in the daily encounters of the police with taxi drivers. Encounters between desi taxi drivers and police have "escalated from racial slurs to assaults and the issuing of false traffic summonses in retaliation for civilian complaints filed against the police for their discriminatory treatment." Seventy-eight percent of reported anti–South Asian attacks occurred in the form of police brutality,[21] mainly against taxi workers. In 1996 a policeman in New York City thrashed a Pakistani taxi worker and yelled, "You immigrants think we're stupid. This is my country. I'll teach you a lesson."[22] On 25 May 1994, the late Saleem Osman spotted a New York Police Department (NYPD) officer harrassing a taxi worker. When he approached the scene, an undercover officer said to him, "There's no black mayor anymore. You better watch out." With David Dinkins no longer mayor, the NYPD reveled in "Giuliani time." They arrested Osman, beat him and detained him at the Midtown Precinct South station. The ongoing struggles of the New York Taxi Workers' Alliance (NYTWA) reflect a long-standing tussle between the immigrant workers (more than 50 percent are from South Asia; the bulk of the rest are from Africa and the Caribbean) and the establishment. These taxi workers are the current vanguard against the racism that structures Americans' lives.[23] The taxi workers are joined in this pioneer role by the domestic workers, who are slowly being organized under the aegis of Workers' Awaaz (New York City).[24] Taking inspiration from these movements, organizations of students and progressive professionals (such as the Forum of Indian Leftists) emerge to openly combat both white supremacy and the pathetic supremacy of those desis who feel they may be allowed into the white club if they too demean working people, blacks, and Latinos.

If life is so bad here, we immigrants are sometimes asked, why bother to come? For one thing, most desis who return for vacations to the subcontinent exaggerate the wonders of our lives here in order to make our very presence here into success.[25] We tend to forget the contradictions of our lives, the troubles, the weariness, the racism. On the plane ride home "we change completely, like chameleons," and we measure our worth in the superior purchasing power of the dollar as compared to the rupee:

> multiplying one with twenty-five
> our pockets feel heavier
> changing our entire selves
> and by the time we get off the plane
> we are members of another class.[26]

The rumors of success, of rapid mobility, and of full scholarships traverse the corridors of colleges and the *adda*s (hangouts) of working people. The wonders of "America" are flaunted in "Bollywood" films, such as Subhash Ghai's 1997 blockbuster *Pardes* and Rishi Kapoor's 1999 *Aa Ab Laut Chale*. In the former film, in fact, a chorus of young children sing a song demanding, "We want to go—America." "My film is about American dreams and the Indian soul," says director Ghai; "America is 'Big Brother' for us here. And every young person is dreamy about the place. But only on reaching there does he realise that there are things about himself that he cannot change."[27] I will address that realization later, but for now let us simply acknowledge that "America" continues to radiate a sort of light for those who try desperately, under its hegemonic shadow, to make some light of their own.

This image of "America" comes to the subcontinent through the good graces of expanding "global" media, whose reach is worldwide but whose content is frequently the fantasy of the American Dream. Can those who are fed a diet of *Dynasty, Dallas,* and *The Bold and the Beautiful* fail to be taken in by the values of avarice preached by Hollywood? To those living in relative deprivation, the gold-plated glory of the United States still shines like a beacon. The U.S. state is party to this fantasy image, which it uses to justify its contention (so beautifully sketched by Francis Fukuyama) that history ended in the consumer-friendly United States. Since

92

this image is by now familiar in film, advertisement, political statement, and article, it intensifies the desire, particularly among those
who feel their own lives have reached an unsatisfactory plateau, to
come to this paradise. The media does not manipulate reality; it
simply frames U.S. life to show it at its best. Also, if the audience re-
jects the values of the shows (especially the avaricious values of the
prime-time soap operas), they may still absorb the images of U.S.
opulence.[28] The impress of wealth is not entirely false, since the U.S.
middle and working class can certainly see more goods on the store
shelves than do most of those living on the subcontinent, and the
wages and credit mechanisms allow people in the United States to
afford more than people on comparable salaries can on the subcontinent. Imperialism does have its perks. Finally, there are many migrants who come to the United States under the family reunification
scheme whose first visit was just a vacation. Holidays do not reveal
the conditions of daily life, for they are a respite from the rigors of
everyday life. A story in the desi community bears upon this directly: God gave a man a choice between Heaven and Hell. Before making a choice, the man asks God for a tour. God takes him to Heaven,
a place of soft music, serene angels, and an atmosphere of peace. He
then goes to Hell, a place of dance, drink, and debauchery. The man
says to God, "I would like to go to Hell because it looks like more
fun." And so, when the man dies, he is taken to Hell, where he is immediately thrown into a cauldron of hot oil. Steaming with anger,
he asks God why Hell is now different. God replies, "last time you
were on a tourist visa, now you are on an immigrant visa."[29]

There is an additional reason most desi migrants disregard the
fact of racism in civil society. Many tend to follow an old tradition
that groups Indians with whites in a racial family called "Aryan,"[30]
believing that if they are joined in this racial fantasy and can only
explain this to the bulk of the population, then they will be accepted. The acts of violence against us, desis seem to say, are in error;
hit the real people of color, not us. Bharati Mukherjee's revelation
is an appropriate example: "I am less shocked, less outraged and
shaken to the core, by a purse-snatching in New York City in
which I lost all of my dowry gold—everything I'd been given by

my mother in marriage—than I was by a simple question asked of me in the summer of 1978 by three high-school boys on the Rosedale subway station platform in Toronto. Their question was, 'Why don't you go back to Africa?'"[31] Mukherjee's anxiety is repeated occasionally, mainly when one is not being observed by those thought to be outside the racist hermeneutic circle. Desis realize they are not "white," but there is certainly a strong sense among most desis that they are not "black." In a racist society, it is hard to expect people to opt for the most despised category. Desis came to the United States and denied their "blackness" at least partly out of a desire for class mobility (something, in the main, denied to blacks) and a sense that solidarity with blacks was tantamount to ending one's dreams of being successful (that is, of being "white"). Of course, even the bluster of Aryanness is denied by arch–white supremacists like David Duke, who was stunned during his 1971 visit to India by the "degeneration" of what he considered the Aryans, a people who had lost their "healthy racial values" to miscegenation. Since India had "passed the point of no return," Duke could only take his racist message back to the United States as a warning.[32]

Dinesh D'Souza has suggested that desis have a strong racist consciousness that is independent of U.S. racism.[33] He says this in order to acquit the United States of racism (he wants to show that though the entire world is racist, the United States demonstrated by ending slavery that it is more committed to freedom than anywhere else). There is indeed a consciousness of color among desi peoples, but is this the same as racism? Are these older awarenesses of color differences identical to the racial divisions and hierarchies that plague the United States? I've always known of the word *"habshi"* in the parlance of north India—it is an unsavory and racist term for Africans. I also knew the adjective *"habshi"* from the delicious *"habshi gosht,"* a Hyderabadi lamb dish, and from *"katra habshiyan,"* a locality in the old city of Delhi. The word *"habsh"* comes from Abyssinia, and its occurrence on the subcontinent reflects the presence of Africans in the world of the Indian Ocean trade and as generals in the Delhi Sultanate (1206–1526), in which an African was consort to Raziyya Sultana (1236–39). Is the word *"habsh"* within Islam an adjective of distaste? I contacted my teacher C. M. Naim and my friend Mir Ali Raza, and both informed me that in Islamic folklore the word *"habsh"* refers to Bilal-e-Habash, one of the first five Muslims and a favorite of Muhammad. Muhammad thought Bilal's *azaan* (the call to prayer by the muezzin) beautiful, and he noted that if Bilal "does not give the *azaan*, God does not want it to be dawn." The adjective *"bilal"* is now used for anyone with a melodious *azaan*. Islam, from its roots, did not sanction differentiation, but that did not mean that Islamic societies came without prejudice or slavery. "The important fact," Naim noted, "is that nowhere in the Islamicate lands did the slave population become ghettoized; they mingled with the rest of the community, married and became assimilated." The African population remains on the subcontinent in some areas, including Hyderabad, Janjira (near Bombay), and the Makran coast in Pakistan.[34]

Even in more modern times, there are stories of fellowship between Africans and Indians. When Indian peasants traveled as indentured servants to the West Indies, many lived alongside descendants of Africans in a relatively convivial manner. Solidarity was produced socially (during the Hosay, or Muharram, festival to commemorate the martyrdom of Husain at the Battle of Karbala), economically (in the "Creole gangs" in which African and Indian children worked), and politically (during the ceaseless struggles against the plantocracy). Walter Rodney, the Guyanese historian, argued that evidence from British Guiana of the previous century "does not sustain the picture of acute and absolute cultural differences coincident with race."[35] The 1882 Cedar Hill Estate strike in Guyana and the 1884 Hosay riots in Trinidad offer intimations of solidarity (these unities, however, must not be seen as strong class unity). The British made every attempt to drive a wedge between the two, particularly by making the Indians do more menial tasks than the Africans and separating them into racialized work teams and residential areas. By 1897 a planter informed the West Indian Commission that the Africans and Indians "do not intermix and that, of course, is one of our greatest safeties in the colony when there has been any rioting. If our negroes were troublesome every coolie on the estate would stand by one. If the coolie attacked me I could with confidence trust my negro friends for keeping me from any injury."[36] In other words, the divisions between Indians and Africans were energetically manufactured by imperial policy and facilitated European rule.

We still have not explained the idea of "race" and skin color as it applies on the subcontinent. If not from Islam, did these ideas come with the Europeans? To accept this interpretation is the immediate temptation, but it is a very limited way to proceed. What about the obvious suggestion that "race" has something to do with "caste"? "Caste" comes from the Portuguese word "*casta*," which itself derives from the Latin *castus,* meaning "pure" and "unstained," notably in terms of sexual purity, that is, "chasteness." In the late 1700s the Europeans used this word to describe the *varna* and *jati* systems because these social organizations appeared to be perfect copies of the neo-Aristotelian classification system being pioneered by Carolus Linneaus in Europe. *Varna* is an ancient textual depiction of a social hierarchy (in which four *varna*s, Brahmin, Kshatriya, Vaishya, and Shudra, represent ideal types of status groups). *Jati* refers to community formations whose principles are localized and various. Some *jati*s are united by occupation (as in artisanal communities), others by marital ties (endogamous or exogamous relations, as in *gotra*s, the filial form of caste), yet others by principles of eating and drinking, still others by totems or by historical cultures. The word *"jati"* was used in the nineteenth century to refer to "nations," and if we borrow from recent theories of nationalism, *jati* itself might be seen as an "imagined community" founded in opposition to other "imagined communities" and linked by relations of power and production. There is no single principle for *jati,* so there can be no single theory of caste.

Such complexity did not matter to H. H. Risley, a colonial bureaucrat and commissioner of the 1901 census of India. In his wide survey of the Bengali peoples in 1891, Risley argued that "the principle of Indian caste is to be sought in the antipathy of the higher race for the lower, of the fair-skinned Aryan for the black Dravidian."[37] Risley was wrong on a number of counts. First, the ethnology of Aryan/Dravidian is misleading; the terms are more useful in the field of linguistics than in that of the social relation of caste. Second, the idea that skin color is an indicator of caste (here seen as a substitute for "race") is erroneous. Risley is able to make this correlation because of the unique meaning of "*varna.*" It literally translates from Sanskrit as "color," and thus many see caste as a scheme of skin colors. However, considerable scholarship shows that *varna* may refer to something akin to feudal colors or standards.[38] Words such as "*suklatva*" ("whiteness") refer not to skin color but to classes of things. Certain things are therefore rendered in the camp of "white" and others in other camps without a hierarchy of value imputed to this classification. In ancient Greece, the idea of blackness was ascribed not to cultural inferiority but to death. Though neither *varna* nor *jati* can be reduced to "race," it is already evident how discourses of whiteness and darkness coalesced neatly with European racist ideas, thereby fashioning an "ancient heritage" for contemporary South Asian racism.

Does this then mean that the obsession with skin color awaited the arrival of European racist ideas? I'm still not sure. All of us have seen the matrimonial advertisements in Indian newspapers and their elaborate codes for skin color (wheatish, fair).[39] The men in demand are to be handsome, well educated, and of particular castes, faiths, and habits. Both "matrimonial female" and "matrimonial male" advertisements describe women (the former are placed by those in search of a husband and the latter by those seeking a wife). The women in both are fairly similar; though they also mention specific castes and faiths and educational qualifications, they offer indices of beauty such as height, weight, skin color, and statements of value ("homely" in Indian usage means one who keeps home properly). A number of ads, it needs to be said, either mention none of these variables or explicitly deny their importance ("caste no bar" or "religion no bar" or "broad-minded"). In most ads, the desired skin color is specified. Irawati Karve, for instance, tells us that there is "among all castes a definite preference for a fair bride against a dark bride," but she does not tell us why.[40]

The idea of desire and skin color, I hazard, is not the same as "race" because concepts of beauty do not necessarily ascribe qualities of behavior (although this is sometimes the case). To be theoretical for a moment, skin color as beauty is not about the essence of determinate Being, but it is a quality of determinate Being (despite the prevalent European idea that utilizes quality as a measure of essence). In the Hindi film *Laawaris* (1981), Amitabh Bachchan's famous song "Mere Angane Mein" (composed by Anand Bakshi) offers a wide range of aspects of beauty—height, weight, size, and skin color. Both fairness and darkness are offered as useful to the bridegroom. Fairness is a quality most often demanded of women.[41] I believe this has to do with the woman herself (beauty), but it also has to do with the generations that follow. Women in general are considered responsible for their progeny—if a boy is born, the woman is congratulated, and vice versa. The man is not considered responsible for either the sex or the beauty of the child, since that burden is borne solely by women who are seen, in many settings, as the conduit of children. The woman-fairness-children link does imply some notion of biology, but I think that it is not the same as the idea that one's entire place in the world is governed by one's "race." A dark man or woman is not socially shunned (even though a dark woman will not be able to marry without the barbs of social stigma). To reduce an unhealthy obsession with skin color to the idea of "race" does not enable us to grasp the historical dynamics of skin color on the subcontinent.[42]

There is a real uncertainty over the question of race and racism, much of which has to do with the lack of attention paid to race in South Asian scholarship, obsessed as it is with caste.[43] Of course, like all traditions of thought, there is no single South Asian approach to other people of color. In the United States too there are contradictory tendencies. Some (as we've seen above) wish to distance themselves from things black.[44] Some ask for occasional alliance with other U.S. minorities, sometimes from fellowship, but sometimes simply to gain some of the resources for advancement guaranteed to historically oppressed minorities by the state. In 1977, for example, the Association of Indians in America successfully lobbied to add Indians to the U.S. Census Bureau's nonwhite category. Even this was ambivalent, for it did not entirely disassociate itself from the 1920s "nonwhite Caucasian" formula, nor did it call for the formation of a complex civil rights coalition against white supremacy.[45] Such an alliance was formed among some sections of those who lived in Britain among desis from the West Indies and Africa, all known as "black" in the parlance of the United Kingdom. This alliance was cognizant that the complex intersection between race and class produced a formidable front against supremacy. "We come from all kinds of families," Aziz of Leicester noted, "but when it comes to our rights we are black."[46]

There is much to be gained from a glance at the earlier experiences of South Asians in the diaspora, particularly the experience of desis in the British Isles. In the 1950s in Britain, a familiar slogan rent the air of the pubs: "The darker the sky, the blacker the faces" as if to remind those of Asian and African ancestry of their current fate, to toil the night shift. Eager to do well, even the merchants took to putting in extra hours, keeping shops open through the night. "The English are not the only nation of shopkeepers," Abdul Lateef said, "we are too. And we're proving it daily in England."[47] In 1963 J. Enoch Powell, the conservative MP who had done some time in India during the raj, praised Indian doctors who "provide a useful and substantial reinforcement of the staffing of our hospitals and who are an advertisement to the world of British medicine and British hospitals."[48] Things seemed well for the subcontinentals, just as they seem well for us on occasion in the United States. Five years later, the axe fell. Powell, at Birmingham on 20 April 1968, described South Asians as dirty breeders of unruly children. A few months later at Eastbourne, Powell agreed that Asian doctors "made it possible to expand the hospital service," but he went on to claim they "have no more to do with immigration than have the *au pair* girls admitted for a year or two to give domestic help." The Asian doctors came, he argued, to get "a few years of post-graduate experience in England." Now, they can leave or else "rivers of blood" will flow in the streets of England.[49] Powellism was realized in the 1968 Immigration Act, which distinguished between "British citizens" (those who could claim ancestry in the British Isles, or, in other words, who could claim "whiteness") and "overseas British citizens" (those who came from the former or current colonial possessions of Britain). The former enjoyed all the rights and privileges of the state, whereas the latter were entitled to passports to enter Britain as workers but without access to any benefits. Powell showed us that we were nothing but probationary residents in what some still see as white lands.

The anti-Asian trajectory in Britain ran parallel to the anti-Asian sentiment in eastern Africa. When Kenya won independence from the British in 1963, *"uhuru"* ("freedom") began to mean "Africanization," with the Asians and Arabs seen as external to Africa. Petty-bourgeois Asian merchants feared that the state was going to confiscate their commercial gains, so many began to seek avenues out of Kenya. In the early years, the government gave loans to African entrepreneurs to break the Asian hold on trade, but after 1967 the laws became more stringent. The state passed an Immigration Act and a Trade Licensing Act, both of which gave it the power to rearrange the role of Asians in the Kenyan economy. An exodus of Asians began toward Britain, India, Canada, and eventually the United States.[50] On the heels of the Kenyan "expulsion," Idi Amin of Uganda began his own campaign against the Asians. As his virulence increased, the Aga Khan (leader of the Ismaili community) remained "confident that in due course we shall succeed in being accepted as full and true citizens of Uganda in every sense of those words. That is what we understand integration to mean."[51] The illusion of acceptance is clearly reminiscent of our own context. On 5 August 1972 Idi Amin informed his country that "Asians came to Uganda to build the railway. The railway is finished. They must leave now." The state shortly thereafter expelled 50,000 Asians. We tend to remember this act only as an example of Idi Amin's heinousness, and we forget the hand of the British, who did two things: They created the idea that desis are only temporary workers whose culture is so transient that they can only make their lives in their homeland, and second, they made it very difficult for the Asians to enter Britain (whose "Commonwealth" was shown to be an utter sham by this episode).[52] The social being of the desi is structured by this imperial racism.

Given this history, there is every reason to hope for widespread resistance among desis to racism against all peoples. That is one response to the fact of a racist civil society. However, this is not something that is plausible in a mass sense among desis in the United States, given the nature of the class dynamics and the class cultures from and in which many desis live. Most desi migrants come from the professionalized middle class, mostly from towns and cities in India. Few hail from families with vast wealth, so that most rely upon their skills and social capital to facilitate their station within the slowly emerging class of the technocrat. According to the U.S. Census Bureau, the median measured net worth of Asians in general and of South Asians in particular is significantly lower than that of whites, though the income levels are roughly comparable for those who hold technical jobs.[53] That is, the professionals in the post-1965 migration came without access to or holdings of large amounts of capital (in dollars), thereby ensuring that their place in the middle class was to be secured entirely by current income (and the moderate savings from that income). Despite predilections toward radical activity (and, anecdotally, I find many of these folk to have been members of progressive organizations in college), few are able to act radically given the structural vise that entraps them. This is the root of the political conservatism of many desis, but it is not a sufficient condition for conservatism. I will pick this up in "Of Authentic Cultural Lives," but for now it is adequate to sense this real problem in the lives of many desis.

In the United States the bulk of the desi community seems to have moved away from active political struggles toward an accommodation with this racist polity. The bargain revolves around the sale of the desi political soul in exchange for the license to accumulate economic wealth through hard work and guile. They seem to be oblivious of their decline into a realm of pure commerce, one that leaves them politically powerless (disorganized and without allies). They live *in* America, but they are not *of* America. The desire for community draws desis to socialize with each other, to seek solace from the rigors of corporate America and to share a common vision born of this abdication from U.S. society—to make enough money, educate their children, and then return to their respective homelands.[54] Retirement in the homeland is viewed as liberation. Implicit in this narrative is a fundamental critique of the work ethic of corporatist America. Work, central to the accumulation of capital, is the evil that the desi economic migrant must escape. Even for a community integrated into the networks of professionalism, the very foundation of the system (work) is anathema. But it is worth enduring the rigors of work and the travails of society to achieve the reward of a pension and the status in the homeland of having returned from abroad.

This strand in desi culture needs to be developed further, for it provides us with a way to bridge a number of gaps—the antiwork ethos (idealized into the future) is in lived contradiction with a workaholic ethos (lived in the present). The social form of the consciousness of the South Asian migrant is structured around this contradiction. Retirement, however, is not opted for as often as it is discussed; as savings are reduced by increased spending, particularly on college tuition, few can afford to retire. A few desi migrants succeed, and the ethnic media accords them the status of role model, which itself is not a generalizable condition. Retirement in the homeland gradually ceases to be a goal and becomes a dream. The feeling of being socially detached from U.S. life justifies withdrawing even further from the social and political life of the United States. The desi migrants most commonly enter U.S. political discourse by complaining about the lack of individual economic growth (which will enable them to realize their retirement utopia). Few actually return to the homeland, and the discussion becomes more and more urgent, sometimes succumbing to political and social problems on the subcontinent. If the conversation is turned to problems in the United States, two statements are made: first, that desi social relations are far superior to those elsewhere (so desi kids do not do drugs or have premarital sex), and second, that there is no racism against desis (desis don't *earn* racism, the suggestion runs, but blacks and Latinos do).

This abdication is rather dubious, since desis do live in the United States and do interact with the society they wish to flee. It is made tenable only by deploying that vision of desis as spiritual and therefore otherwordly, outside the vocabulary of the U.S. republic. Desis are too busy within the realm of the family to extend themselves to the domain of civil society (this despite the resilient civil society in the subcontinent). The Association of Indians in America was founded in 1967 to nurture the idea that Indians are immigrants and not sojourners. "If we could collectively do something to aid India that would be fine," said one of the founders, "but our main purpose, as we envisioned it from the beginning, was to get involved in the social issues and politicial process of this country."[55] *India Abroad* (the leading desi weekly paper) founded the India Abroad Political Action Center in Washington, D.C., in response to this abdication from U.S. political life, but in its earlier years it was more keen on lobbying Congress than on creating the organizations to enrich the lives of Indians in the United States (its current incarnation seems to be moving toward an engagement with our lives).

The real sense of abdication appears among first-generation migrants who claim to be exiles. Like Rama, Sita, and Laxman, or indeed, like the Pandava brothers and Draupadi, they wend their way in the forests of Dandak, serving their economic *tapasya* (ordeal), waiting for the time when they can reenter the kingdom of Ayodhya in triumph (the sad irony of Ayodhya will be revealed in a later section dealing with Yankee Hindutva ["Hinduness," or the ideology of the Hindu Right]).[56] "Home" is over there; the United States is just an unpleasant place in which to work. When

Indian workers went to Fiji under the indenture regime, they signed an agreement *(girmit)* that allowed the *girmitiya* (the signer of the *girmit*) to return to the homeland in ten years. Departure is always in the future as the *girmitiya* waits through multiple generations for the epic return to the homeland. Their retirement is their liberation. The implication is that the *girmitiya* is unhappy in this land of wealth. In three-quarters of Indian American families in 1975, at least one spouse held onto Indian citizenship in order to facilitate an eventual return to the homeland.[57] The percentages are almost unchanged today. A few years ago, Pakistani TV ran a serial entitled *Mirza Ghalib in America*. One character says to another, "Yeh mulk theek nahi hai. Yahan ke green card se, apne watan mein discard zayada behtar hai [This country is no good. Better to be a discard in one's country than to bear a green card]." But few actually return.

Whereas retirement is the salvation promised as the reward of an unhappy present, refuge in the "home" is one way to make the present bearable. Racist civil society is abandoned in favor of the domain of the home. The retreat into the home is not an unfamiliar resolution to life in a society dominated by racism, for that was the content of British India as well as the strategy adopted by the emergent bourgeoisie in India. In the United States the desi sunders the world into two: the outside world, the world of the workplace, is a world of capital that must be exploited as much as possible, and the inside world, the world of the home, is a world of culture that must be protected and cherished. The external world, the workplace, is (in the terms of the Transcendentalists) the world of the practical Occident, and the internal world, the home, is the world of the spiritual Orient. The translation of the orientalist divide is identical, but the project for which it is utilized is rather different. Whereas morality is protected by the desi migrant within the world of the home and culture, immorality is virtually sanctioned in the world of capital. What the migrants want is the best of both worlds, and since the migrants deem themselves superior in the world of the home, the mistreatment by white society is salved. The desi takes cultural refuge in the "home," a place in which the desi might feel sovereign, superior, and dignified. The desi can protect and preserve tradition at home and at the same time be culturally safe when in the domain of capital (commerce and science).

The desi woman emerges within this logic as the repository of tradition, and as long as she is able to reproduce "India" in the home, she too is encouraged to go out and work to enhance the capital sums of the family fund. The woman is here responsible, in large measure, for preventing the acculturation of the children, a heavy burden in a society far more complex than this simple and sexist separation of domains is allowed to bear.[58] Many young desi women raised in the United States "feel oppressed by the traditional Indian image of an unmarried female that others impose upon them." Regardless of whether this "traditional" image is altogether common, one young woman complained that "so much is expected of us. We are supposed to excel in school and careers and still be demure and delicate, good mothers, wives and daughter-in-laws."[59] The violence visited upon women within the confines of the home reveals both the depth of women's resistance to this construction and the fervency with which some men attempt to police the domain in order to restrict women's right to moral autonomy. Across the United States there are now organizations set up for South Asian women to take shelter from circumstances of abuse and for desis to fight the phenomenon of "domestic" violence.[60] "All batterers need to be exposed," all families that protect batterers "need to be exposed for the kind of criminality they are sheltering," said one activist, and, in addition, the ideology of the "dutiful wife" needs to be countered.[61] Although this form of violence is pervasive in most communities and on the subcontinent, I maintain that the special divide made by desis between capital and culture provides the context for the violence visited upon desi women in the United States.

The instability of the strategy of abdication is revealed by the continual threat to the existence of desi peoples in the United States. Violence continues; it does not abate. Despite the attempt by desis to depoliticize their cultural withdrawal, the reaction to the desi is articulated in political, social, and economic terms: There are too many of them, it is said; they are taking jobs from "real" Americans, they are destroying American culture and civic religion, they are dirtying U.S. cities. In spite of the fact that most desi migrants do not live in "ethnic ghettos" (they live around their workplaces, such as hospitals, universities, hotels and motels, technology parks, in large urban areas), the desi presence in the United States is linked to the existence of these "ghettos," these visible reminders that desis exist in this country. They create symbolic communities in areas devoted to shops and places of worship (such as Devon Street in Chicago, Jackson Heights and Flushing in Queens, Edison in New Jersey).[62] These symbolic communities function in a different way in the worldview of non-desis in the United States: They are places of exoticism (where nondesis can go to taste the culture of the subcontinent without leaving the United States) and places that represent the loss of *native* control over the cities. (It is no wonder these are the sites of much of the anti-Asian violence.)

The dominant classes in the United States do not accept the terms of the *girmitiya* resolution, that desis are here to work hard and make money, and not to interfere in political matters. The very presence of the desi is construed as an interference, and the act of making money is itself an act of violence against those who want to guard the *nativist* economy. "Throughout the history of economics," Georg Simmel wrote in a landmark essay, "the stranger everywhere appears as the trader, or the trader as stranger."[63] In other words, the indelible immigrant is seen as a merchant out to cheat the native peoples of their hard-earned money. The murder of Vincent Chin (a Chinese American man bludgeoned to death in Detroit by two whites in 1982 as part of an anti-Asian wave enlivened by U.S. jingoism against the Japanese automobile industry) or of Navroze Mody, the hostility to the kiosk merchant, the jokes at the expense of Apu (the clerk of the Kwik-E-Mart on *The Simpsons,* always trying to cheat his customers), and other such incidents are part of that same nativism, which believes that even the minimum postulate of the *girmitiya* resolution (that desis are

Manavi demonstration, New Jersey (1980s). Courtesy of Shamita Das Dasgupta, Manavi.

here to make money) is unacceptable. In Gary Okihiro's useful account, the Asian presence in the United States is treated as a peril
of the body ("yellow peril") and a peril of the mind ("model minority"). The former refers to the fact of exponential Asian bodies
entering the territory. The latter refers to the fact of Asian success,
that is, the fact that Asians are no longer assumed to be "coolies"
but are instead successful, something unacceptable, once again, to
nativism.[64] This analysis exposes the two bankrupt responses to
nativism: first, voluntary repatriation, and second, further burial
in the morbid *girmitiya* resolution. One available and progressive
response is to create alliances to combat the institutions and the
ideology that structure this problem in the first place, just so that
we appreciate that the United States cannot have our labor without our lives. But how do we propose to understand the nature of
these "lives"? That is the task of the following section.

OF AUTHENTIC CULTURAL LIVES

Back in the days when I was a teenager
Dazed and confused was the status of my nature
Desi, pardesi what was I? "Just crazy?"
Easy said my daddy, stop sweatin' 'bout your future
Be hittin' all your books like there be no tomorrow
Straight As, it pays, that'll drown your sorrow
"Oh bhai," said I, must give this shit a try
So EE [Electrical Engineering] was to me, like the Nile was to
the Pharaoh
. . . .
We be to rap what raga be to veena
'Cause we're cool like that, we're cool like that, we're desi like
that, yeah we're desi like that . . .

—Desi Jersey Mafia, "Desi Like Dat"

The lives of migrants to the United States came under special
scrutiny from those who fashioned themselves as guardians of its
cultural inheritance. Benjamin Franklin, for instance, was struck
by the entry of Germans into his "anglo-saxon" domain, so much

so that he worried that they would "soon so outnumber us that [despite] the advantages we have, we will, in my opinion, not be able to preserve our language, and even our Government will become precarious."[1] Anything less than total assimilation to the core of "anglo-saxon" culture was tantamount to treason. Since "assimilate" means to "make similar," there is an expectation among some U.S. residents that those who are different may be transformed into those who are similar, or, indeed, identical. There are some who cannot become even similar (let alone identical), so the attempt to assimilate is futile for them. This is indeed the tenor of Thomas Jefferson's remarks about blacks in *Notes on the State of Virginia* (1787) and, notably, in a letter Jefferson wrote to James Monroe in 1801: "It is impossible not to look forward to distant times, when our rapid multiplication will expand itself and cover the whole northern, if not the southern continent, with a people speaking the same language, governed in similar forms, and by similar laws; nor can we contemplate with satisfaction either blot or mixture on that surface."[2] Without "blot and mixture," the United States was to be a homogeneous realm for the free enterprise of the "anglo-saxon." Of course, the United States was never homogeneous, given that the early Republic already contained within it Amerindians, blacks, and Catholics—all "blots" on the surface of the white, Protestant Republic.

In the early part of our century, sociologists and public policy experts understood that the attempt to forge a homogeneous culture was not only fallacious but also posed certain problems for the creation of social solidarity. Faced with the influx of working-class and peasant immigrants from Europe in the 1880s, the U.S. state attempted many forms of social integration, but found that this policy was not entirely successful nor universally desired (this despite the Englishman Israel Zangwill's hopeful 1908 play, *The Melting Pot*, and the rise of nativism in the 1920s). Assimilation failed because most immigrants (for social, linguistic, and economic reasons) flocked to areas where they could recreate, in part, the lifestyles they had inherited. One of the least-known facts of the European conquest of the Americas is that, despite the pieties of assimilation, the Europeans failed to assimilate to the staples of the New World (maize, possum, raccoon, sweet potatoes, and white potatoes) and reverted to those of the Old World.[3] The branding reproach of assimilation is levied against those non-Europeans who do not dissolve themselves into Euro-America's image of itself. Robert Park and H. A. Miller, in their 1921 classic *Old World Traits Transplanted*, responded to the failure of assimilation and wrote that "a wise policy of assimilation like a wise educational policy, does not seek to destroy the attitudes and memories that are there, but to build on them."[4] In many ways ahead of his time, Park argued that cultural communities must be allowed to develop their own cultural resources, but not entirely in a state of anarchy. That is, this cultural growth must proceed as long as it does not clash with certain agreed-upon principles, including the democratic right to dissent.

The formal roots of multiculturalism may be seen in these sociological visions. Each cultural community is accorded the right to determine its destiny, as long as it does not clash in some fundamental way with the social contract of the state and its citizens. The United States is already some way from the strident chauvinism of the cultural purists. This is not to say that such chauvinism has disappeared, for it remains in the programmatic racism of such as Pat Buchanan and the pragmatic racism of such as Nimi McConigley (the Indian American woman who ran for the Senate from Wyoming on an "English only" platform).[5] Yet the fact of a multicultural United States cannot be denied, even by people, such as Dinesh D'Souza, who acknowledge that other knowledges may be used "to complement" the study of the "anglo-saxon" world. "The great works of other civilizations, like those of our own," notes D'Souza, "can broaden our minds and sharpen our thinking."[6] And this from the man who wrote *Illiberal Education* (1991), the New Right's antimulticulturalism manifesto.

The problem with U.S. multiculturalism as it stands is that it pretends to be the solution to chauvinism rather than the means for a struggle against white supremacy. Whereas assimilation demands that each inhabitant of the United States be transformed into the

norm, U.S. multiculturalism asks that each immigrant group preserve its own heritage (as long as it speaks English). The heritage,
or "culture," is not treated as a living set of social relations but as a
timeless trait.[7] "As an Asian or African," an Iranian intellectual
complained, "I am supposed to preserve my manners, culture,
music, religion and so forth untouched, like an unearthed relic, so
that the gentlemen can find and excavate them, so they can display
them in a museum and say, 'Yes, another example of primitive
life.'"[8] Desi schoolchildren encounter this "encyclopedic" notion
of culture, as an inert set of artifacts that can be saved and preserved, when their teachers ask them to wear "Indian clothes" to
school as part of show-and-tell. Consumerism seems to be the
main drive for this kind of multiculturalism, with all that is seen as
"fun" adopted while all that is deemed to be "fundamentalist" is
abjured. The hijab and falafel are welcome, but the "Arab-type" is
to be feared.[9] "There is difference and there is power," June Jordan
noted, "and who holds the power shall decide the meaning of difference."[10] There is an expectation and eagerness of cultural difference in every avenue of life, as reported in this example by Gita
Sahgal:

> Having abandoned an egalitarian ideal for a policy of recogniz-
> ing cultural differences, [the multiculturalist policymakers] tend
> to have to codify, implement and reinforce these differences (as
> British colonialism did in relation to family law). For instance, a
> well-meaning social worker, enquiring into cooking arrange-
> ments in the [Asian women's] refuge, was told that there were
> two kitchens. "Ah, yes," she said knowledgeably, "one vegetari-
> an and one non-vegetarian." "No," we said, "one upstairs and
> one downstairs."[11]

Rather than straddle the hard contradiction between difference
and similarity, there is a tendency to move in one or the other direction. Either people are all the same, or they are fundamentally different. There is little patience with the strategy that though people
share much they are also dissimilar. The idea of "culture" that operates in standard multiculturalist and in chauvinist statements is

similarly static: Both see "culture" as a thing rather than as a process. "It is good to swim in the waters of tradition," Gandhi wrote, "but to sink in them is suicide."[12] Tradition or culture must bend to the will of people rather than keeping them captive to its nuances. Tradition itself is a peculiar thing, a set of customs and rituals that are handed down through history. But they are not handed down without being changed. People adapt and incorporate artifacts from the past in the context of their own particular historical conjuncture, fighting their own battles and struggling with their own contradictions.

U.S. multiculturalism joins with desi conservatism to invoke certain aspects of desi culture as desi culture *tout court.* The well-meaning multiculturalist hails the first generation migrants as representatives of an "Indian culture" that is itself not homogeneous. Multiculturalism draws its own ideas of India from U.S. orientalism and sees it as fundamentally spiritual (represented by certain icons); this India resonates in the classroom and on celluloid. Thus there is an expectation that desis must be spiritual (and so spirituality is authorized for them, as in the presence of temples and mosques).[13] Desi culture, in imperial eyes, is to be fundamentally a sort of religious culture, since religion is seen as the subcontinent's cultural essence.

But though desis do raise temples, gurudwaras, and mosques, many of them serve as community centers as much as religious havens.[14] Anyone who drives around the northern suburbs of Detroit will see the Bharatiya temple, or in south Houston the Sri Meenakshi temple, or in Nashville the Ganesha temple. In Palatine, Illinois, one will find a hexagonal gurudwara, and in Bartlett, Illinois, one will see the new Jain temple.[15] Just because these centers are "religious" does not mean that they are used solely as such. Desis are able, at least to some extent, to manipulate the forms foisted upon them by history. But there is an eager expectation that desis will be religious, an expectation fostered by the votaries of Hindutva as much as by naive multiculturalists. The sentiment that religious buildings should also be used as community centers continues, but it is hard to do so under the shadow of

Hindutva. In Connecticut, desis fought the immigration authorities for five years to bring workers from India to construct the Sri Satyanarayana temple in Middletown. Completed in 1998, the temple is dedicated to eleven deities in the hope of being comprehensive. "We wanted to bring the entire community together," said Rao Singamesetti, "to feel like a big family."[16] The point was to make the temple a refuge for desis, but after the destruction of the mosque at Ayodhya in 1992, it is unlikely that a Hindu temple can represent a home to all desis (notably to those of other faiths than Hinduism and those who are faithless).[17]

Singamesetti Rao has a point, the desire to bring the community together "to feel like a big family." Migrants do create all kinds of spaces for fellowship, from the legion of associations that exist even in remote towns (such as in Fredericton, New Brunswick, Canada) to the informal circles of friends who meet weekly to socialize.[18] Arthur and Usha Helweg correctly note that most desis, like many immigrants, really let down their hair among themselves. Among whites, they tell us in their condescending prose, the desis "are superb imitators and behave properly, tell the right jokes, laugh at the correct time and assume the correct posture, but the smiles are not as wide, the laughter not as loud, and the hug not as hard as when they are among Indians."[19] In the safe space of a desi gathering, alliances are made through shared sorrows and joys. These groups enable forms of rivalry, as men and women offer stories of their successes and of the wonders of their children. The desi stores and Hindi movie theaters act as anchors in the daily lives of the migrants. When new migrants arrive, they turn to these centers for information and help with their transition. Help is, almost without exception, warmly given.

The fact of multiculturalism permits non-Europeans to put their own cultures on display rather than feeling obliged to hide it and adopt the ways of Europe. There is now some license to difference, a position that is vastly better than the project of sameness. Desis in the United States can be colorful now. The *masala* (spiciness) can be on display. On special occasions, it can be presented in parades or on the proscenium stage—Diwali, Id, Gandhi Jayanti,

Independence Days. With color and confidence, migrants stage versions of the community's special forms of expression. These events are the extraordinary flourishes of cultural life, for they come rarely and they enable people to turn bland existence into something festive.

What sorts of things are put on display? Of the entire panoply of cultural events and forms, what is chosen to be enacted in the United States? Migrants mainly reproduce the kinds of activities they experienced in their youth on the subcontinent or during trips to visit relatives in the various nation-states. Those from India borrow from the kind of integrated diversity produced through the construction of state official culture in the 1950s. The Sangeet Natak Akademi, the Lalit Kala Akademi, and the Sahitya Akademi poured resources into those cultural features deemed worthy of the new nation. They elevated special regional dances and songs to the national stage, such as Rabrindrasangeet (Bengal), Bhavgeet (Maharashtra), Garba-Dandia Ras (Gujarat), Bhangra-Gidda (Punjab), Kathak (Kerala), and the newly re-created Bharatnatyam (Tamil Nadu), among others. Dances, songs, speeches, and lately fashion shows comprise the program for endless Diwali or India Day parties. Those from Pakistan celebrate Jashn-e Eid or Pakistan Day with very similar events; the only difference might be that instead of an *aarti* (Hindu blessing), they begin with the Al-Fateha (Muslim blessing) and the crowd sings "Dil, Dil Pakistan." The Association of Indians in America, the Pakistan American Cultural Association, and the various other organizations of regions on the subcontinent host these extraordinary cultural shows, which often end with the national anthems of the United States and a subcontinental nation. A considerable portion of these organizations' efforts goes toward networking and professional development, a legacy that has traveled across the generations through such groups as Network of Indian Professionals (Net-IP).

In these events, culture operates less in the anthropological sense, as "what we do," and more in the normative sense, as "what every person should know." That is, these events encourage a kind of cultural literacy among the community members as

Pageant of an Indian Wedding, Rockland County, New York (1998). Photograph by Kala Dwarakanath. Courtesy of *India Abroad*.

well as helping create fellowship through these nationalist leisure activities. There is, it needs to be said, a great difference between national chauvinism and national fellowship. In the heart of whiteness, national fellowship is a worthy sentiment because it prevents an utter capitulation to imperial culture and at the same time it allows migrants to treasure meaningful cultural forms. These forms not only mark off some space from the tyranny of dominant cultural forms, but they are also emotionally meaningful for migrants, who feel a tingle of familiarity at such events, far from the rigor of their everyday lives. Even more, these events enable migrants, especially from the hitherto colonized world, to cultivate pride in their past through the official cultures (a legacy of the well-worn attempt by nation-states to create internal solidarity). That is, it allows such migrants to feel worthy of the cultural heritage of which they can boast. There is something pitiful in having to feel grand by identification with the grandeur of the nation and its officially constructed glorious past. The public pride also has a corporatist side, since the "leaders" of the community use these festivities to adorn themselves as unelected representatives of the people at large in order to fashion links with those politicians, executives, and media celebrities whom they invite to the events as guests.

The immigrants from South Asia may cloak themselves in a high culture even though on the subcontinent such an act might accord ill with their own class position. As people of the middle class, on the subcontinent the fantasy of the feudal _rais_ (nobles) does not fit, but in the United States it fits quite well. Here we act as ex officio representatives of a civilization rather than as members of a class community. As ambassadors of the Old World, desis (like the Irish and members of other communities) take to the streets to put the dominant classes on notice of the community's presence, cohesiveness, and strength. The first reported such event was the 1974 Indian Festival Day in Central Park, New York, where the community organized fashion shows, food stalls, and music shows. But the parades that are now held are the real public cultural show. "New York City is a city of parades," said the organizers of the desi-run Muslim World Day Parade, "we saw other parades show their communities' strength, so we thought we have to do this too."[20] New York City now hosts two parades in mid-August, an India Day Parade as well as a Pakistan Day Parade. The bourgeois thrust of these public events means that any potentially destabilizing, nonmainstream element is forbidden. Therefore, in 1994, though Miss Universe Sushmita Sen and the Hindu Right (Bharatiya Janata Party) float enthused part of the crowd at the India Day Parade, the organizers had forbidden the South Asian Lesbian and Gay Association (SALGA) from participating. In its quest for embourgeoisement, the "leadership" of the community demonstrated its boundaries, which were further revealed by the protest by Sakhi (a women's organization) and SALGA.[21] In 1998 various groups committed to social justice and liberation held Desi *Dhamaka* (Explosion) as an alternative to the parade, an event that promises both to promote the vitality of South Asia in the United States and to show its vibrancy from the standpoint of its social justice traditions (and not from that of congealed authority).

One must keep in mind here that not all nonwhite communities have the same access to "culture" and to the authentic. Some U.S. black intellectuals pushed the Black Pride movement in the 1960s in the direction of an Afrocentricity to locate a great African culture. Certainly, like other such movements, this pursuit also neglected the peasants and workers of the continent in its search for an identification with an aristocratic past (Nubian kings and queens, as well as the Pharaohs). Like immigrants, U.S. blacks do not recover this tradition as a prelude to repatriation (that is, they do not envision a trip to Liberia or a resurrection of Marcus Garvey's "Back-to-Africa" project). Rather, they seek to translate ancient greatness into cultural capital here. In 1967 James Baldwin noted that white immigrants (Irish and Jews) cling "to those credentials forged in the Old World, credentials which cannot be duplicated here, credentials which the American Negro does not have."[22] These migrants, as desis do now, used their past glory as currency to purchase respect here. The recent attempts by blacks to create a past is in line with this strategy, but it has come under strong resistance from the U.S. academy, which refuses to even permit Africa's past to have cultural worth.[23]

It is easy to empathize with the longing for some cultural resources in the United States. To be lost at sea in the midst of a relentless corporate ethic and a passionate consumer society is not comfortable for our souls; people seek some sort of shelter. Always afraid of being mass produced, individuals want to make some sort of statement of distinction, some cultural statement. Whitman, for example, could not bear the sense that he was only a product of the contemporary and of technology, so he invoked the "Past," making its passage from India to heal the modern soul. Migrants fear the loss of their culture, just as much as the young whites fear (falsely) that they have never had a culture at all. Just as white Americans don the robes of the East or reinvent their ethnicities of Europe, just as blacks seek connections with Africa in name, religion, and food, just as Latinos find links with Latin America, so too do desis seek some icon in their homeland for solace. Those who came to the United States as part of the technical-professional wave found jobs all across the country, and many came to live in "vanilla suburbs" (in the words of Parliament Funkadelic). The isolation of this existence has led many to take refuge in such forms of interaction as the Internet. In the landscape of e-mail, all tangible traces of identity can be evacuated, yet it is a zone suffused with congealed forms of identity (religion, ethnicity). People insist on coming together to reconstruct the same categories that bind them and bend them in the physical world. The newsgroups (soc.culture.india; soc.culture.pakistan; soc.culture.bangladesh) and the chat rooms are spaces of belonging, a real "home" held in place by aggressive forms of conformism.[24] In these places, the isolated individual expresses his or her opinions on historical events and cultural icons and spews bigoted sentiments about other communities (topics include "Why are Muslim men bad in bed?" "Hindu Kush mountains are evidence of a historical genocide of Hindus," "Muslim pride," and "Indian gals and American guys"). We are lonely in the belly of our corporate employers, so lonely that we hide in the warm embrace of our reinvented culture, here cultivated in the electronic pathways. The entry of the desi petty bourgeoisie in the late 1970s facilitated the formation of numerous organizations and stores in the cities, especially in the Indian ghettos. Such spaces made tangible the community that is otherwise re-created in private and in remote venues. These folk, whom I will present in the section "Of Yankee Hindutva," offer their services as the channels of the "authentic culture," notably through the organs of the Hindu Right.

The link to the homeland is fostered partly by a desire to maintain one's credentials as a member of a worthwhile people with a great past in the Old World. The attachment is also fostered by ties to family members that remain in South Asia. Occasional visits to the homeland are de rigueur, particularly when one has children, for the pilgrimage is a way to keep them connected to their ancestral pasts. Our migrants feel a sort of responsibility toward the cultures of the homeland, an issue that I will elaborate at length later. But there is yet another reason, and it has to do with a sense of responsibility toward the people who live in those left-behind lands. If technical-professional desi workers are asked why they left the subcontinent, there is often an awkward pause. Migrants are embarrassed by the question. When they finally answer, they often use a collective pronoun to speak of their own individual, personal decision, such as "When we came . . ." or "we decided to leave because . . ." This use of the collective pronoun takes a personal sense of guilt and makes it a collective issue; it is a way to project one's guilt onto a collectivity and hence to forgive oneself. It is one small way to deal with the constant discomfort of being part of the "brain drain" from countries that gave one a sense of purpose and the means to realize that sense.

The nation-states of the subcontinent recognize this insecurity, and they harvest it to draw the cultural and economic capital of their compatriots overseas. The nation principally hails the emigrants to garner coveted foreign exchange, and in the process it interpellates them into a community, such as the "Non-Resident Indian" (NRI) or the "Overseas Chinese." From 1979 to 1993, about 77 percent of the total foreign direct investment into the People's Republic of China came from 50 million Overseas Chinese. The Indian state created the NRI in the 1970s to draw in such funds, but the 15 million NRIs (with an estimated savings of $8 billion) did not invest with the same gusto as the Chinese; from August 1991 to December 1994, only 8 percent of foreign direct investment into India came from the NRIs, and after this initial burst of muted enthusiasm, the amounts have decreased.[25] "Indian communities abroad are noted for their hard work, initiative, and enterprise. As a result, they have accumulated large resources of investible funds," noted Planning Commission member Manmohan Singh at the Overseas Indian Jaambo Association (Bombay, 12 November 1982). "It is reasonable to expect that both as a part of a viable strategy of management of their investment portfolio and their sustained interest in India's development, many persons of Indian origin would be interested in investing a part of their assets in India provided they are able to obtain a fair and reasonable return on their investment."[26]

Apart from the nation-states, charity organizations that raise money for specific projects on the subcontinent also draw the desis' savings and spare time. Secular charity organizations include the many U.S. chapters of Child Relief and You (CRY), Association for India's Development (AID), India Development Service (IDS), and on the Left, there are the India Relief and Education Fund (IREF) and the Secular India's National Growth and Harmony (SINGH) Foundation.[27] Staffed by hard-working volunteers, outfits like AID and IDS garner money to support individual projects (such as hospitals, schools, and institutes for the specially challenged).

The display of culture in the public domain is one thing, for migrants do deploy "culture" in another, more mundane way. Anxious about the capacity of U.S. cultural forms to entrance them, migrants cherish what they conceptualize as their cultural forms in the home (and impart these with persistent care to young children). The home, that domain that many U.S. desis see as the refuge from a racist polity, becomes the place for the enactment of culture (or, in other words, the preservation of heritage). Many desis concede that the West is superior in the arts of techno-management but hold that it is inferior in the arts of family management. For example, a young person wrote to the desi media that "dating was out of the question, we could not even see our friends outside of school too often because again, it would interfere with our studies."[28] A gentleman responded with the following:

> You want to date. But why? Generally dating is done (a) to seek a suitable partner for marriage, (b) to obtain sexual gratification without being married, or (c) to "enjoy" the opposite sex's company in total privacy for whatever reasons. These reasons for dating do not have any place in this time in your life when you

are trying to build your future. Haven't you heard about date rapes and teen-age pregnancies?

His question reminds us of the middle-class anxiousness over civil society in the United States. But the man went further, noting, "Can't we have the best of both worlds—enjoying America while preserving our culture and identity?"[29]

Lest one mistake this debate as an intergenerational disagreement, one might want to turn to the kinds of statements made increasingly by young desis, such as a young man from George Washington University who touted India as a "spiritual refuge. What defines the essence of India," he wrote in an e-mail to the Indian Students Association (2 September 1998) "lies in that which is not restricted by time. And this is the spiritual essence which pervades the humble facade we have all come to joke about, ignore, or even repress from our memories." The conceit that desi cultural values are superior leads to a disdain for the collapse of civil society. The belief that there is a coherent Indian family tradition apart from the travails of modernity allows desis to disregard the *modern* dilemmas of family struggles (and even of the very *modern* way in which the family is deemed to be the last resort against the wiles of capitalism). The bifurcation of Indian tradition (family) from U.S. modernity (civil society) disregards both the interpenetration of the two domains and the rapacious dynamic of global capital as it seeks its own reproduction through the production of consumer desire in each crevice of social life. The "family" has become the haven for many, not just for desis, but it is a false security. We need to struggle for the reconstruction of civil society, a struggle against the drive to commodify each and every sphere of our lives. To engage in such a fight means, for example, abjuring the illusion that "Indian family values" are a resilient bulwark against capitalism. Sheltering behind family values is tantamount to the sort of hidebound approach of those who take refuge in orthodox religion to fend off commodification or those who use *ayurveda* (the science of life) as the answer to what is seen as one's "personal" dilemma.

Such a bifurcation assumes that the territory of the United States is already a homogeneous fabric. This puts enormous pressure on migrants, who seek to "assimilate" but find themselves confronted with a forbidding racism. This leads them in at least two directions, either into the shell of "national culture" (that is, to retreating from an abandoned "outside society") or else into an intensified desire to "assimilate" and gain acceptance (that is, to seeing the earlier attempt as insufficient, as having made mistakes that need to be remedied for a successful assimilation). Many of those born in the new land first try to assimilate in a one-dimensional way (to become "American"), discover the resilience of their own "pasts" as well as of racism's present, and then recover the resources within "national cultures" in a process that we may name "reverse assimilation." Though young desis may reject things Indian in the teen years, the ethnically segregated college experience draws them to India, to which they might even go on a "cultural mission," to learn from it as a font of spiritual and ethnic authority, to gauge one's roots.[30] The reversal of assimilation is not itself without problems. "It becomes difficult," R. Radhakrishnan correctly noted, "to determine if the drive towards authenticity is nothing but a paranoid reaction to the 'naturalness' of dominant groups. . . . If a minority group were left in peace with itself and not dominated or forced into a relationship with the dominant world or natural order, would the group still feel the term 'authentic' meaningful or necessary?"[31] Do young people embrace the dance, food, and religion of the "national culture" as a reaction to alienation from "America" as well as because of white Americans' positive valuation of the exotic and spiritual East? This is a hard question that cannot be answered here, but it must be kept in mind.

To turn to the homeland for "culture" returns to a problem I began to unravel earlier. Desis, we often hear, must adopt desi family values. This is argued in two ways: Either desi family values are superior to U.S. values, or else being desi requires one to adopt desi values. Either way, children are asked to adhere to certain desi rules. If children wish to challenge these rules, they are informed that they are being "American" and are not in keeping with the norms of their homeland. To be an "American" in this context is a mark of shame. If children say that they are gay or lesbians, the desi parents sometimes counter that the children are victims of a "white disease."[32] To be desi, it seems, is to be socially conservative, something that is perhaps inexplicable to the social rebels on the subcontinent. There is a denial that young desis might use drugs or belong to gangs. These are immediately associated with life in the United States ("But then again, this is America, and what you see is what you get") and not with problems of capitalist modernity.[33] Drugs and gangs, of course, are not alien to desi life on the subcontinent. In 1995 Sunil Hali's *Mausam*, a thirteen-part Hindi soap opera on desi life in New Jersey, was broadcast in New York City and its New York, New Jersey, and Connecticut suburbs. The story line was as complex as any soap opera, so it cannot be distilled. One of the characters, Raj, is married to a white woman, Jenny, first seen in a negligee sipping a glass of whiskey. Jenny, the bad and blond U.S. temptress, ruined Raj's relationship with his family. "You come here with nothing in your pocket, you drive a cab, you work at Hudson News and then you become successful," underscores Hali, "but then your son marries an American and you have a heart attack. Life is like that." Through a series of complex maneuvers, Raj leaves Jenny and marries Rashmi, the perfect desi bride. "We come here to promote our financial needs and our educational needs," says Lalit Ahluwalia, who directed the series, "but our traditional values are still with us. You should remain what you are no matter where you are."[34] This is precisely the problem: What are desis? What are their values? Are docile women and diligent men the sole models available to desis?

It seems so, at least to some. Desi "culture" is treated as an ahistorical trait, a fetish, that must be inhabited to avoid being suspected of cultural treason. The assumption that "Indian women" must be subordinate is widespread. A desi from Texas said that when it comes to marriage he "wants to get someone from a village—someone subservient."[35] This is also the sense offered by Apache Indian's otherwise wry song "Arranged Marriage": "Me want me arranged marriage from me mum and daddy, me won gal to look after me, me wan gal a say me can manage, me won gal respect me mum and daddy."[36] Girls are made to feel that certain "customs" cannot be challenged or elaborated; as one girl put it, an arranged marriage is "a lot like rape. But you do it because it is expected of you."[37] That desis cultivate arranged marriages of boys and girls unknown to each other and that men are expected to dominate the marriage is an idea promulgated in much of U.S. media, including an atrocious show by Oprah Winfrey in 1988.[38] U.S. orientalism joins with U.S. desi conservatism to enable such illiterate comments as that Benazir Bhutto "flouted tradition" by seeing her husband before her marriage.[39] There is little recognition that the concept of "arranged marriage" is not the only form for desi marital relations, and there is little sense of the vibrant changes that have occured in sexual and gender relations on the subcontinent.[40] Finally, when one accepts that men are culturally authorized to dominate women, it is not far before even violence is sanctioned. The so-called cultural defense argument for domestic violence is deemed to be legitimate in U.S. courts, so much so that wife killers earn lighter sentences if they can convince the judge and jury that their "culture" sanctions violence to make the wife obedient.[41]

The divide between "India" and "America" makes dissent impossible if youth want to retain their desiness. Can one be a desi rebel and transform family life as a desi? "In the end [after much soul searching] you realize that you are neither Indian nor American," says Vindu Goel, "you are simply yourself, an amalgam of cultural contradictions."[42] The failure to offer a better account of the cultural capacity of desis in the United States leads either to this form of acultural individualism or else to a turn to a fetishized U.S. or desi culture. There is little sense of the complex project of cultural production from multiple lineages, a project that is ongoing in some corners of South Asian America, such as at the annual Desh Pardesh festival, at the Youth Solidarity Summer and South Asian Solidarity Seminar for Youth camps, in the work of the New York Taxi Workers' Alliance, and in Workers'

Awaaz. At the Youth Solidarity Summer school in August 1997, a young woman asked why desis worry about protecting "Indian culture." "There are enough Indians in India to do just that," she said wryly. Of course, those on the subcontinent are also in the midst of a cultural struggle between those who want to "preserve" certain cultural traits as representative and those who want to produce cultural forms worthy of the complex moralities alive and well on the subcontinent.

Those desis who reside outside the territory of the subcontinental states are rendered somewhat incapable of fully experiencing a shared destiny and equality of citizenship with those who live under the daily rule of the states.[43] Their national culture will not be culture as the lives of the people but as something of a fantasy-culture, a nostalgia of distance, without the creative contradictions that provide the lively cultural forms negotiated by the peoples still on the subcontinent. When one is divorced from the subcontinent's geography and history, one cannot simply hope to replicate the totality of desi culture with its many resplendent contradictions. Of course, migrants can try: They can build temples, identify geological formations with mythical figures (as a rock formation in Fiji was chosen as the image of Naga), open shops like those of a subcontinental city.

Nevertheless, even these attempts to import culture are selective. Rather than worrying about importing desi culture *tout court,* migrants must worry about which aspects of desi culture to select. They need to imaginatively account for the origins of the various "cultural" resources and draw from them with care to solve our contemporary problems. There are other visions of the homeland (and consequently of desi culture). One need not go very far to see such visions, for they are available in the United States among the few thousand Punjabi men who traveled here during the previous fin de siècle; their leitmotiv was patriotism, which has only now reverted to its lonely status as an emotion to be cynically derided. In those days, patriotic struggle was a cherished value. People struggled to make a better world, and for that they turned to their "homeland" for inspiration. Rather than making them chauvinistic, their turn to the "homeland" was geared toward making them all the more concerned about social and political justice globally. Here is one of their songs, from a 1916 collection:

> Let the rascal tyrant cut my hands
> Let him deprive me of pen and ink
> Let him sew my mouth with stitches
> Let my tongue not work to utter my sentences
> Even then I will send the thundering waves of my heart in every
>   direction
> Saying, "I am a servant of my country
> I will die for her."[44]

In 1913, on the West Coast of North America, radical Punjabi migrants founded the Ghadar Party. "*Ghadar*" means "revolt" or "rebellion," and the party drew inspiration from the *sipahi* (soldier) and peasant rebellion of 1857 on the subcontinent.[45] The radical Punjabi men used the name as a means to renew the spirit of rebellion, of *ghadar*. Their newspaper *Ghadar* explained the purpose of the party: "Today in a foreign country, but in the language of our own country, we start a war against the British Raj. What is our name? Ghadar. What is our work? Ghadar. Where will Ghadar break out? In India. The time will come when rifles and blood will take the place of pen and ink."[46] An important figure in the Ghadar Party, as well as in the Indian Communist movement, was Baba Sohan Singh Bhakna. In 1904, when Sohan Singh arrived in Seattle, an immigration officer asked him about polygamy and polyandry in the Punjab. Sohan Singh did not deny the existence of both sorts of marital practices. When the officer pointedly asked him how he could say that he was against this sort of thing if it happened in his village, Sohan Singh replied, "Everyone has the right to reject a particular tradition or custom which he does not like."[47] This statement tells us much about the notion of "culture" that operated among the Ghadarites of the West Coast.

Migration allows communities to selectively appropriate traditions and customs. The weight of previous generations continues to weigh heavily on the minds and practices of the migrants, but territorial separation makes some customs impossible and others inadequate to the new location. Given that the Punjabi community in North America was almost entirely male, the men could not follow their various endogamous marital traditions; given the anti-miscegenation laws and given their proximity to Mexicans on the fields of the West, most Punjabi men married Mexican women. Without access to the sacred geography of their childhood (the host of shrines to *pirs* (saint-teachers), to saints, and to such preceptors as Sakhi Sarvar, Baba Farid, Nanakdas, Ghulam Mohammad), the Punjabi men began to turn to the gurudwara at Stockton, California, which functioned as a social, political, and theological center. They negotiated customs within the new landscape. By the time Sohan Singh met the immigration officer, his encounters with progressive movements in Punjab had already taught him to judge cultural practices and choose from them. In America the act of choosing was a necessity.

Of course, as Kartar Dhillon pointed out recently, migration does not necessarily produce a more progressive society. Her elder brother insisted that she return to India to marry the "right person." But she had met a Punjabi man who had impressed her "by his fiery speeches at meetings of the Gadar Party."[48] Kartar Dhillon's younger brother, Bud, went to the Soviet Union in his teens to struggle against injustice and to free India; he, Kartar said, was her main ally in her struggle for personal and human freedom.[49] At the Desh Pardesh festival in May 1995, Kartar emphasized the difference between her two brothers. The elder brother was wedded to what he considered was tradition (which included the subordination of women to the men in the family), and the younger brother was wedded to an alternative tradition (which included the freedom of women to struggle for more power in the family and society). These two brothers looked back to India with different eyes. The former sought a place to gain strength for his own insecurities in a racist land, whereas the latter wanted to win liberty for the homeland to create the possibility of justice everywhere. Bud and Kartar embody the values of the

Ghadarites—patriotism, fellowship, sacrifice, and a strong instinct against global injustice.

Of course, actions of struggle themselves are no guarantee of progressive politics. The image of India was the "Mother" who had to be saved by her bold and noble sons:

Bud Dhillon (right) and Daswanda Singh Mann at Gadar Ashram, 5 Wood Street, San Francisco, on the eve of their departure for a Freedom for India mission (1924). Courtesy of Kartar Dhillon.

My darling sons, come to the battlefield
Carrying the power of knowledge in one hand and a sword in
    the other

. . . .

Extinguish the fires of selfishness
By pouring over it the waters of patriotism.[50]

Her daughters were not to be called to her service until Mahatma
Gandhi took leadership of the freedom movement. To gender a
colonized nation female is to do two contradictory things: to replicate the patriarchal notion that a community's men need to protect their women from foreigners, and to produce an image of a
fiery and militant woman ("Mother India") who exhorts her sons
to battle (but in other songs, "friends" are called upon to save the
"Mother"). The "Mother" image opened up space for activism
by women. If the nation was to be saved, women were needed as
much as men. Different parts of the nationalist project called
upon women in their own characteristic manner: The bourgeois
faction called women to ensure the spiritual and political health
of the next generation of boys; the Gandhian faction called
women to purify the nonviolent movement by what Gandhi saw
as their necessarily nonviolent participation; the militant faction
called women to act as Durga for the community and as Kali
against the British (the anti-British "terrorism" in the early 1930s
of Shanti Ghosh, Suniti Chaudhary, Bina Das, Preetilata Wadedar,
and Kamala Dasgupta still awaits memorial). The doors to active
political work opened via the image of "Mother," but that image
came at a price for the women. The women participated in the
struggles, but they carried the burden of national tradition and
honor as well. Further, the image of "Mother" reinforced the notion that women, like the nation, must be protected from the will
of the colonizer. At its best, the Janus-faced image of "Mother"
allowed for contradictory usage, whereas the one-dimensional
South Asian American image of the submissive woman as the pro-
tector of a conservative tradition allows for only grief and resentment. If desi "culture" is to be relevant in the United States, it

must entertain the contradictory notions embedded in South Asian history to ground its own struggles in the heart of whiteness.

Struggle is seen in South Asian American terms as antidesi. Don't get involved in radical activities, desis are often told, for those are not in keeping with desi traditions. Desi traditions are imagined to be dedicated hard work and cultural conservatism. The ideas of social justice are rarely considered: The global desi bourgeoisie has put Gandhi, the icon of struggle, in mothballs and retired his activities to another time, another place.[51] Conservative thought is wedded to the idea that history has ended and that now people must get on with the job of making a living and ensuring a similar future for their children. For the first generation to be born in the United States, the "homeland" is a place of dread and of awe. Their parents, lost in the welter of the United States, enforce a rigid notion of "culture" in order to keep the children in line. On occasional trips back to the subcontinent, their naturally jealous middle-class cousins taunt them about their "incomplete Indian-ness." Then there are the new migrants who use the ponderous and overused acronym ABCD (American-Born Confused Desi)[52] to emphasize to the accidental Americans that they are "confused." The "homeland" is wielded by all these people against the next generation, who are forced to feel culturally inadequate and unfinished. As Sunaina Maira correctly noted, the push to view culture as a static trait "leads to a dismissal of the experiences of second-generation adolescents who grow up in multiple realities." These young people, she continued, "learn to expertly navigate different cultural worlds and to call on different models of behavior in different settings."[53]

Despite their virtuoso cultural literacy, many young people go in search of their culture as a trait, and they turn to those aspects proffered by orientalist educational institutions, by their untutored parents, and by rapacious groups such as the Vishwa Hindu Parishad and the Hindu Students Council. These various agencies are unable to introduce the next generation to the complexity of their situation, to the difficulties inherent in their pastiche cultural location. To do that one must go in search of other traditions, such as the histories of struggle that allow us to tend to our current contradictions rather than those histories of "culture" that force us to slither into inappropriate molds. The latter tradition dovetails with the politics of identity, whose only tactic appears to be a false search for coherence. Rather than falling prey to the culturalist notion that all "races" must take their place on the U.S. spectrum of high cultures, we must fight to forge complex cultures of solidarity. To "assimilate" implies that one must lose oneself in something else, to annihilate one's own cultural history and absorb that of someone else. Du Bois, in his 1903 masterpiece *The Souls of Black Folk,* was torn between the need to be treated as "equal" (in all senses, including culturally equal, thereby American) and the need to be true to one's heritage (to be black or, here, to be desi). Instead of this false choice, Du Bois argued that black people must be "co-worker[s] in the kingdom of culture, to escape death and isolation, to husband and use [their] best powers and [their] latent genius."[54] In this vein, rather than turn to India for the pure tradition, we must be able to turn to the complexity of India in order to take elements of the tradition that are meaningful solutions to our own local questions. Before we recover that instinct for struggle, let us go further into the search for authenticity, into the world of the Hindu Right in the United States.

OF YANKEE HINDUTVA

I can understand your [South Asian American] dilemma, but keep your Indian soul even though your exterior may be American. Bring balance in your life, get out of the confusion that comes by living in a foreign land. . . . India may have problems, but she also has intellectual and moral powers and resources that will one day teach the world. There will be a day when the world will bow at the feet of India and seek knowledge from India. You may live here, but if your motherland hollers for you, I know that you will run for her succor.

—Uma Bharati, quoted in *India West*

When I think of my perceptions of Vedic literature, I'm like, these people are priests, like, the Vedic dudes are just out of control . . . is this because I've grown up in this culture . . . that I think these Vedic people are freaks, or does everybody think that the Vedic people are freaks? . . . or is it that my exposure to this Western stuff has been so pro-[Western philosophy]?

—Manjali, quoted in Sunaina Maira, "Making Room for a Hybrid Space"

In recent years, the most significant element of "national culture" among Indian Americans has been the turn to religion, especially a syndicated form of Hinduism. Today, most community gatherings feel emboldened to relate themselves in some way to religion, either by holding these events at one of the many temples, by celebrating more and more religious festivals, or by token gestures of solicitude to a faith whose intricacies are forgotten. At a time when many deracinated desis felt incapable of enacting desiness, an organization arrived on the scene to coordinate cultural transfers. The Vishwa Hindu Parishad of America (VHPA) offered what Biju Mathew calls "cultural information packages," kits of such information as Hindu names for children, selections from Hindu texts, and answers to frequently asked questions about Hinduism. The VHPA was met at each turn by the Jamaat-e-Islami, an orthodox Muslim organization that did the same sorts of things for young Muslims as the VHPA did for young Hindus. Both organizations translate a cultural dilemma into a religious solution. This section will concentrate on the VHPA rather than the Jamaat because I believe that the former is far more powerful (demographically and financially) and is far more liable to create divisions within the desi community than to draw us toward an engagement with our location as desis in the United States.[1]

In 1964 the Vishwa Hindu Parishad (VHP) was founded in Bombay as a mass organization to draw heterogeneous Hindu sects to a united Hindu platform. In the 1980s the VHP came into its own as the militant wing of the Hindu Right, which comprises a political party (the Bharatiya Janata Party, BJP), an ideological outfit (Rashtriya Swayamsevak Sangh), and a violent "street gang" formation (Bajrang Dal). As part of a political strategy to take control of the Indian state, the Hindu Right pushed its agenda forward on two issues, the destruction of a sixteenth-century mosque at Ayodhya and an end to compensatory discrimination to oppressed castes (the dispute over the Mandal Commission's report on compensatory discrimination or affirmative action). The VHP recognized early in its career that the desis in the United States might provide it with capital and legitimacy for its mission and that it would have to appeal simply to their "patriotism" and to their sense of guilt. This, indeed, was prescient. Its kin outfit, the VHPA, set up shop in the United States in the early 1970s and began to make inroads into the community by posing as a "cultural" organization. In its early years the VHPA worked through the good graces of those few committed ideologues who migrated for technical-professional work (committed in the sense that they may have participated in the student organizations of the Hindu Right while in college) as well as the slowly growing community of petty-bourgeois merchants (who were located in the strategic center of the shopping districts for desi groceries). These people gave their time to the erection of centers of worship, took crucial positions in the boards of religious organizations, and started to offer themselves as the translators of a homogenized Hindu culture into what they considered the wasteland of U.S. society. The VHPA fed off the energy of the VHP and related organizations in India, so it was not until those groups came close to power that the VHPA exerted its power in the United States.

The Hindu Right in India became strong in the 1980s through a virulent campaign against Muslims and oppressed castes (as well as Christians, the Left, and women). Its conspiracy to destroy the mosque erected at Ayodhya by Mir Baqi came to a head on 6 December 1992, when fascistic hordes were spurred on by their leaders (who appealed to them in terms of "masculine virility, national pride, racial redemption, contempt for law and order") to set upon the historic building.[2] After the carnage at Ayodhya, blood flowed in the streets of India, from the outskirts of Delhi to the center of Bombay. The event earned the eternal gratitude of a fragment of desis who called themselves the "Concerned NRIs" and ran advertisements in Indian and Indian-American newspapers to congratulate the Hindu Right. In the wake of the anti-Muslim Gulf War, these desis found an avenue to make an alliance with the U.S. state against what the United States called "Muslim fanaticism." Some even used the conjuncture to argue that India could be the Israel of Asia, a U.S. fortress against Islam (Pakistan) and communism (China).[3] Many of these desis participated, by purchasing symbolic bricks, in the movement to raise funds for the erection of a Ram temple on the site of the mosque. For them the destruction was no surprise; on the contrary, by 1992 it was the fruit of their aspirations.

The Hindu Right's dynamic followed in the footsteps of earlier movements that communalized the desi polity in the United States. The Khalistani crusade to create a Sikh homeland made the gurudwara virtually out-of-bounds to non-Sikhs, a situation quite at odds with the role of the Sikh temple as a social and political haven for Punjabis of all faiths (the Stockton gurudwara, after all, was the home of the Ghadarites); in Berkeley and Yuba City, California, militant Sikhs began to wear black turbans to signal their alienation from other desis. Alongside this logic sits the slow Islamization fostered in Pakistan (exemplified by the promulgation of the Hudood ordinances in 1987 that made women culpable for rape against them) and in Bangladesh. This Islamization was also evident in India, the home of the movement against Salman Rushdie (a movement that climaxed in Bradford, England, with the bonfire of *The Satanic Verses*).[4] In search of respect in terms of realpolitick and power politics, many desis on the Hindu Right were further pleased when a minority government led by the BJP detonated five nuclear devices in May 1998; when Pakistan responded with its explosions, some migrants from Pakistan felt an identical zeal. These folk took the explosions as a transnational dose of Viagra, as jingoism became a substitute for the traditions of anti-imperialism and antiracism fostered by previous regimes. Chandrakant Trivedi (president of the Federation of Indian Associations) led an effort to raise funds for India as a symbolic attempt to overturn hypocritical U.S. sanctions, and he was joined by several bourgeois U.S. desi organizations, including the India-America Chamber of Commerce and the Indo-American Political Foundation.[5] India used to respond to white supremacy as the land of Gandhi that would fight with moral force; now India simply flaunts its nuclear weapons and tells the world to back off.

The virulence of this kind of pride may make it easier to live as a subordinate population in the United States, but it certainly does not transform the fact of subordination (as a minority in the United States). These events severely compromised the moral capacity of desi peoples to fight for social justice. In turn, the cleavages created between peoples from the different subcontinental states has widened on religious lines as Indians are pressured to be aggressively Hindu and Pakistanis are asked, in turn, to be publically Muslim. The president of the VHPA favored the name "American Hindus" to differentiate Hindus from Muslims, since for the latter, in his estimation, "Muslim identity is more important than their Indian identity."[6] And, indeed, on 22 August 1998 the VHPA organized a Dharam Sansad (a Parliament of Righteousness) at which it designed a ten-point *Achar-Samhita* (Code of Conduct) for Hindus in the world. The Sansad asked Hindus not to be "apologetic" about their "values," and one item in the code was concerned with "how to instill and cultivate the appropriate level of assertiveness and aggressiveness among Hindus."

To widen identities on religious lines is an insult to the diverse reality of social and cultural life on the subcontinent. Under the direction of K. Suresh Singh, the Anthropological Survey of India has begun to publish a series entitled The People of India (the first volume appeared in 1992) that shows the enormous diversity of life on the subcontinent. There are forms of religious practice that borrow from every major tradition, there are enormous numbers of languages and dialects, there is every kind of social custom and taboo. The huge and creative sedimentation of custom does not seem to deteriorate over time. Rendering this diversity into such terms as "Hindu" or "Muslim" tells us less about the people in question than about those overdetermined categories. Further, to assume that Indians are Hindus and Pakistanis are Muslims does a disservice to those who do not belong to these faiths but live within the states. There are more Muslims in India than in the Persian Gulf states, and their cultural traditions are as integral to the subcontinent as are those deemed to be Hindu. And finally, demarcating these territories in terms of a religion erases the presence of a vast number of agnostics and atheists who live in these lands. These tendencies are hardly modern or derived from Europe, since they can find their ancestors in such people as Kanabhuj (the "atom eater") or Kanada, who formulated the Vaisesika system, or in the Mimamsa philosophical system, or indeed in the materialism of the Lokayatas and the determinism of the Ajivikas. With so many deeply rooted traditions, it is hard to sustain the fallacy that India is Hindu and Pakistan is Muslim.

The desire to posit some kind of high culture before the eyes of white supremacy is nothing new for desi peoples in diaspora. Taraknath Das, a respected desi figure in the early decades of this century, lifted up an orientalist vision of India to prove that Indians belonged firmly in the camp of humanity, that they had high cultures that might stand the U.S. elite's test of worth. Working-class migrants, such as the Irish, came under special censure in this "melting pot" test in the crucible of nativism. On 11 January 1926 Das wrote a long letter to the Indian nationalist Lala Lajpat Rai to commend him on the formation of the Hindu Mahasabha in India, an organization committed to bigotry and violence but useful for an Indian American in search of an organization of "Hindu Culture."[7] Presaging contemporary conservatives who turn eagerly toward the unsavory *Hindutva* project, Das wrote to Lajpat Rai that the "greatest work for the regeneration of the people of India is yet to be undertaken by the Hindu Mahasabha movement." The "Hindu people" needed "regeneration," one might imagine, because they had been made less than human in European terms; their "regeneration," in other words, was to be precisely in the image of Europe. Perhaps for this reason (and despite the anti-Catholicism of the United States in the 1920s), Das urged "Elders of the Hindu Mahasabha" to "come to Rome for a winter or a summer" to study "the greatest and most powerful organisation of the Catholic Church and the institutions of the Vatican." This apprenticeship would not turn "Hindus" into Catholics but would allow the Hindu Mahasabha to learn how to mobilize and discipline a populace unseasoned to obey singularity.

The Hindu Mahasabha, founded in 1915, came to life in 1922–23 when it called for the formation of "Hindu self-defence

Taraknath Das and Mrs. Das (1920s). Courtesy of the Bentley Historical Library, University of Michigan; from Box 10 of the Jabez T. Sunderland Collection.

squads," not to combat the British forces but to organize the "Hindus" against the "Muslims" and others. As Das wrote his letter, the Mahasabha was in the midst of a distasteful struggle against the mosques of Allahabad (the Mahasabha rejected each offer from the Muslim clergy and fomented a deep sectarian divide in the city). It was precisely these violently divisive political projects that led Das to write to Lajpat Rai. Unhappy with democracy, Das did not want the Mahasabha to educate people; so he urged them to avoid the formation of "a mass movement of the character which Mahatma Gandhi started on the question of Charka, etc." Instead, the Mahasabha must produce leaders who would demand absolute loyalty from a benighted following. From whom should the Mahasabha's leaders gain their wisdom? "I have noted," Das wrote, "that the Mahasabha keeps close contact with the Pundits of the orthodox school. It is a very good thing." Let the organization bend, Das suggested, to the medieval values of that orthodoxy. In contemporary conservatism a similar tendency is evident in the types of sects flourishing in the United States and in the people in control of the many theocratic institutions.

Das's complete identification with Hindu orthodoxy led him toward an anti-Islamic stance whose virulence is not unfamiliar among those who adopt the trappings of *Hindutva* today. Here is a stunning quotation:

> I regret very much that since the ascendancy of Mahatma Gandhi, the Congress has been reduced to a communal organization to promote Moslem interests against the interest of all the people of India. I do not believe that there can be a genuine Hindu-Moslem unity by catering to the Moslems and by sacrificing the sound principle of Nationalism. I have seen enough of the Indian Moslem patriots in all parts of the world, and I happen to know something of their international work on the basis of Islam First and use India for the cause of Islam.

Perhaps Das, living in Europe and the United States, had no access to the events of Non-Cooperation and Khilafat (the anti-imperialist upsurge in India after World War I), for these movements hardly resembled his description. In addition, Das failed to appreciate the moral and political need for an a priori unity of oppressed peoples and of the complex cultures of the Indian subcontinent (themselves impossible to sector into "Hindu" and "Moslem" with such ease). The bourgeois nationalist dynamic toward monoculturalism took on a vehemence in the United States in the 1920s, and it is evident in Das; this same dynamic is alive and well today within the *Hindutva* movement both in India and in the United States. Political projects of the Right fail to conceptualize the inherent multiculturalism of states and the need for multinationalism to be the cultural logic of state formation (a project of the Left).

The turn to religion, therefore, is not itself unusual within that cumbersome phenomenon known as the desi diaspora. Early indicators of this appeared in the 1890s, when Arya Samaj missionaries and Muslim clerics traveled to Trinidad to take charge of what the British saw as a loss of moral compass among the indentured workers. The British were responding to a vibrant festival known as Hosay (loosely based on the Muharram), which was celebrated by those of African, Portuguese, and Asian ancestry. Indentured life segregated these peoples by race, and it also prevented the free movement of laborers to meet others on the small island. But on Hosay each plantation created its own *taziya* (a replica of the graves of Hassan and Hussein, martyrs in the struggle of early Islam) and took to the byways and streets in a fantastic competition of color and sound. In 1884 the Hosay came at a time of labor struggle, and the British plantocracy cracked down not only on that year's celebrations (which turned to militant struggle) but also on the festival itself.[8] The British encouraged the entry of religious leaders to divide the developing solidarities. Hosay was to be restricted to Shias, while the clerics offered Hindu customs to the Hindus, Christian to the Christians, and so on. The complexity and secularization of everyday life was being directly challenged by the British planters and officials as well as their friends of the cloth (of green, black, and saffron). The battle was on for the hearts and minds of the indentured workers. India was recentered in the lives of the migrants, who sought language, culture, and religion. "Culture," here, is already being used to index the customs of spirituality and domesticity and not the actual life experiences of the people (such as the brutality of indenture, the monotony of plantation work, the attempt to find solace in religious and nonreligious traditions, the attempt to form family lives and other social networks in the hostile plantation, and the creative move to make the landscape more familiar and sacred). "Culture" is seen as particular high cultural traditions as constructed by religious elites. Islam becomes a faith of the Quran and the *Sharia* as interpreted by conservative and orthodox clerics; Hinduism is what the Brahmin priest decrees. The chain of reasoning is simple: "Culture" is religion in the interpretation of the elite priests who sanction it.

The indentured workers in the Caribbean left their homes in eastern India with a firm sense of folk religious practice, something attested to in many accounts.[9] Without temples and mosques, these workers re-created religion in concord with their new lives, a dynamic disrupted by the entry of the Arya Samaj missionaries in the late 1890s. The post-1965 desi migrants to the United States came without a well-developed sense of cultural forms. Most studied in secularized institutions cut off from the world of "traditional" culture and more in tune with the English-medium world of techno-culture (such as the Indian Institute of Technology [IIT], Indian Institute of Management [IIM], All India Institute of Medical Science [AIIMS]).These schools provide an extensive but narrow education, without a liberal training that might offer a nuanced idea of "culture" and of one's cultural history. Desis absorbed such things as songs, stories, practices, and beliefs, but unsystematically. Desi cultural resources offered a fairly good understanding of how to live, but that practical understanding was not necessarily raised to the level of a conscious philosophy. Some children of the migrants feel frustrated with their parents' religious literacy. "Our parents just practiced whatever their parents had inculcated into them," noted a young Hindu Right militant. When he asked his parents why they pray to Kali or who Ganesh is, they did not know. "Nobody had answers! Parents don't know; they're lost. They don't know where to look. Kids are really desperate to know who they are, the meaning of their customs."[10]

The turn to "culture" or "religion" created a problem of knowledge, since few migrants felt secure enough to maintain and transmit culture in isolation. The cultural organizations (many organized on the basis of language and region) helped in this process, notably by providing confidence, mutual aid, and safe spaces for the enactment of cultural practices. Friends also helped each other reinvent things only partially remembered, particularly such things as marriage rituals, which are rarely experienced. In the mid-1980s my cousins invited me to share a Diwali evening with them. We ate sweetmeats in a room adorned by *murtis* and enveloped in the smell of a familiar incense. The little girl of the family, dressed in fine desi clothes, picked up an *Amar Chitra Katha* (popular comic books that recount, frequently from a Hindu chauvinist standpoint, the history and mythology of South Asia). She sat before a diorama of the last books of the *Ramayana* made of small figurines and a few old posters, and she read from the comic. In the New World, I remember thinking, comic books serve as our scriptures. This was a premature thought. By the late 1980s organizations from South Asia were entering the United States to authorize syndicated forms of religiosity. Since desis are under obligation to present themselves before the eyes of white supremacy as a cultural commodity, many turned to such self-described purveyors of "culture" as orientalist textbooks and their authors and the organizers of Yankee Hindutva.

U.S. desis may desire a "culture," but not one that openly challenges the cultural hegemony of white supremacy. Therefore, Yankee Hindutva operates in "private" domains, such as temples and homes, but notably through the Internet. The information superhighway provides a safe space for an expression of nationalism and identity that has little place in the corporatized nationalism of the United States. Although the nets are safe and "free," they are also isolated. An India-related newsgroup rarely attracts a non-Indian (or non–South Asian); a Hinduism-related website attracts only those interested in Hinduism (for that matter, a Gujarati Samaj mailing list only occasionally contains non-Gujaratis). Thus, these "isolated" sites become spawning grounds for the technocratic migrants who need to reinvent their identity each night after having sold their souls to corporate America during the day. In the 1970s the VHPA relied upon the ghettoized petty bourgeoisie to manage its organization, but now it has widened its leadership net to include isolated professional-technical workers who can do their religious-political work through e-mail. The Internet became a place for migrants to learn about their culture from convenient websites with brief statements on static customs and rituals. "This is the story of . . ." "This is how you do this ritual . . ." These recipes for culture flood the websites and newsgroups as folks now take permission from barely known political and cultural organizations with their own firm, but rarely discussed, agenda.[11]

The Sangh *lafang*s (Loafers), in Subir Sinha's felicitous phrase, seized the time and the possibilities offered by mainstream multiculturalism and conservative desis. To win over the desis, the VHPA put itself forward as the solution to all the migrants' social anxieties. The VHPA acts multiculturally through its student wing, the Hindu Students Council (HSC), which champions a syndicated Brahmanical Hinduism (or Hindutva) as the neglected culture of the Hindu Americans. The HSC subtly moves away from the violence and sectarianism of related organizations in India and vanishes into the multicultural space opened up in the liberal academy. The HSCs and Hindutva flourish in the most liberal universities in the United States, which offer such sectarian outfits the liberty to promote what some consider to be the neglected verities of an ancient civilization. The VHPA and the HSC claim to be simply "cultural" organizations, far from the political parent groups that spawned them. For older migrants, the VHPA offers the ethic of "a strong family," and it emphasizes "special programs [to] support the needs of Young Americans, thus aiming to mould the ideal citizens fired with zeal and Patriotic spirit. [The VHPA] is working to instill a true Human pride in its members thus bringing closer to reality the American dream of a Kinder, Gentler Nation." "Strong family," as we shall see, is code for a strong father in a patriarchal household. On patriotism, the text is deliberately ambiguous as to whether the patriotism is to be directed toward India or the United States. What is very clear is that the VHPA claims to do "cultural" work, to add "enrichment and cultural awareness to American society, based on time-tested Eternal Hindu values."[12] "The VHP pretends to be a cultural organization seeking to instill 'Hindu cultural values' among the youth," says a secular and democratic organization from Massachusetts, "yet a large part of its work here has been to raise funds for activities that lead to communal riots in India."[13] I will discuss the money later, but for now it is sufficient to recognize that the VHPA disassociates itself from the political work of the VHP. It inserts itself through the channels of multiculturalism, and it claims to do only "cultural" work (despite its financial and formal links with political groups in India).

Is the work that the VHPA does in the United States solely "cultural"? On a surface level, the VHPA welcomes Indian politicians and organizes their tours across the United States. In this sense it is very political. Further, the Hindu Right fosters a close relationship with the transnational elite who have considerable influence over public policy in India and in the United States. The Hindujas, a UK-based family conglomerate, continue to donate considerable funds to Columbia University in New York City to maintain a Vedic studies center, and they expend funds to create a moral politics in India (that is, they support the BJP in many different ways); it needs to be said that much of this money probably came from the Hindujas's alleged nefarious role as middlemen in arms trades (such as in the Bofors scandal).[14] A pro-Hindutva management consultant in Maryland posted two letters on the web in 1996, one from Ashok Singhal on the letterhead of the government of India (from his thirteen days as home minister in the first BJP government), and the other from Jay Dubashi, a BJP economic consultant. The management consultant leveraged his access to these people through his location in the United States (itself the center of transnational capitalism). The VHPA allows such people to make contacts for business and political reasons. Hence, on this obvious score, it is hardly *merely* cultural.

Also on the surface level, the VHPA participates in fund-raising for the Hindu Right within India. Two years after its formation, the VHP in India enunciated its global strategy. It was to open associations "outside Bharat having similar aims and objects or affiliate such associations with the Parishad." The VHP's board was authorized to "collect funds and donations from Hindus residing outside Bharat."[15] At the Tenth Hindu Conference in New York City in 1984, a resolution urged "all the Hindus of the world—back home and abroad—to act in a broad and nationalistic manner rising above their personal beliefs and creeds, parochial languages, and provincial and sectarian considerations such as Gujarati, Punjabi, Tamilian, Telugu, Bengali, Jains, Sikhs, etc." The VHPA offers the Hindu (and Sikh and Jain) migrant an easy task: to give money for work in India, to help those Hindus who are in "distress." The money rolls in. Between 1990 and 1992, the average annual income of the VHPA was $385,462. By 1993 its income had gone up to $1,057,147. An allied group of the VHPA, the India Development and Relief Fund, raised almost $2 million in the 1990s (some of it via the United Way). This money is discreetly transferred into India. It is common knowledge that during the wave of Shilapujan ceremonies across the globe toward the erection of a Ram temple at Ayodhya, millions of dollars in cash and kind reached India. It is also common knowledge that VHP and BJP functionaries carry huge sums of money in cash or kind from the United States to India.

One aspect of the financial relations of the Hindu Right can be documented through two of its programs, the Vanvasi Sena and Support a Child. The Hindu Right transfers money to nongovernmental front organizations on the subcontinent. Compared to the volume of industrial investment flowing into India, a few million dollars under the Service program appears to be insignificant. However, that sum enters the country in a sector that draws money from neither the Indian state nor transnational capital. This sector is made up of organizations that battle for the spoils of the liberal elements in the advanced industrial countries as well as of the domestic bourgeoisie. The Hindutva groups' pipeline of funds automatically put them among the elite of these groups, and they are therefore able to exert their influence among subaltern populations. In addition to the financial significance of the U.S. groups, the U.S. desis offer their Indian allies *legitimacy*. Imperial domination began a tradition in India of valorizing anything "foreign"; the BJP frequently refers to its U.S. allies in order to reaffirm its legitimacy as the party that appeals even to those who live overseas. These sorts of activities are patently political by any definition of the word.

But let us go further. Can one do merely "cultural" work? Isn't all "cultural" activity also in some ways political? For example, Yankee Hindutva offers a way for the migrants to reconstruct their dignity in a racist society. Through their activities, they try to show that Indians have a great culture, one even superior to U.S. culture (as Uma Bharati, a BJP member of the Indian Parliament, said in the speech quoted at the beginning of this chapter).[16] Yankee Hindutva fights a bigoted culture with its own bigoted worldview: "If you say your culture is better, we'll say our culture is better." Rather than negotiate the weaknesses in all our cultural experiments, Yankee Hindutva reinforces the idea of the separation of "Hindu" and "American" and thereby further segregates the consciousness of the Hindu migrant from U.S. society. It intensifies the ahistorical dyad between East and West to position the former as worthwhile and great in order to stand tall before the dominant latter. The divide is accepted by the U.S. state and dominant classes, since it allows them to shore up the desis over blacks. U.S. racism opens the door toward a valorization of the forces of Hindutva by both the Hindu bourgeoisie and by a U.S. society that is superficially impressed by the antiquity of the subcontinent and its philosophical heritage, notably the monotheism of the Upanishads and of Buddhism. "American children visit their in-laws only for Thanksgiving dinners," said Mahesh Gupta (chair of the Overseas Friends of the BJP), "but in Indian arranged marriages the young couples spend months with the parents and parents-in-law."[17] Whom does he wish to fool? Murders of brides over dowry are only one indication of the grief that young brides have to endure from their in-laws; their fate is as cruel as that of some young Americans who lose their family ties under pressure from their work schedules. Yankee Hindutva goes further, since it encourages Hindu women to avoid professionalism and warns Hindu teenagers to eschew sexual and social relations with non-Hindu youth.[18] Hindu men are urged to live epic lives that serve as a mode of social control of the youth as well as women.[19] The youth are alienated from the resources that might help them live in a multicultural nation and a complex world.[20] "The main purpose of our functions," said one VHPA volunteer, "is to transmit our culture to the younger generation."[21] What is this "culture" that is to be transmitted? Does it draw from the lifeworld of the youth, and is it therefore, able to respond to the youth and to be developed by them?

U.S. society is under attack from the rapaciousness of transnational capital, which knows it can sell whatever someone will buy regardless of ethics. Parents of all stripes are fighting a defensive battle against the weight of these corporations. Rather than join what should be a collective battle to reconstruct society along the lines of compassion and fellowship, Yankee Hindutva asks desi children to withdraw into Hindu enclaves to learn the ways they are greater than others. At its summer camps, the VHPA trains youth in a syndicated Hindu dharma (righteousness).[22] There is nothing wrong with learning *shlokas* (Sanskrit stanzas), stories from epic literature, Hindi, yoga, *bhajans* (devotional songs), and dance. There is, indeed, nothing wrong with the Gita reading groups, the *mahila sabhas* (women's organizations), the informal baby-sitting groups, the temple-based functions, and *pujas* (prayers). There is, however, everything wrong with learning them as if they are the heritage solely of Hindus and not part of a complex shared history that includes those who are not Hindus. Suneeti Kulkarni defended her son Udayan's time at a VHPA camp by saying that "everyone should know about religion. After they grow up, they can decide their stand."[23]

How do they decide or make a choice when they have not been given a story filled with different versions of the past? The Hinducentrics (such as the VHPA) want to create homogeneous

VHPA activists attack Youth Solidarity summer participants, India Day parade (1998). Courtesy of Sunaina Maira.

identities for our youth. Despite their claim that they want to create harmony, they produce chauvinism in desi young people. There is everything wrong with teaching "culture" as a set of certainties rather than as an ambiguous resource. "The religious heritage that is being projected here and sought to be preserved and passed on to the next generation," C. M. Naim wrote, "is closer to an ideology than a faith or culture. It has more certainties than doubts, more pride than humility; it is more concerned with power than salvation; and it would rather exclude and isolate than accommodate and include."[24] In the United States there are mosques and temples but no *dargah*s (shrines), "not the kind where a South Asian Muslim and a South Asian Hindu would go together to obtain that special pleasure of communion or that equally special comfort of a personal intercession with God."[25] U.S. desis, Shamita Das Dasgupta perceptively noted, "are developing what I call 'Hindi cinema Hinduism,' portraying 'pativrata' women, who may not be reality based at all. There's this mythical, homogeneous Hindu culture that is evolving. Rituals and activities are emerging in the name of 'our' traditions."[26] Instead of this syndicated Hinduism, we desis need to tend to the core of mundane secularism, one that is an "everyday critical life-practice."[27]

Religion-as-certainty was the theme of the centenary celebration of Vivekananda's visit to the United States. The VHPA organized a conference in Washington, D.C., entitled Global Vision 2000 (6–8 August 1993), and it was a signatory at the World Parliament of Religions held in Chicago (September 1993). Busloads of young desis arrived in the capital, many soon to don T-shirts distributed by the Hare Krishnas ("Be Udderly Cool: Save a Cow," said one) and caps distributed by the VHPA (a blue baseball cap with "VHP" embroidered on it in white). Such leading lights of Indian culture as Sonal Mansingh, Hariprasad Chaurasia, and Anuradha Paudwal ironically celebrated Hindutva with cultural acts devoted to the complex heritage of the subcontinent. Several controversial politicians of the Hindu Right gave speeches at the show, including Ashok Singhal (head of the VHP) and Uma Bharati. Their statements made it clear that they saw the occasion as "an obscene celebration of the demolition of the Babri Masjid [the sixteenth-century mosque at Ayodhya], the induction of religion into politics, and the creation of a 'Hindu vote-bank.'"[28] The carefulness and honesty of Vivekananda's U.S. tour was lost by this strident use of his image for what is essentially a local imperialism. Singhal noted that 6 December 1992, the day the mosque at Ayodhya was demolished, should be inscribed in "letters of gold," and Bharati told liberal Hindus that "WE are ashamed of YOU. After December 6, the tiger has been let out of the cage." K. Suryanarayan Rao offered a paper with the title "Rashtriya Sevaksangh Fulfils the Mission of Swami Vivekananda," and Romesh Diwan celebrated the "New Economic Order."

Some people who attended the event came filled with religious exuberance; Neelam Gandhi, for instance, said, "As a Hindu, I love Ram, I love Krishna, and anything Bharatiya." She was certain that "the VHP did not do anything wrong" in Ayodhya, a statement remarkable for its ignorance (the VHP was, at that time, banned in India for its unconstitutional destruction of a national heritage site and for incitement of violence against Muslims and Dalits [untouchables]). The virulence of the proceedings was at variance with the sentiments of others among the young audience, one of whom told Arvind Rajagopal that she was there because "it's more a matter of self-confidence than of culture. You know you're not crazy, you're not alone. The things you're worrying about are not abstract. If you believe you have a right to be a particular way, people will respect you."[29] In search of a sense of being in a racist society, this young woman stumbled into racism's mirror image. The anti-Muslim and antiblack undertones of the event remained hidden from this young woman by the simple claim to a worthy culture. Rather than drawing her into a movement to combat the foundations of white supremacy, Yankee Hindutva gives her a bigoted pride and an obscene hatred for one of white supremacy's current foes (Islam).

The VHPA and the HSC fail to grasp the complexity of the crisis in the United States because many of the leaders are bound to the political imperatives of the subcontinent rather than to the lives of people here. The typical local HSC is organized and run by a male, first-generation immigrant, graduate student connected to the Hindutva ensemble in India. Many HSCs are now being organized and run by second-generation youth, male or female, many of whom have family ties to VHPA. These local leaders work within a strict hierarchical chain of command that extends through regional coordinators to the National Council of Chapters (operated out of HSC headquarters in Needham, Massachusetts). The insistence on a congealed hierarchy reveals much. As a disillusioned young man who once held local HSC office in Ann Arbor, Michigan, put it, "The top leadership of HSC has long ceased being students, but they run the show and work in close cooperation with their 'superiors' in VHPA."[30] Subcontinental matters so dominate the agenda that they wipe out the very real dilemmas of life in the United States. Those crises are sacrificed to a movement whose sole purpose seems to be to create authoritarianism on the subcontinent. The semiwilling detritus of this is the desi community in the United States.

The tragedy of the Hindu migrants is their inability to reconstruct traditions to suit a difficult context. Faced with the ritualization of desi life in Britain, Suresh Grover and others inserted themselves into the space of culture to create resources drawn from desi and British cultural forms. They chose Diwali as the festival to be reconstructed, and they offered "Diwali against Communalism" as their event.[31] Diwali (*Dipawali,* the row of oil lamps, the festival of lights) was the ideal event to reconstruct.[32] There is no single story that explains Diwali, for some traditions tell of Vishnu's victory over the anti-God Naraka or over Bali, other traditions exalt Krishna, and yet others, the most popular, tell of the return of Rama to Ayodhya after his long exile and his campaigns in Lanka. The day of Diwali is seen as a day of renewal, as the start of the new year. Tulsidas's sixteenth-century poem *Ramcaritmanas* tells us that the "arrival of Ram in Ayodhya was like the rising of the full moon over the ocean. . . . Beautiful women filled golden plates with fruits, flowers and curds and flocked to the streets singing songs of welcome. Men surged forward in vast numbers, eager to pay respects to their beloved Ram" (*Uttarkand* 1.2). Diwali refers specifically (in these traditions) to the creation of a new kingdom, but more generally to a renewal. Diwali functions, therefore, as a metaphor rather than as the commemoration of any specific event. The tales of Diwali function as a *smrti,* as the process of remembering the past to gain wisdom.

Yankee Hindutva celebrates Diwali each year through Brahmanical Hindu rituals, whether at the grand pageant in the South Street Seaport in New York City or elsewhere. The VHPA's motto, "Dharmo rakshati rakshitah [If you protect your religion, it will protect you]," drives the festivals—they aim to preserve a vision of Diwali rather than to use the festival as a way to express one's own dilemmas. The VHPA remembers Diwali thus:

> In northern parts of Bharat, Deepaavali is associated with the return of Sri Rama to Ayodhya after vanquishing Raavana. The people of Ayodhya, overwhelmed with joy, welcomed Rama through jubilation and illumination of the entire capital. Well

has it been said that while Sri Rama unified the north and south of our country, Sri Krishna united the west and the east. Sri Rama and Sri Krishna together therefore symbolize the grand unity of our motherland.[33]

Indian territorial nationalism and an implicit suggestion that Hinduism is the heir to nationalism crowns this description. Because of these sorts of definitions, but also because of recent events, the festival of Diwali is slowly being drawn into the orbit of Yankee Hindutva. Invoking the story of Rama these days, then, puts one in an unhappy predicament. The forces of Hindutva have made the figure of Rama into a fierce warrior who leaves his beloved conscience behind at preadolescence. From the start of the Ayodhya agitation, the beneficent Rama was replaced by a severe and cruel Rama. While the VHP "*kar sevaks*" (ritual volunteers) demolished the mosque at Ayodhya, a person at a microphone chanted "Shri Ram Jai Ram, Jai Jai Ram [Praise to Rama]." The wanton destruction of a building was serenaded with the name of Rama. The massacre of Dalits and Muslims that followed was also glorified with passionate cries to the honor of Rama. The blood that has been spilled in the name of this deity makes me wonder if there is any need to remember Diwali through him. Are there no other stories for our *nyasa* (identification by homology)? Fortunately, the forces of Hindutva invoke only one marginal tradition of Rama, for the multiple forms *(bahurupa)* of Rama offer a history full of the complexities of life rather than the simple Bunyanesque tale proffered by the theocratic fascists.

The story of Rama comes in many packages. The *Ramayana* (400 B.C.E.–300 C.E.) presents the character of Rama, an avatar of Vishnu, who is to be the model of righteousness, but not a righteousness familiar to the authors of the Vedas and of the Dharmashastras. Rama does not keep to his *varna* domain but consorts with various members of oppressed castes and outcast tribes. Rama, further, does not appear as an abstract Vedic God but as the personalized figure whose presence inaugurates the *Bhakti* (personal devotion) tradition, which is commonly found

in devotional poetry as well as in the common north Indian greet-
ing, "Ram, Ram." The *Ramcaritmanas* draws from this latter notion and transforms the figure of Rama from a commonplace hero
into a personal God accessible to the masses (the text, after all,
was written in Avadhi, not in Sanskrit). The various texts offer the
story of Rama to make pedagogical and moral points: the
Ramayana argues for the colonization of the peoples of the subcontinent, whereas the *Ramcaritmanas* argues for the worship of
an iconic figure rather than, for instance, a consideration of the
Upanishads' metaphysics.

Diwali commemorates one event in the life of Rama: his triumphant return to Ayodhya after his exile and his defeat of Lanka.
The return, however, comes in the midst of a relentless campaign
of terror against Sita, which bears recollection. After Rama's army
liberates Sita from her captivity in the palace of Ravana, Rama demands an ordeal of fire, an *agni-pariksha,* to test her sexual purity
as well as her fidelity. "I have suspected your character," Rama
says (*Yuddhakandam,* 117). "You were taken by Ravana on his
lap, beheld by him with sinful eyes; how can I, taking you back,
bring disgrace upon my great family? . . . I have got no attachment
for you—do you go wherever you wish, O gentle one." Sita, the
Ramayana says, "trembled like a creeper torn by the trunk of an
elephant," and she wept. Sita goes through the fire and emerges
unscathed, and Rama declares that "if I would take the daughter
of Janaka without purifying her, people would say that Rama the
son of King Daçaratha is lustful and ignorant of the morality of the
people" (*Yuddhakandam,* 120). He accepts Sita and they enter
Ayodhya. He rules in Ayodhya, but his mind is still nettled with
suspicion. To restore his reputation among his councilors and citizens, Rama asks Lakshman to take Sita into exile. Sita, in the forest, learns of her fate, and she cries aloud "with the notes of pea-
cocks" (*Uttarakandam,* 58). Exiled, Sita gives birth to twins.
When Rama finds her later, he forces upon her a third trial: This
time, she enjoins the earth to part and accept her (in much the
same way as Kalidasa's Shakuntala enters the earth to seek refuge
from the betrayal of men). Rama's Rajya, the time of great peace,

is disturbed by the citizenry's demand that the loyalty of women be constantly tested.

The test of loyalty is not unfamiliar even today. Like the roots of Diwali, history is marked by the tales of many *Sitas*—women, Dalits, *adivasis* (tribals), Muslims, the working-class, blacks, Latinos—who have had to face tests of loyalty, ordeals of fire. There is no need to repeat the well-known litany of barbaric ordeals inflicted upon the oppressed and the exploited. A string of dates marking riots and police brutality does not adequately capture the pain inflicted upon the subordinate. We accept our guilt in the face of murder, we console our shame with our sophism. We justify the murder of Muslims by some false argument about their disloyalty; we justify the harassment of women by some specious claims about dharma; we justify the exploitation of workers by recourse to the double-entry account book (which now stands in for reason). The *agni-pariksha* of the multitude continues unabated. Like Rama, we constantly demand that the powerless face the ordeals that establish the dominance of the powerful. We have made our pact with history and rejected the cultural struggle for wisdom. Ram at least grieved when he enjoined the endless and ruthless ordeals, but we have rejected that too; all that most of us have expressed is the sense that certain unseen forces compel us to stand aside and watch as the vast masses endure poverty and death for the sake of "development" and "profitability." When Sita descended into the earth, Rama returned to Ayodhya "stricken with sorrow and grief . . . with his eyes full of tears, with his face downwards and with a dejected mind" (*Uttarakandam*, 111); he is a figure capable of remorse and mercy. Such emotions seem to have vanished from an elite who have taken the verities of neoclassical economics as *sruti* (primary scripture), which is *apauruseya* (impersonal), abstract, and beyond human intervention. Such an attitude to life betrays the vast mass to ceaseless toil without the hope of economic subsistence and cultural sustenance.

When the indentured workers celebrated Diwali in their localities, they rejoiced in their complexity and the richness of the story of Rama.[34] "Diwali against Communalism" in England was also an interesting way to tread the terrain of cultural complexity. The organizers insisted that the festival was not to belong only to Hindus; rather, the organizing committee and all kinds of shows on the program must be open to all non-Hindus. They found sponsorships from African, Pakistani, and Indian associations, and they drew in artists, playwrights, puppeteers, and actors. The theme of the event, following from the exile in the Dandak jungle, was to be forests. About a thousand schoolchildren from Hounslow carried puppets and candles in a demonstration for a secular Diwali, a show of force for peace and justice and a memory of the secularized rituals that dot the landscape of South Asia. As Grover noted, multiculturalism can be used by progressives, since the organizers of "Diwali against Communalism" went to the schools and offered their program as one gesture toward the elaboration of desi culture. There was no objection from the teachers.[35] Such a festival does not make a chauvinistic statement about any one "culture" as opposed to any other. Rather, it produces forms for the expression of multiple dilemmas of people who find in these arenas some resources for hope and further struggle.

Those in India too struggle with the reconstruction of culture. The only advantage they have over the desi diaspora is that they do not have to labor under the illusion that there is a distant land that is the home of pure religion, of the dharma that Hindu American children are told to long for. Hindu children in India are told of a Vedic age, an age textually re-created not a century ago by orientalist scholars, a distant age whose purity was lost over time. Both of these distant purities—the Vedic age or India— are attempts by certain elements to enforce their versions of culture and tradition on all people. Tradition and culture are not givens; rather, they need to be constantly remade in ways that enable us to live creatively, to struggle in the creation of a good society of the future.

OF ANTIBLACK RACISM

Peculiar circumstances have kept Indians and American Negroes far apart. The Indians naturally recoiled from being mistaken for Negroes and having to share their disabilities. The Negroes thought of Indians as people ashamed of their race and color so that the two seldom meet. My meeting with Tagore [in 1929] helped to change this attitude and today Negroes and Indians realize that both are fighting the same great battle against the assumption of superiority made so often by the white race.
    —W. E. B. Du Bois, *Against Racism*

Desis seek out an "authentic culture" for complex reasons, among them the desire not to be seen as fundamentally inferior to those who see themselves as "white" and superior. To be on a par with or at least not beneath these people, desis, like other subordinated peoples, revel in those among them who succeed in white terms. There is a sotto voce knowledge among nonwhites of their various forms of greatness. Parents instruct their children to recognize all kinds of people valued by Europe, a ubiquitous theme not just among desis but also among Jews and those of African ancestry.[1] Vijay Singh won a golf tournament; Kalpana Chawla may go into space as a NASA astronaut; Murjani designed Gloria Vanderbilt jeans; Bose is the electronics magnate; Vishwanath Anand is a chess grandmaster; Kabir Bedi acted in a soap opera. The ambit of this knowledge among desis is extensive, even among those ignorant or disdainful of the activities in which these people excel. I hate golf, but I couldn't not know of Vijay Singh's triumphs; I never watch soap operas, but I somehow knew that Kabir Bedi was to be on *The Bold and the Beautiful*; I relish the fact that Freddy Mercury of Queen is from Bombay and was once Freddy Bulsara.[2] To take pride in these figures is a hallmark of the desire to say to someone, "I am worthy, I am worthy, respect me."

There is something wonderful in the care that parents take to inculcate their children with a sense of pride in their heritage and of possibilities in themselves. Success in the United States is not just something that is touted for the benefit of children; it is also used as a means to create pride among the multitude on the subcontinent. In Rajkot, in Gujarat, Chief Minister Keshubhai Patel told a meeting of doctors that "Gujarati medicos in San Francisco were more trusted by Americans than their own white physicians." The crowd was amused and happy.[3] There is also something pathetic in this tendency to celebrate only those who succeed in terms set by white supremacy. Only if desis appear in the *New York Times* or on CNN do we consider them admirable. Those who are successes in other value frameworks but are not so recognized rarely find themselves felicitated or held up as role models for the children. Those who struggle silently for social justice, for instance, find few memorials to them (except when they memorialize themselves, as in the 13 May 1998 taxi workers' strike in New York City or in the agit-prop Urvashi Vaid expressed during her encounter with George Bush).

When we tell ourselves and others that we are great, do we mean to imply that there are some who are not so great? White supremacy judges certain people greater than others, and some are frequently denied the capacity to be great at all. This is the root of antiblackness, for it is "blacks" who are mainly denigrated. I've put "blacks" in quotes deliberately, since it is not a self-referential category. Blackness signifies emptiness, failure; it does not refer directly to "black bodies" (of which there are really none). Rather, it refers to a projection onto certain peoples who are deemed to be "black." This idea of blackness does not necessarily refer to those of African ancestry; it is white supremacy's attitude toward people whom it designates as "black" and who are then assumed to be inferior in various ways.[4] During British rule in India, for instance, the word "nigger" was used liberally to refer to Indians, as in E. M. Forster's phrase "buck niggers" and in an etiquette book that pleaded with the English not to call their Indian servants "nigs," since they are, after all, "fellow creatures."[5] The word "nigger" does not refer directly to Africans but to those who are seen to be black in countenance (skin color) or demeanor ("nigger" comes from the Greek *anigros* [unclean-impure], itself close to *knephas* [darkness] and *knephaios* [dark, as somber]). Then there is the hideous 1899 account by Helen Bannerman, *Little Black Sambo*, about a "black" child (Indian/African) who outfoxes a marauding tiger. Despite the apologies by her biographer, it is clear that for Bannerman "black" refers to Indians as much as to Africans, in line with her milieu.[6] In addition, in the United States during parts of the nineteenth century, southern Europeans and the Irish were somewhat "black," a phenomenon only now being exposed in some very useful histories.[7] Such accounts show us that "black" itself does not refer to peoples from any specific place or time. Rather, white power determines who is to be black at specific periods of time for various reasons. If "black" is contingent, so too is "white," but the power relations between "black" (inferior, bad) and "white" (superior, good) are not provisional.

White supremacy denies blacks any greatness, past, present, or future. Certain historic peoples feel the edge of this racism with unbridled vehemence, for instance, Amerindians, Australian aborigines, and sub-Saharan Africans. Hegel, for instance, argued that these people made no contribution to universal history. "We have information," he wrote of the Aztecs and Mayans, "but it imports nothing more than that this culture was an entirely nationalistic one, which must expire as soon as Spirit [the Europeans] approached it." The arts of ancient Egypt did "not belong to the African spirit. What we properly understand by Africa," he wrote, "is the Unhistorical, Undeveloped Spirit, still involved in the conditions of mere nature."[8] That he had only limited information did not stop Hegel, like most Europeans, from denying these peoples their cultural treasures and denying them the capacity to enact sublime cultural forms. Indians, however much denigrated as nether peoples, did not suffer this kind of denunciation. White supremacy's relationship to India was far more nuanced than its relationship to Africa. It was, for instance, acknowledged that in the ancient past the subcontinent had produced worthwhile artifacts and ideas, but time and a lack of historical development had either ritualized them or left them in ruins. Even Lord Curzon, the conservative viceroy of India, was keen to preserve its monuments, in which he saw value. It is, of course, far better to be acknowledged as having some value than to be denied any at all. This is the nub of the problem I will explore in this section. White supremacy does not endow all of Asia with equivalent value. With the advent of southeast Asians and the shifts in the class position of Asian migrants to the United States, the media began to differentiate between those Asians with cultural worth and those whom they saw as less worthy. "As a rule," declared *Time* magazine in 1993, "Asians in America have reflected extremely well, especially those who have drawn from the wellsprings of the older civilizations of India, China, Japan and Korea."[9] The so-called boat people—the Hmong, the Laotians, the Cambodians, the Vietnamese, all members of venerable civilizations—find themselves seen as the lesser Asians not just by the Klan (who reemerged spectacularly in 1981 to fight the Vietnamese fisherfolk in Texas) but in the liberal imagination.

To be given some value; to be seen as worthwhile, if only for one's ancient wisdom; to be seen as deeply spiritual and capable of wisdom about the ethereal world—this is the hallmark of the desi in the eyes of white supremacy. Deepak Chopra's burlesque speaks directly to this tradition; so too does Dinesh D'Souza's val-

A working-class Sikh, an "unmodel minority," British Columbia, Canada (early 1900s). Courtesy of Vancouver Public Library, Vancouver, British Columbia, Canada.

orization of ancient Indian texts. Indians are great. Others are not so great. Others, in fact, are mediocre, subordinate. We are indeed far from statements of simple cultural difference and in the midst of statements of cultural hierarchy and value. For three centuries, white supremacy has fought a campaign to elevate "whites" (and "Western Civilization") to the top of the totem pole, while simultaneously degrading "blacks" to the bottom of the pile.[10] The idea that "white" is supreme was consolidated, new historical work shows, in the early eighteenth century through a complex set of forces, mostly centered around issues of land (as the main source of wealth) and imported labor (in the main, from Ireland and Africa).[11] "Black," as culturally lesser, was forged in the smithy of agrarian relations; white supremacy treated black people as chattel, with little consideration for their cultural sentiments and political desires. The U.S. state created legal and punitive mechanisms to keep blacks at the bottom of the totem pole. It also relied upon competition from white workers and upon their disdain for blacks.

This was particularly so for those who migrated from Europe to the United States in the late nineteenth century. These migrants came with a fresh set of ideals, ideals that began to characterize the entire "American experience." The migrants left the shores of Europe to arrive in the United States with the idea that "here labor could become emancipated from the necessity of continuous toil and that an increasing proportion could join the class of exploiters, that is those who made their income chiefly by profit derived through the hiring of labor."[12] Ideas such as the collective emancipation of the entire working class came only in fits and starts, sometimes with groups that lived in socialist communes (such as the Icarians), but at other times in the uneasy socialism of particular trades (whose limited strength was made clear during the 1877 railroad strike).[13] These workers, in their early tenure in the United States, opposed slavery, either for moral reasons or else for fear of being economically driven to the level of slaves. But the opposition was in small circles (for example, among German workers, the "Red 48ers," and the Communist Club of New York). When Daniel O'Connell, from Ireland, offered his support to blacks, Irish mine workers in the oppressive pits of eastern Pennsylvania wrote to chastise him. We are citizens, they said. The racism of these workers, Mike Davis argued, must be seen "as part and parcel of their rapid and defensive 'Americanization' in a social context where each corporatist lower class culture (native-Protestant versus immigrant-Catholic) faithfully reflected through the prism of its own particular values the unifying settler-colonial credo that made them all 'CITIZENS.'"[14] During Reconstruction, Du Bois argued, "as succeeding immigrants were thrown in difficult and exasperating competition with [freed] black workers, their attitude changed."[15] The immigrants' prosperity (or potential mobility) was gained on the backs of the black workers, especially when the West provided the migrants with land for exploitation (the great "frontier thesis" of Frederick Jackson Turner, another wonder of the 1893 Columbian exposition). The black workers provided the bulk of the surplus value, the means for the economic mobility of the white, migrant workers. The tortured history of trade unionism in the United States with regard to black workers illustrates the contradiction between the knowledge of white exploitation as well as black exploitation and of white immobility because of black stasis.[16]

In an important 1993 article, Toni Morrison wrote that the immigrant must participate

> freely in this most enduring and efficient rite of passage into American culture: negative appraisals of the native-born black population. Only when the lesson of racial estrangement is learned is assimilation complete. Whatever the lived experience of immigrants with African Americans—pleasant, beneficial or bruising—the rhetorical experience renders blacks as noncitizens, already discredited outlaws.[17]

"In race talk," she continued, "the move into mainstream America always means buying into the notion of American blacks as the real aliens." And the Indians from India tend to the side of the Yankee cowboy, whose title to this soil was won on the backs of Amerindians and blacks. With blacks at the bottom, there is every indication that any migrant has a good chance both of being above the nether end of society and of experiencing some mobility. Recognition of this fact illustrates the acceptance of structural racism against blacks in U.S. society. Even if one does not read the census reports, one can guess that the black population in the United States is in dire straights. Between 1973 and 1993, incomes of white families rose by 2 percent, whereas incomes of black families fell by 3 percent. Black men of every educational group earned a lower hourly wage in 1993 than they did in 1979.[18] This deterioration of income allowed many immigrants to see themselves as immune to poverty, which appeared to be endemic to blacks. Indeed, the media and the political rhetoric made it seem as if the "underclass" was not a general economic condition but was somehow the cultural inheritance of the black (or those of African descent) poor. Stereotypes of black criminality and of laziness abounded just as *Time* announced the birth of the "underclass" in 1977. The presence of these stereotypes and of the urban rebellions led many migrants to fear the black masses.

The tragedy of this stereotyping and of the frustrations of black youth do not enter the framework of migrants such as Dinesh D'Souza. According to D'Souza, one is allowed to be prejudiced against blacks in the United States because blacks are (in his dubious opinion) statistically dangerous.[19] Without a theory of structural racism and without an appreciation for the history of U.S. blacks (whose struggles produced the limited freedoms we, as migrants, enjoy in the United States), there is every indication that the migrant tunes in to a benign form of racism: an adoption of stereotypes rather than a compassionate look at the enduring forms of racism.

Racism, in its most persistent form, exists in the structure of social life, and it is sustained by the reduction of "racism" to its overt form. Most people eschew the cultivation of hate; they are not like those egregious racists who dragged James Byrd down a dirt road in Jasper, Texas; they exculpate themselves from what they consider is a vulgar, lower-class kind of racism.

Racism, however, refers not just to social oppression but also to the way structures of exploitation have been sedimented in the United States. The history of legal slavery, of Jim Crow, and of a decapitalized existence produced an unequal world validated after the fact and guaranteed as private property. Racism, in this account, is not merely an irrational prejudice that remains at the level of abuse and stereotype; nor is it capable of being defeated by the tonic of education alone. There is no false innocence in structural racism, since it refers to the historical appropriation of values and the monopolization of power by an elite that is wedded to class privilege and to white supremacy.[20] Martin Luther King Jr. was well aware of the power of this form of racism toward the end of his meteoric life:

The plantation and ghetto were created by those who had power, both to confine those who had no power and to perpetuate their powerlessness. The problem of transforming the ghetto, therefore, is a problem of power—confrontation of the forces of power demanding change and the forces of power dedicated to the preserving of the status quo. Now power properly understood is nothing but the ability to achieve purpose. It is the strength required to bring about social, political and economic change.[21]

The state in liberal democracy fails to address the problem of structural discrimination, since it pledges to stand for equality and to stand apart from the differences in civil society. "Far from abolishing these *factual* distinctions," Marx argues, "the state presupposes them in order to exist, it only experiences itself as *political state* and asserts its *universality* in opposition to these elements."[22] The state can preen in its universality, in its adherence to the Enlightenment tradition, if it ignores the inequalities of civil society. To stand apart from civil society, the state accepts its inequalities and therefore acts on behalf of those who have already secured power over society (the state may, in fact, also actively participate on behalf of those in power, but only by saying it is helping the *public* or *general* interest—as in the theory that with deregulation "a rising tide lifts all boats," though only the yachts found themselves afloat). The state may want to be impartial and may indeed see itself as impartial, but it cannot *be* impartial if the social relations that found it are partial. Its actions must impact upon the partiality of civil society, so that its laws cannot be "color-blind," "gender-blind," or "class-blind." To act upon inequality with equality is to allow unequalness to persist. To quote King again:

> Anatole France once said, "The law, in its majestic equality, forbids all men to sleep under bridges—the rich as well as the poor." There could scarcely be a better statement of the dilemma of the Negro today. After a decade of bitter struggle, multiple laws have been enacted proclaiming his equality. He should

> feel exhilaration as his goal comes into sight. But the ordinary
> black man knows that Anatole France's sardonic jest expresses
> a very bitter truth. Despite new laws, little has changed in his
> life in the ghettos. The Negro is still the poorest American—
> walled in by color and poverty. The law pronounces him equal,
> abstractly, but his conditions of life are still far from equal to
> those of other Americans.[23]

When chattel slavery was abolished, lawmakers considered
unequal economic policies on behalf of the ex-slaves (rather than
on behalf of the slavers) to ensure some means to create free exis-
tences. The proposed reparations (forty acres and a mule) would
have served as capital funds to generate some measure of equality.
These did not appear, so black America was given "equality"
(only in its constitutional form) in the state (which did not act
upon it until the 1960s) and was thus condemned to the inequality of civil society. For this reason, King called for a "poor people's
movement" to liberate the working class and the poor from
hopelessness, and Whitney Young called for a domestic Marshall
Plan to transfer capital sums to the poor. This did not happen.
Further, even such mild forms of redress as affirmative action are
being dismantled. By all accounts, Asian support for California's
Proposition 209 (to end affirmative action) was rather strong; the
anti-immigrant sentiment amongst desis was equally firm. Both
Newt Gingrich and California governor Pete Wilson began to
spout the slogan "Asian Americans are hurt by affirmative action." That the chancellor of the University of California at
Berkeley, an Asian American, was fundamentally opposed to an
end to affirmative action did not change the mind of too many
members of the Asian community, and certainly not the desis.[24]
Structural racism constitutes desis' lives in the United States;
desi attitudes toward its structures allows us to be genteel in our
bigotry.

Structural racism is screened off by seeing its effects as the responsibility of those who are poor rather than of the political
economy. For example, in the mid-1960s, just as the Civil Rights

Acts passed through Congress, the liberal government under Lyndon Johnson ceased to talk of redressal or of state complicity in racism; it now spoke of the effects of racism (poverty and violence) as "circumstances present in the family within which [the black man] grows up." The "black family," specifically the black man (as absconder) and the black woman (as the insufficient patriarch), came under attack as the locus of the "black problem";[25] that the "black family" was constituted in a variety of nonbourgeois ways was precisely the handle for the revanchist idea that black people are responsible for their own poverty and immobility. In his landmark 4 June 1965 address at Howard University, Johnson noted that the "breakdown of the Negro family structure" meant that "all the rest: schools and playgrounds, public assistance and private concern, will never be enough to cut completely the circle of despair and deprivation."[26] This story of the pathologies of blackness emerged from Moynihan's 1965 report as well as from Johnson's speech; it was constituted by the media in reaction to the 1965 Watts uprising; it was sustained as a way to counter any criticism of the inadequacy of the political rights restored to blacks in the Civil Rights Acts of 1964–65.

Also in 1965, an important year in U.S. history, the new immigration law was promulgated; it allowed scores of techno-professional workers to enter the United States. The Asian entry into the United States was used in direct opposition to the blacks. I have already mentioned the famous *US News & World Report* (26 December 1966) story that heralded the supposed independence of the Asian in comparison to the blacks. This is an instance of the model minority thesis, which says that some "minorities" are able through their own efforts (that is, without state support) to be socially mobile, whereas others seem to be constitutionally unable to do so. In the mid-1960s, the former included east Asians and the latter the blacks. The Chinese, once fundamentally oppressed by white supremacy, are transformed in the context of the Black Liberation movement into a pliant and worthy "minority." Chinatown was a colony prior to the 1960s, not an ethnic arcade for tourists. Only when the Chinese became a "model" did Chinatown itself become a place to eat and stroll.[27] The transformation was astounding, given the anti-Asian sentiment (against all Asians—Chinese, Korean, Japanese, . . .) during World War II. As Watts burned Pearl Harbor receded, and the Asian appeared as one ideological weapon against blacks. Look at the Asians, every black activist was told; they seem to make it on their own; what's wrong with your people? Can't they also make it?

In 1966 Irving Kristol penned a remarkable story entitled "The Negro Today Is Like the Immigrant Yesterday," in which he asked the simple question (with a special code word) "Can the Negro be expected to follow the path of previous immigrant groups or is his a special, 'pathological' case?"[28] He put the word "pathological" in quotes because he disingenuously claimed that anyone who labels the entirety of black America "in an extreme psychiatric and sociological condition" is liable to be called a racist (but one certainly is a racist if one implies that this condition is a result of one's Being and not of one's being exploited). After a long description of the perilous state of black America, Kristol noted that "the real tragedy of the American Negro today is not that he is poor, or black, but that he is a latecomer—he confronts a settled and highly organized society whose assimilatory powers have markedly declined over the past decades."[29] The readers who are puzzled may congratulate themselves on their perceptiveness. "Latecomers" to what? Certainly, latecomers to the feast of capital, since most blacks worked to produce the bounty that was divided among some whites in an earlier time.

Having structured that wealth as protected private property, white people can now revel in their liberality toward blacks (even though the labor of black people produced much of the values appropriated by white America). Implicit in the kind of genteel statements made by Kristol is the suggestion that some migrants can "assimilate" and can make it. He referred fleetingly to the Jews and often to the Irish, but in 1966 others spoke candidly of the real model among the minorities, the Asians. The Asians may have come late to the feast of capital, but, it was said by such as

Kristol, they carry with them cultural (or biological, depending on whom one reads) capital, an inheritance sufficient for advancement. Most Asian immigrants saw this narrow welcome and, immorally, accepted it (D'Souza's theories are a lame attempt to validate this defensive Asian racism as a defensible policy itself).

The entry of desis in large numbers *after* the passage of the Civil Rights Acts not only brought them into the model minority category but also set the terms for the desi view of Black Liberation. It did not take long for the media to add desis to the model minority category. Here was a community with phenomenal demographic data: Almost everyone had an advanced degree, and almost all the migrants imbibed bourgeois values of education and a work ethic. There was little recognition in the media that this was an artificial community, that most of those who migrated here came through the filters of the INS. This was the cream of the bourgeois South Asian crop, and it was certainly going to make an impact despite its small numbers. Further, all the migrants seemed to be part of nuclear families and thereby proved Moynihan's and Johnson's thesis. There was little discussion of the fact that the migrants formed "nuclear" families because they could not bring in their extended families; nor was it mentioned that divorce was impossible for many spouses (given their precarious visa situation, a condition ameliorated by the Battered Spouse Waiver of 1990).[30] The 1950s fantasy of white family life (as illustrated on TV shows like *Leave It to Beaver*) erased the fact of Jim Crow segregation (the black domestic servant, for instance) and the sorts of oppression (against white women) that produced the phantasm of the family.

"Family" itself cannot be an index of social stability, since it exists within a matrix of social relations (whereby social costs are often passed on—blacks enabled white stability, and black domestics even enabled the "liberation" of elite white women from the late 1950s onward). The issue of "family" also ignored the massive investment made by the *family* left behind by the migrants, a network of relatives who produced the bourgeois techno-professional with love, capital, and energy. This "family" included the postcolonial state, whose own investment in the migrant was immense. The United Nations has determined that between 1960 and 1990, the United States and Canada accepted more than a million techno-professionals from postcolonial states; these states lost an investment of about $20,000 per skilled migrant.[31] Such facts are erased as the ahistorical "Asian" is set beside the equally ahistorical "black" to make the simple claim that the former shows that the problem of the latter is either genetic (though few lack the taste to say so) or cultural (the collapse of the family and so on). In a chapter entitled "Blacks and Asians in America," Francis Fukuyama compared Asians to Jews and blacks to the Irish. Such a comparison reproduces standard stereotypes of the hardworking and family-oriented Jew-Asian and the lazy and irresponsible Irish-black.[32] To elevate "Asians" at the expense of "blacks" is a specie of inferential racism that refers to "naturalized representations of events and situations relating to race, whether 'factual' or 'fictional,' that have racist premises and propositions inscribed in turn as a set of *unquestioned assumptions*."[33] Inferential racism, in general, is "invisible" because it is not considered to be offensive. Given the enormity of the structural crisis in the United States, the media still tends to view blacks as the source of the problem (this is so in the 1965 Moynihan Report, which blames black women for poverty, and it is so in the attack on young black men, who are blamed for a breakdown of civic life). Blacks are only applauded as musicians and athletes, standard stereotypes from the days of slavery.[34] Attacking blacks by paying tribute to "Asian intelligence" makes one immune from charges of racism, and the model minority thesis is thus a pillar of inferential racism.

This stereotype was a godsend for desis. It provided them with an avenue toward advancement, despite its negative impact on blacks and its strengthening of white supremacy. In the throes of an intensified Black Liberation movement, the white establishment pointed to its civil rights legislation as the ceiling for state action. The rest, they said, was to come from the initiative of the oppressed themselves. This implied that the oppressed did not take initiative, a notion as condescending as it was erroneous. Blacks did not have the power to enact their initiative, which drew many urban blacks into the poor people's movement as well as the Black Power movement. For desis, much of this was bewildering. Most had little idea of the Jim Crow atmosphere: Since they migrated mostly to northern cities after the enactment of the 1964–65 Civil Rights Acts, they did not experience the worst of the overt racism felt by the small number of desis who migrated to the United States before the mid–1960s. Further, that many did not participate in the Civil Rights movement meant that they did not cherish the rights won by those who could not really benefit from them.[35] Most desis, too, had not participated in the freedom struggle against the British, so they did not feel the fist of white supremacy, nor had they experienced the vitality of freedom through struggle. They came as techno-professionals to a land that emancipated its state from direct racism, transferred antiblack racism to civil society, and used them as a weapon to demonstrate U.S. blacks' inability to rise of their own volition. Racism, in this form, is not simply about culture; it implies biology as well. The 1990 U.S. Census, for instance, reports that African-born migrants enter the United States with the highest rate of education (88 percent come with a high school degree or more; for Asians the rate is 76 percent, for Central Americans it is 46 percent, and for the U.S.-born population it is 77 percent; 46 percent of the African-born migrants come to the United States with a B.A., whereas only 20 percent of U.S.-born citizens hold a B.A.).[36] These Africans are not presented as a model minority, an indication perhaps of the resilience of biologistic thinking among the media and the general population in the formulation of antiblack racism. Where these Africans are discussed, they are used in a manner similar to the Asians, again without any consideration of the INS filtering that only allows techno-professionals to enter the United States.[37]

The lack of connection between desi advancement on the backs of blacks and of the use of desis in a war against black Americans comes at the expense of a tradition of solidarity and fellowship that began at least a hundred years ago. The legacy of links between desis and Africans, whether in the Caribbean, in Africa, or indeed in the United States (in Salem in the late 1700s), needs to be revisited so that we might reconstruct some resources for an antiracist fight. Two poems will help me set up this tradition.

Mighty Britain, tremble!
Let your empire's standard sway
Lest it break entirely—
Mr. Ghandhi fasts today.

You may think it foolish—
That there's no truth in what I say—
That all of Asia's watching
As Ghandhi fasts today.

All of Asia's watching,
And I am watching, too,
For I am also jim crowed—
As India is jim crowed by you.

You know quite well, Great Britain,
That it is not right
To starve and beat and oppress
Those who are not white.

Of course, we do it too,
Here in the USA
May Ghandhi's prayers help us, as well,
As he fasts today.[38]

Come, I have heard the drum's rhythms
Come, my pulse races
Come, Africa.
Come, I have lifted my forehead from the dust
Come, I have scraped the despondent skin from my eyes
Come, I have freed my arm from pain
Come, I have clawed through the web of helplessness
Come, Africa.
In my grip, the chain has become my mace
I broke the fetter from my neck and made it into a shield

Come, Africa.

In every swamp, the radiant spear ends burn

The enemy's blood turns the dark night red

Come, Africa.

The earth throbs with me, Africa

The river dances and the forest keeps time

I am Africa, I have taken your shape.

I am you, my walk is your lion's walk,

Come, Africa, come with your lion's walk,

Come, Africa.[39]

The first poem, written in 1943 by Langston Hughes, follows at least three decades of support by the U.S. black press of the struggle for Indian liberation, particularly of Gandhi. New York City was a hotbed of interaction between blacks and Indians. When Lala Lajpat Rai was in exile there, he courted black leaders (including Booker T. Washington), and when Marcus Garvey made the city his home, he made firm alliances with Indian rebels. Garvey left Jamaica in 1916, the year indenture ended (it ended largely because of much militancy in the islands by those of Indian and African ancestry). Haridas T. Muzumdar, a Gandhian, came to the United States in the 1910s and became a close associate of Garvey after he "read an account of a lynching in the South. After reading that account I could not eat for two days."[40] From India too came Hucheshwar G. Mugdal; he migrated to Trinidad and then emerged in New York, where he became the editor of Garvey's *Negro World* in 1922.[41] Another figure in this world of complex alliances is Kumar Goshal, an artist and a regular political contributor to the *Guardian* who fought alongside Paul Robeson, Henry Wallace, the Council on African Affairs, and South Africans like Ashwin Choudree for freedom for the colonized peoples of the world.[42]

In 1919 Du Bois asked that "the sympathy of Black America must of necessity go out to colored India and colored Egypt," for "we are all—we the Despised and Oppressed—the 'niggers' of England and America." Du Bois was part of the black tradition set in place by David Walker's *Appeal to the Colored Citizens of the World* (1829–30), Martin Delany's *Blake* (1859), and Frederick Douglass's spirited sentiment that freedom was indivisible. Not content with the solidarity of purpose, Du Bois (like Bhim Rao Ambedkar in India) sought a congress of blood to bind the oneness. "The blood of yellow and white hordes," he wrote, "has diluted the ancient black blood of India, but her eldest Buddha sits back, with kinky hair." Empathize, Du Bois pleaded, with "the suffering of unknown friends. . . . Only our hearts pray that Right may triumph and Justice and Pity over brute force and Organized Theft and Race Prejudice from San Francisco to Calcutta and from Cairo to New York."[43]

In 1928 Du Bois published a social realist novel, *Dark Princess,* which is sadly neglected despite its refreshing look at the travails of black social and political life.[44] Neither politically bleak like Ralph Ellison and Richard Wright nor a pessimistic social realist like Upton Sinclair, Du Bois offered a structural view of the peculiar character of the U.S. haute-bourgeois state as well as of the noble and ignoble struggles of U.S. blacks for freedom. An even more startling part of the novel is the central role played by Kautalya, a princess from India who provides important financial, ideological, and emotional support for the central character, Matthew, the black man who is snubbed by his country and his community for his radicalism. When Matthew meets Kautalya in Berlin, she invites him (as a representative of the "American Negroes," for "You are a nation!") to be "part of a great committee of the darker peoples; of those who suffer under the arrogance and tyranny of the white world."[45] At the end of the book, the child of Kautalya and Matthew, Madhu, is crowned the maharaja of Bwodpur, and he is left as the hope for the future struggle against "brown reaction and white intrigue."[46] Du Bois, who studied in Germany, knew of the community of Indian radicals (under the leadership of Virendranath Chattopadhyay, who founded the League against Imperialism in 1928) and he certainly knew Lala Lajpat Rai. These Indians provide the social and historical basis for Kautalya, but the historical figures are not in any way aristocratic. If Du Bois was able to grasp the significance of these radical Indians, perhaps he felt the need to exoticize them and to gender Asia female. Nevertheless, from the standpoint of black America, India entered as a site of struggle against imperialism and racism. This is a significant difference from the world of the orientalists.

The second poem, written in 1955 by the desi poet Faiz Ahmed Faiz, indicates the view of Black Liberation from the subcontinent. The poem is both beautiful and distressing. It reveals a strong sentiment of solidarity with an oppressed continent, but it is also ambiguous in terms of its tactics for emancipation. Is Africa to follow ("come") the rest of the rebellious world, or is Africa to accompany ("come along") that world? Further, the imagery of the "natural world" and of primeval energy does not threaten stereotypes of Africa at all. Nevertheless, I would still argue that such poetry reveals some measure of fealty to the idea of anticolonial struggle. The first African nation to wrench itself from colonialism was Ghana in 1957, the year after this poem was written. The spirit of Bandung (the Afro-Asian conference of Newly Independent States held in 1955) and of this decolonization produced a strong emotional link between continents, a feeling that moved Chuck Berry to add a line about Bombay in his 1955 "Brown-Eyed Handsome Man."[47] This feeling is also captured in the different receptions Carl T. Rowan and Martin Luther King Jr. received on their trips to India in the 1950s. When Rowan tried to underplay the role of Jim Crow, he was treated with disdain.[48] King, on the other hand, was received with ebullience:

> Virtually every door was open to us. We had hundreds of invitations that the limited time did not allow us to accept. We were looked upon as brothers with the color of our skins as something of an asset. But the strongest bond of fraternity was the common cause of minority and colonial peoples in America, Africa and Asia struggling to throw off racialism and imperialism. We had the opportunity to share our views with thousands of Indian people through endless conversations and numerous

discussion sessions. I spoke before university groups and public meetings all over India. Because of the keen interest that the Indian people have in the race problem these meetings were usually packed.[49]

There remains a powerful, if demographically small, tradition among desis of seeing Africa as an ally of the liberation movement and of seeing black America as the harbinger of freedom within the belly of the beast. During his travels in the U.S. South in 1894, Vivekananda was shocked by "the condition of the Negro in the South, who is not allowed into hotels nor to ride in the same cars with white men, and is a being to whom no decent man will speak."[50] In 1929 Du Bois wrote to Gandhi asking him for a message "to these twelve million people who are the grandchildren of slaves, and who amid great difficulties are forging forward in America." Gandhi responded that "let not the 12 million Negroes be ashamed of the fact that they are the grandchildren of slaves. There is no dishonour in being slaves. There is dishonour in being slave-owners."[51] Such a strong endorsement by Gandhi was met with even stronger statements by Nehru, who, for instance, refused to allow the U.S. State Department to influence Indian celebrations for Robeson in 1958 and whose own public statements of support for the Black Liberation movement deserve to be remembered. In 1946, for instance, he criticized the "assimilation" policy of the United States, which claimed to "make every citizen a 100 per cent American"; nevertheless, "negroes, though they may be 100 per cent American, are a race apart, deprived of many opportunities and privileges, which others have as a matter of course".[52] This is, of course, the context of the Indian government's support of the 1952 *We Charge Genocide* petition of the Civil Rights Congress (submitted to the United Nations by the Communist Party of the USA [CPUSA] leader William Patterson) as well as of the Indian government's unwavering commitment to Black Liberation in Africa.[53]

Does all this mean that there is an unproblematic unity between Africans, U.S. blacks and Indian peoples? Certainly not. In his 1928 novel Du Bois wrote clearly of the prejudice Indians evinced toward blacks. When Matthew asks one of Kautalya's courtiers about her, the man talks of the high hopes her subjects held for her. "And now, now finally, God preserve us," he says, "the Princess is stooping to raise the dregs of mankind; laborers, scrubwomen, scavengers, and beggars, into some fancied democracy of the world. It is a madness born of pity for you and your unfortunate people."[54] The condescension is pervasive; reading the text I had to put the book down because it reminded me of the attitude one hears from South Asian Americans toward blacks. Unity between them can certainly not be presupposed. Indeed, on the contrary, in too many desi households one hears sotto voce racism and stereotyping of blacks.

Why do desis participate in antiblack racism, especially with this tradition behind them and given the racism that they also experience? There is a temptation to assume that desis know the net effects of antiblack racism and see that it is to their benefit to trumpet the model minority thesis (this is the kind of "rationality" developed by D'Souza).[55] There is also an attraction to the thesis that desis have a racist tradition that can be seen in the mysteries of the caste complex. It may be that some desis are rational in their discrimination (to gain at the expense of blacks) or that some simply live within a racist cultural matrix (forged by an adherence to the stereotypes of blacks as culturally inferior). The majority do not hold these views but simply go in search of a coherent identity as a way to be desi in the United States. Since the conservative desi culture that is being created in the United States tends toward forms of racism, those who go to that conservative culture in search of desiness either come away repulsed by it or else make accommodations with racism. If we desis are racist, we tend to think, then we must either reject desiness entirely or else come to grips with this as a part of our culture. Though there is little that a book such as this can do for those whose calculations show that the model minority thesis is beneficial, it can do much for those who are morally committed to Black Liberation but find themselves unable to be so and to be desi at the same time. To proceed, I want to take some lessons from the philosopher Lewis Gordon, whose own work on antiblack racism comes to the heart of the matter.

The search for identity, Gordon reminds us, is a delusion. Our selves are protean, never at a state of rest (Being), but always in a state of Becoming, unfolding into what it wills and cannot will. Our lives are not in statis, even if we sometimes try to be at peace with ourselves. There is no identity that can be found and then inhabited outside continual change. There is always a journey into the many possibilities that are simultaneously constrained, imagined, denied, and produced. Some people (for reasons of class, gender, national, or racial power) can imagine that their possibilities can indeed come to pass; others find they cannot even allow themselves to think of certain options. Choice is circumscribed, but the fact that we choose in the world is not. "Implicit in having found myself," Gordon noted, "is the denial of continued choice."[56] If there is no stable identity, then we have some measure of choice in our lives (these are, of course, curtailed by power relations—but these are never negated entirely). If we have a choice, then we are to some extent responsible for our views, if not our situations.[57] The poor cannot walk away from poverty through thought (a specie of voluntarism), but they have a choice over their perception of poverty (they can see it as the only condition available to them, they can try to protest, or they can try to better themselves). Given this theory, antiblack racism is also something of a choice. Oftentimes we hide from the choices we have made (such as the choice to participate in or accommodate antiblack racism); we tend to betray bad faith or "the effort to hide from human reality, the effort to hide from ourselves." The antiblack racist, in this case, "is a figure who hides from himself by taking false or evasive attitudes toward people of other races."[58] The desi, in many cases, is an antiblack racist in this sense.

It is hard to think that one is in bad faith given the enormity of the structural racism that sets in motion many of the other forms of racism. Gordon calls this weak bad faith, since we as individuals cannot do much to fight structural racism. If we hold racist beliefs and act in a racist manner, we can be held accountable for our acts, and we can be asked to change (this is the case of the "stubborn racist"). But we do make a contribution toward structural racism, since our weak bad faith "expresses itself in the systems of beliefs manifested by people in their everyday activities, their folkways and mores, and because such a system's maintenance and perpetuation depend on a collectivity of choices that may or may not be efforts to hide from responsibility."[59] Desis are faced with a situation, as "latecomers" (in the language of Irving Kristol), wherein "reality" and "the way things are" are held up as a guide toward how they must act. "You cannot change anything," desis are told in effect, "since you are a foreigner and, besides, can you show that you have not benefited from the system (you in your fancy car and with your college degree)?" Faced with these congealed values, "reality" takes on a cosmological significance, and migrants are tempted not to touch it lest they trigger a debacle of enormous proportions.[60] Desis can, of course, risk their values and fight against "reality" as well as their own construction as the model minority. One easy task in that regard is to commit model minority suicide, to demonstrate against "reality" and re-create a form of Asian misbehavior that is as desi as Gandhi.

Some young desis, however, do not find the model minority category useful in their social lives. Children of the techno-professionals are expected to identify with white, bourgeois values, but, says Uttam Tambar, if you hail from the working class or urban petty bourgeoisie, "you identified with black culture." Ravi Dixit, a young desi from Boston who participated in the Youth Solidarity Summer of 1997, noted that "for many South Asians, myself included, city life and culture have been the most welcoming and adaptable culture in the United States. Of course, Hip-Hop is definitely more of a medium of living and expression for people of color and I, being Indian, feel more like a person of color than white."[61] Many young desis in England and in North America have fashioned their cultural politics around several of the icons of the black diaspora culture, which itself seeks a way to prevent being culturally normalized at the same time that blacks are economically disenfranchised. The bhangra, jungle, ragga,

Five young people in New York City (1997). Courtesy of Amitava Kumar.

and D.J. sounds of Birmingham and Southall fill the headphones and the parties of the youth with the music of XLNC, Asian Dub Foundation, Apna Sangeet, Apache Indian, and Safri Boys and with the sounds of DJ Ritu, DJ State of Bengal, and Bally Sagoo.[62] In Britain young urban children of desi migrants used the beat and the songs of bhangra (a form of Punjabi music based on the beat of the double-faced drum, or *dholak*) alongside the dance hall sounds of Caribbean music and New York hip-hop to produce a vibrant sound that is unique to the complexities of inner-city Britain. In the United States there are DJ Rekha and DJ Siraiki (two who are not derivative), innovative bands like the Chicago-based Funkadesi (created in 1996), and the voice of Penn Masala.[63] In the world of jazz, innovators like Vijay Iyer and Rudresh Mahantappa explore and meld a variety of musical heritages; "my music," says Iyer, "would be nothing without the history of African Americans and the music that they brought to this country and made here."[64] This musical fusion allows for a certain amount of social fusion, but one must not mistake it for the creation of political solidarity.[65] One must be wary of the easy expectation that these new cultural products will create a creolized, "hybrid" youth.[66] In December 1994, for example, a desi boy was beaten up by a group of white youth in Providence, Rhode Island, for playing a bhangra tape.[67] The sounds of music are not a passport into the New World.

Though inner-city South Asian, Caribbean, and white Britons forge cultures to combat the disenfranchisement of their localities, they also create ethno-racial subcultures that both enrich their lives and pit them against each other. When the South Asian American music scene exploded in 1996, the first observers noted that "the only black people [at the parties] are security guards."[68] In an astute analysis, Sunaina Maira showed how the adoption of black styles by young desi youth is less part of a rebellion against the structures of power and more, perhaps, a generational stance against their parents. One young woman told Maira that blackness was a short-term fashion that would be shed once the young desi walked into the arms of corporate life. But even at the parties, Maira noted, the adoption of "bhangra moves" allowed the desi youth "to assert their ethnic identity" and distinguish themselves from blacks.[69]

Music and other cultural products enjoin us to listen to the youth's disenchantment with the false utopias of the past. As various class fragments of the desi community meet, there is an appreciation that the parental utopia has failed. When I write of various class fragments, I include the meeting of the Indo-Caribbeans and the subcontinentals in places such as Queens, New York, which has its own history of conflict and its own indices demonstrating the shallowness of such myths as model minority.[70] With almost 50 percent of the taxi drivers in New York City being South Asian, the myth of Asian success is threatened and the utopia is put at risk. Much of the anxiety of the youth over the present is being organized into gang activity, whose radicalism is more than questionable. From Queens, New York (Malayali Hit Squad; Medina) to San Jose, California (Asian Indian Mob [AIM]) to Toronto, Ontario (Pangé Lane Wale), urban desi boys (and some girls) are forming gangs in order to protect their communities and to transmit the culture of the community to the next generation. As an "original gangsta'" from AIM put it, "we want to help the younger kids get involved in the community. We help them learn about their culture. They get to hang out with others like them."[71] What is this "culture" that the gangs are transmitting? What is the notion of "protection" they deploy with regard to the community? What kind of solidarity are these young gangs trying to craft?

To answer these questions, the experience of the Southall Youth Movement (SYM) and gangs such as Holy Smokes and Tooti Nung needs to be shared on this side of the Atlantic. SYM was founded in memory of Gurinder Singh Chaggar (who was murdered in 1976) as a defensive mobilization against neofascist elements such as the National Front, the skinheads, and the British police. "The street has been appropriated by our youth and transformed into a political institution," writes Tuku Mukherjee, an SYM worker. "It is for them at once the privileged space of confrontation with racism, and of a relative autonomy within their own community from which they can defend its existence."[72] A convenient alliance was formed between the Asian commercial bourgeoisie (who did not want to lose control of their neighborhoods and marketplaces) and the local Asian lumpen proletariat. The alliance was not radical but defensive, intended to protect the bourgeois aspirations of the community.[73]

The gangs and SYM are fraught with an internal contradiction; they accept a rigid and racist notion of "culture," and they seek to protect this culture and its community against all odds. Part of this protection must be from internal elements who wish to transform the cultural practices in line with principles of justice and freedom. SYM accepts multiculturalism's racist dictum that each culture has a discrete logic that must not be tampered with. Culture, as I showed earlier, is not a fixed set of practices that are determined without history and power. Culture is a field upon which some of the most important political battles are fought, such as questions of gender relations, the status of faith and of religious practice, the question of education, and questions of elitism and prejudice. To close off these discussions is to narrow the rhetoric of freedom mobilized by the youth.

The culture upheld by these gang formations is mainly a specific Jat masculine culture (represented by the massive hit song "Jat De Dushmani" [Animosity of the Jats], by Dippa), which has very negative effects on women.[74] Women are seen as the repositories and showcases of culture. Just as culture is to be preserved, so too are women. This means that women are denied moral equivalence with men, and they are denied permission to make autonomous decisions. Women are more often the physical and psychological targets than the beneficiaries of this culturalism. Writing from the standpoint of the Southall Black Sisters (SBS), Pragna Patel speaks of the need to channel the male youth into radical activity alongside their sisters to produce "a culture in which violence and degradation do not exist."[75]

SBS provides us with a model that is replicable and necessary. An organization of Asian and Afro-Caribbean women, SBS was founded in 1979 and has struggled against domestic violence, fundamentalism, Thatcherism, sexism, and racism. In the United States there are many groups that do the kinds of work done by SBS, groups that find their hub in the Center for Third World Organizing in Oakland, California. More must be written about these groups, which are drawing in young desis and training them to fight for social justice rather than for narrow identity interests (which, as the model minority stereotype shows, often leads to antiblack politics). There is a need to formulate a theory of political work that will allow us to leave the language of political expediency behind.

Demonstration against the National Emergency in India and imperialism, Berkeley (1976). Courtesy of Dr. Sharat G. Lin.

OF SOLIDARITY AND OTHER DESIRES

A parrot knifes
through the sky's bright skin,
a sting of green.
It takes so little
to make the mind bleed
into another country,
a past that you agreed
to leave behind.

—Imtiaz Dharkar, "Exile"

I'll be sowing the seeds of community
Accommodating every colour, every need
So listen to my message
And heed my warning
I'm telling you now
How a new age is dawning.

—Asian Dub Foundation, "Rebel Warrior"

In December 1994 the city authorities of Providence, Rhode Island, planned to erect an incinerator in an area that predominantly housed the black, Latino, and Hmong working class. A full decade after Union Carbide's criminal policies murdered thousands in Bhopal, India, Providence (like most U.S. cities) conducted its own brand of environmental racism. The struggle against the incinerator proceeded apace, led by Direct Action for Rights and Equality (the predominant community organization) and joined by the Communists and the Greens. A demonstration at the plant was to be a tribute to the dead of Bhopal and to the ongoing crime of ecocide. The Alliance for a Secular and Democratic South Asia (Providence) and the South Asian Students Association (SASA) (Brown University) jointly sponsored the event. Afterward, a student came up to me and said that he was pleased with the memorial and somewhat sympathetic to the issues, but he felt that I was more of a leftist than a South Asian. The sentiment is startling, since I was born and raised in India. But he did not mean that I had no claim to the "homeland," only that my essential desiness was suspect. There was, for him, not enough pliancy, spirituality, or desire to succeed in corporate terms. What is it to *be* South Asian? In his eyes, one is not South Asian racially (since there is only a very loose sense that "we" are a "race," and besides, few Brahmins would identify themselves genetically with Dalits, and sometimes vice versa). He, like many, sees "South Asian" as a cultural designation that refers to the kind of desi constructed by such white gazes as I have delineated in this book. The desi is to be spiritual and cooperative but driven to succeed in commercial terms.

The construction of the desi as essentially docile ignores the deep roots of radicalism, both in the subcontinental past and in the United States. Volumes could be written on that tradition, which stretches from the Sramanic revolt against Brahmanism to the emergence of the anticolonial Indian national movement and to today's tireless striving of the Communists, feminists, socialists, and the Greens. In the United States this fiery heritage was imported with the first large group of migrants, those from Punjab who formed the Ghadar Party in San Francisco in 1913. "Tribe after tribe are ready for mutiny," wrote Har Dayal.[1] "Your voice has reached China, Japan, Manila, Sumatra, Fiji, Java, Singapore, Egypt, Paris, South Africa, South America, East Africa and Panama." With branches in many of the plantation colonies, the Ghadar Party emerged as the voice of desi radicalism, calling for an end to imperialism. There could be no dignified life in the United States, the Ghadarites argued, if India was still held in thrall by Britain. "The world derisively accosts us: O Coolie, O Coolie. We have no fluttering flag of our own. Our home is on fire. Why don't we rise up and extinguish it?"[2] The rebellions of 1913–14 pushed the British to end indenture, a condition of slavery that was not overthrown without mass popular struggle.[3] In the former plantation colonies, the legacy of this left-wing struggle can be seen in those elements who work within the late Cheddi Jagan's People's Progressive Party and the late Walter Rodney's Working People's Alliance (Guyana), the Young East India Party and the All Trinidad Sugar Estates and Factory Workers' Union (Trinidad), and the South African trade unions, the African National Congress (ANC), and the Communist Party (South Africa).

In the United States the heritage of Ghadar has continued among people with faith in different ideologies and committed to a host of strategies. There are some who turn their eyes mainly to events on the subcontinent; they create secular and democratic spaces within which people of all generations can develop progressive ideas. Their very existence challenges the model minority myth by propagating the idea that no people are inherently better than or superior to others. Exemplary among these are the groups formed after momentous events in South Asia: After the Liberation of Bangladesh in 1971, the South Asia Forum was formed in New York and Washington, D.C.; after the Indian Emergency of 1975, the Indian People's Association of North America in Vancouver, the Indians for Political Freedom in Chicago, and the Group of Concerned South Asians in Boston; after the emergence of the Khalistani movement, the Punjabi People's Cultural Association in the San Francisco area and the Ghadarite Cell in Bakersfield, California;

and finally, after the destruction of the Babri Masjid, many groups, including Concerned South Asians in New York, Alliance for a Secular and Democratic South Asia in Boston, Coalition against Communalism in the Bay Area, and Coalition for Egalitarian and Secular India in Los Angeles. These groups enshrine the traditions of those, such as Kumar Goshal, who spent their time in the United States absorbed in anti-imperialist work. Perhaps the main limitation of the groups that exist at present is their hesitancy to work on anti-imperialist and antiracist projects on behalf of other places than South Asia and other people than desis. If the struggle on behalf of Mumia Abu-Jamal, the black political prisoner, now a symbol of the U.S. penal industrial complex, represents a moment in the antiracist war, there are few South Asian organizations at the forefront; in addition there are few desi organizations visibly opposed to imperialist onslaughts in Central and Latin America. On the other hand, the sheer global nature of imperialism means that when South Asians work against such treaties as the Multilateral Agreement on Investments or the Global Agreement on Trade and Tariffs, they perforce create some solidarities with nondesis. The Forum of Indian Leftists, for instance, joined with the Democratic Socialists of America to host two panels on the Multilateral Agreement on Investments (MAI) at the Socialist Scholars Conference in March 1998, one on the "Global Economy and the MAI" (which included Jean-Pierre Page of the French trade union, the General Confederation of Workers [CGT], and Mark Levenson of the textile workers' union UNITE) and the other on "Gender, Human Rights and the Global Economy" (which included Lisa McGowan of Fifty Years Is Enough and Joo Huyan of the Audre Lorde Project). Further, if desis work with the International Rivers Network to combat the undemocratic way large dam projects enter India, they perforce must take interest in and work with the people in the vicinity of the Katse Dam in Lesotho or those who live beside the great Biobío River in Chile. When U.S. imperialism acts against countries like Iraq or Cuba, there are a handful of desis in each city who people the picket lines and organize demonstrations (such as the Forum of Indian Leftists [FOIL]-initiated protest in New York City against the U.S. bombing of Sudan and Afghanistan in August 1998). These alliances need further elaboration.

The spirit of Ghadar moves desis to act on behalf of their ancestral states, but it also draws many radicals toward negotiation with the complexity of their lives in the United States. At the forefront of this are the many womens' groups that emerged to create social spaces for women and to fight the many forms of domestic violence within our community. They pose a significant challenge to the patriarchal feudal culture that is being reimagined in the United States, not only to the detriment of women's lives but also to the detriment of the development of personhood among the young. The antisexist struggles remind many that "culture" is not a static thing but, rather, the basis for long-standing conversations about ways of life in congruence with the materials available to fashion our existence. Groups such as Sakhi (New York City), Narika (Oakland) and Manavi (New Jersey) are representative of a movement that covers the entire country.

Alongside these groups emerged the gay and lesbian organizations who support them. "The sadness I find in the Indian community is that we are so judgmental and gossip oriented," wrote a young gay man. "Where are the Indians when you truly need the support? I haven't found one goddamn Indian since I've been HIV positive who has gained my trust to the point where I feel comfortable telling them I'm HIV positive. Yet I feel comfortable telling other people (non-Indians). What does that say?"[4] To respond to this absence, desi gay and lesbian support networks emerged in the mid-1980s, groups such as Trikone (San Jose), SALGA (New York City), Khush (Toronto), and South Asian Lesbian and Gay Network (London), as well as to offer information and advice on HIV-AIDS (Alliance for South Asian AIDS Prevention in Toronto or the Asian and Pacific Islander Coalition on HIV/AIDS in New York). In addition, the gay and lesbian groups urge desis to change their hidebound attitude toward sexuality. On 25 January 1999 SALGA held a press conference in New York City to condemn the attacks by the Hindu Right of Deepa Mehta's *Fire,* a film about empathy in an Indian household and lesbianism. The conservatism of "culture" is routinely challenged by the womens' organizations and by the gay and lesbian groups, both of whom work on the terrain of gender and sexuality. As most South Asians slipped comfortably into conservatism through the 1980s, these organizations in almost every agglomeration of desi peoples fought strongly to keep culture fluid and dynamic.

In recent years young desis have emerged as a visible force on college campuses, where the various ethnicity-based student organizations trod an unsatisfactory dialectic between the desire to participate in the social life (the parties and the hook-ups) and the gnawing desire to do something worthwhile. For children of professionals, an adolescence without too many desi companions or acquaintances is suddenly transformed into a college experience surrounded by those of South Asian ancestry (a consequence of the social segregations on college campuses). The sheer density of desis provides the possibility for "reverse assimilation," the rediscovery of one's ethnicity and the urge to engage that difference in

SALGA at India Day parade (1997). Courtesy of Amitava Kumar.

one's social life. Desi parties on campuses bear names such as Club Zamana, Instant Karma, and Utsav, and the annual meeting of SASA is a general gathering of young people to revel in the numbers and to enjoy the social spaces provided by the festival. This sometimes degenerates into self-commodification, but it is also a necessary response to the bewildering conformism of college life in the United States (this despite the appearance of "official diversity" on campuses).

Many of the leaders of the SASAs feel these events are somehow inadequate, so they are on the road toward establishing at least a charity or community service dimension, if not a political dynamic itself. Urvashi Vaid delivered the keynote address at SASA's Brown University conclave in 1995. The address set the stage for workshops on racism, sexism, homophobia, activism, and the class realities of U.S. life. At the 1999 SASA conference, Shabana Azmi shared her history of activism, the comedian Alaudin made us laugh into struggle, and I was able to debate Dinesh D'Souza on the question of affirmative action. The institutionalization of the Gandhi Day of Service (by the Indian Students Association [ISA] of Michigan) and the creation of a board for the nationwide SASA opens up the possibility that the youth activities will move in a progressive direction. During the Emergency of 1975 in India,[5] several students at the University of California at Berkeley held a meeting of the Indian Students Association and "decided to move away from the former almost entirely cultural and social priorities of the ISA." Though the new ISA continued to host cultural programs, it took leadership in holding "critical discussions of important social, political, and economic issues of the day." At the same time, it sponsored demonstrations against dictatorship in India as well as in solidarity with the Vietnamese and Palestinian freedom fighters and others.[6] The Berkeley ISA struggled to "build solidarity among groups of like interests and objectives" through sponsorship of "progressive programs of socio-political concern to encourage a broad base of interest in humanitarian and social problems in India, South Asia, the Middle East, and the world in general." The ISA considered the epitome of its work to be such things as "the working Indian community in Canada sending money back to progressive political movements in India in recent years, and the instrumental role of some Vietnamese in the US in strengthening the US anti-war movement."[7] The nascent nationwide SASA may not move immediately to the sorts of positions adopted by the Berkeley ISA, but it is very clear that the group's tendency will be toward an active and militant engagement against oppression (and certainly against some forms of exploitation).

In Britain, the killing of Gurinder Singh Chaggar in 1976 "may have been the incident that spurred the Asian youth into or-

Anti-Emergency demonstration, Berkeley (1976). Courtesy of Dr. Sharat G. Lin.

ganising themselves, [but] the basis of their militancy was the racism they experienced at school, in the streets and in the search for jobs."[8] Most of the youth organized into SASA may not experience the kind of overt racism common in 1970s Britain, but they also draw their rage from their own everyday experiences. The problem with a movement based on experience is that it might not be able to create solidarities across groups with different experiences; solidarity is in some cases better crafted through a moral and ideological linkage than an experiential one. The tragedy of experiential or identity politics, in its narrow sense, is that it pushes a person or group not toward identification with the struggles of others but toward an exclusive concern with the identity of oneself and one's group. Rather than being informed of other's struggles and open to other's concerns, such groups claim particular knowledges and actions, some of which may be detrimental to other oppressed groups.[9] Rinku Sen, codirector of the Center for Third World Organizing (CTWO), notes that the Left must go among the bourgeois and petty-bourgeois desis "to engage these people to the extent that it is possible to go against their class interests in many cases." To commit model minority suicide, she noted, we must "identify with the poorest of the poor wherever I'm at." This is what Sivanandan means when he says that "class cannot just be a matter of identity, it has to be a focus of commitment."[10] Commitment and identification are truly important if we are to fashion a politics at a disjuncture from the way we are used by white supremacy as well as against the types of state policies that continue to exploit and oppress the bulk of the population.

In an important analysis, Etienne Balibar argued that the modern state is faced with a problem regarding the children of immigrants who will refuse to submit to the kinds of disciplinary regimes set in place for their parents. The danger, he noted, is that this second generation "will develop a much greater degree of social combativeness, combining class demands with cultural demands." To prevent this, the form of "class racism" enacted by the state and the dominant classes attempts to mark the second generation with "generic signs" of what is deemed to be their culture, which is rendered harmless by the "disqualification of resistances" as a cultural resource.[11] One must, therefore, be scrupulous in one's turn to "culture" and open to the vibrancy and multiplicity of one's cultural past rather than accepting the one-dimensional rituals forwarded by the state and by cultural "leaders." Radicalism is as South Asian as Gandhi.

Several parts of the desi Left in the United States are at work trying to forge a politics of identification. There are those who are going to be puzzled by any suggestion that the term "Left" still bears any meaning after the collapse of the Soviet Union. This criticism is rather Eurocentric, since the Communist Left is still going strong in, among other countries, India, Nepal, Cuba, Vietnam, China, South Africa, and Chile. The socialists, the Greens, and the other progressives are also on the leftist train to some extent. In 1994, faced with the problem of the convergence of political visions into a toothless middle, Italian political philosopher Norberto Bobbio published a book (which became a best-seller in his native land) in which he argued that the distinction between Left and Right "corresponds best to the difference between egalitarianism and inegalitarianism, and ultimately comes down to a different perception of what makes human beings equal and what makes them unequal." The Left, he noted, adopts a maximalist notion of equality as a social good, whereas the Right adopts a minimalist notion of equality. But the Left does not fetishize equality, since it realizes that equality "has the effect of restricting the freedom of both rich and poor, but with this difference: the rich lose a freedom which they actually enjoyed, whereas the poor lose only a potential freedom."[12] The Left must cherish this insight and work with the principle of *égaliberté* (equality-freedom), the belief in the universal and unspecified ideal of freedom to galvanize social action for justice.[13]

To re-create the Left, some of us created the Forum of Indian Leftists and the Progressive South Asian Exchange in 1995 (for details, see the forum's homepage at www.foil.org). This followed from the work of many people in the secular and democratic movements as well as in the antiracist and trade union work done by desis in the United States. We drew inspiration from the Ghadar past, but also from our Canadian friends, whose Desh Pardesh festival is a paean to contemporary radicalism of all kinds.

The desi Left, then, has been party to the creation of a "racial project," one that is "simultaneously an interpretation, representation, or explanation of racial dynamics, and an effort to reorganize and redistribute resources along racial lines."[14] The creation of this "racial project," however, comes at a time when most people are unable to create meaningful collective activities and when our civil and political society is deeply fractured. There is a need in this climate to "build an organizational culture that embraces its different members and to explicitly address the politics of difference."[15] If we do not address the vital concept of difference, we allow the Right to frame our problems in terms of an ahistorical idea of equality (so that those who are unequal now cannot speak of their oppression without it being rendered as claim for "special privileges," when in fact it is nothing other than the cry of the oppressed for justice).[16]

To speak of difference and to mobilize in terms of identities (toward collective action) is not easy, and one feels the impatience of the organizers and activists. "Multiculturalism is a hard row to hoe," noted Alfredo DeAvila, who trains young organizers of color in Oakland, "and people are simply not used to taking the time to make sure that everyone has a common understanding of what the options are."[17] One example of the "racial project" comes from Los Angeles, where Local 11 of the Hotel Employees and Restaurant Employees (HERE) union approached the Korean Immigrant Worker Advocates (KIWA) for assistance in 1992. The Korean owners of the Wilshire Plaza Hotel had just fired a group of workers, many of whom are Latinos. KIWA joined HERE to launch a campaign against the owners, and they now organize Latino workers against the Korean bosses. "We see KIWA as having two goals," noted its director Roy Hong. "The first is to inject a progressive agenda into the Korean and Asian community, and the second is to build bridges of solidarity with other communities of color based on common interests."[18] KIWA, like La Mujer Obrera (El Paso, Texas) or Teamsters Local 175 (Seattle, Washington), offers an object lesson in groups' ability to create a politics of identification that is as wide as possible.

At the start of the campaign of South Asian taxi drivers in New York City, certain organizations (such as Pak Brothers and Unity) worked for the interests of the desi cabbies but against those of the black and Latino residents of the city.[19] "The best way to overcome prejudices between [communities of color]," said Saleem Osman, a pioneer organizer among the drivers, "is to work together in solidarity with each other to build unity."[20] Concerted effort by drivers such as Osman helped reframe the problem, mainly because the drivers refused to be silent about ethnicity. "Rather than see race, gender and sexuality as 'problems,' [this polycultural working class pushed] working-class politics in new directions."[21] "Unlike in the past," Biju Mathew of the Taxi Workers Alliance noted, "drivers from other communities—Haitians, West Africans, Iranians—have come forward to take on leadership positions. We have found that the most successful strategy in dealing with ethnicity and nationalism is to talk most explicitly about it, constantly reminding people that problems can come up."[22] In fact, the richness of national heritages actually worked in favor of the drivers. Bangladeshis brought skills honed in their liberation movement, Haitians imported their experiences of the fight against the dictators Duvalier, and others drew from their experiences of resisting tyranny in their home countries. The taxi struggles in New York in recent years continue a glorious tradition from the 1930s. During the 1934 taxi strike in the city, a black driver from Harlem stood before white drivers in a union hall. "Boys," he said, "when you say you're with us, mean it. Mean it from the bottom of your hearts! We been gypped ever since 1861 and we're from Missouri. If you show the boys up in Harlem you mean what you say, then you're getting the sweetest little bunch of fighters in the world: for them spades driving the Blue and Black taxis up there can do one thing—and that's fight! And when we fights together, us black and white, man, they ain't nobody can stop us!"[23] Here is solidarity produced through race talk, for the black driver reminds the white drivers of the failures of Reconstruction and the strength of black militancy due to that betrayal.

Solidarity is a desire, a promise, an aspiration. It speaks to our wish for a kind of unity, one that does not exist now but that we want to produce. Gihan Perera, trained by the AFL-CIO, at work in UNITE, offered a vision of the struggle: "I desired to come together with all those great folks [in the National Organizer's Alliance] not only to affirm our commonalities, but also to be challenged by them, to challenge them, to venture toward the unfamiliar, to step on *un*common ground. I wanted to explore the gaps and contradictions in our own work, and take a bold leap into the unknown."[24] Solidarity must be crafted on the basis of both commonalities and differences, on the basis of a theoretically aware translation of our mutual contradictions into political practice. Political struggle is the crucible of the future, and our political categories simply enable us to *enter* the crucible rather than tell us much about what will be produced in the process of the struggle. "Some things if you stretch it so far, it'll be another thing," Fred Hampton explained. "Did you ever cook something so long that it turns into something else? Ain't that right? That's what we're talking about with politics."[25]

That this solidarity requires a tremendous act of production shows it is not "natural." That there is a desire to create unity among working class peoples and oppressed peoples of color does not mean unity is waiting to happen. There is no ontological necessity for this solidarity to be produced. History may proceed without it ever emerging, but we on the Left want it to happen. A scrupulous political instinct and theory shows that such a conglomeration of peoples might be a sufficient challenge to the status quo, that it might produce the kind of energy needed to transform what passes for "reality." This knowledge leads to a desire for such solidarity, but to achieve it will require an immense amount of effort. And indeed, too many of the current groups are far too disorganized and so are unable to create the kinds of unified movements that can make far-reaching social change. There are "networks composed of a multiplicity of groups that are dispersed, fragmented, and submerged in everyday life" and they suffer from "short-term and reversible commitment, multiple leadership, temporary and ad hoc organizational structures."[26] These are activities in search of an ideology, people in search of a common project. It will take effort to build the majorities of the future, an endeavor that is meaningful and necessary (and one that even the theorists of new social movements anticipate).[27]

The effort to build solidarity must be directed not just to education but to the entire array of things called struggle.[28] To struggle against prejudices and foes is the best crucible to create the trust and love necessary for the production of solidarity. What does it mean to struggle? Ideological work against injustice is an important part of this fight, since it sets the theoretical tenor for the other parts, the demonstrations, the protests, the rallies. These form the obvious elements of struggle, whose less-obvious mechanism is the creation of the beloved community among those who struggle. Community organizing develops the instincts that come from daily experiences to do the active work of forging communities and building a society founded on social justice and equality (not on exclusiveness, nostalgia, and a negative peace). It is hard to enter a nongovernmental organization and not find a young desi on the staff. There is also significant work being done in small socialist groups across the United States (including the Communist Party, community organizations, and antifascist groups) who fight against militarism, racism, ecocide, and, in sum, capitalism; there are some desis here as well. The most profound bonds are built in the heat of the struggle, especially when one demonstrates to the collectivity that one is prepared to share the burden of other's misery. Sacrifice is a necessary part of struggle, but so too is fellowship. Desis' commitment to reject the model minority thesis and to abjure the idea that desis are essentially spiritual is part of the sacrifice of class privilege afforded by white supremacy. Too much sacrifice might prove to be the grounds for arrogance. Tempered with fellowship, sacrifice shows that one is not in the struggle only for oneself, but also for the ideal of collective mastery.

Sometimes a struggle is victory enough. That was the mood of both the taxi workers of New York and those desi activists who have helped support the taxi militancy. After three taxi strikes in 1998 (13 May, 21 May, and 1 July), the 24,000 taxi workers ride a buoyant tide despite a harsh response from City Hall. That over 50 percent of these drivers hail from South Asia and that they held fast against the city despite the nuclear jingoism on the subcontinent shows precisely what is possible. After 98 percent of the taxi workers supported the strike on 13 May, Biju Mathew, of the NYTWA, declared that "we have the most successful strike in the city's history." The media admitted its surprise at the victory of the demonstration, but Mathew was clear that NYTWA "was not surprised at all. We knew we had a big strike on our hands. We know how to communicate with the drivers." The drivers immediate complaint was against seventeen draconian rules, promulgated by Mayor Rudolph Giuliani on 27 April, that struck at the dignity of the drivers. "This strike," said Louis, a Haitian driver, "is about economic conditions, about our working conditions, about our demand for dignity and justice." Solidarity was produced in the process of the struggle, a process that must be endlessly crafted to endure the phalanx of the Establishment.

At the dawn of the strike, Azad Hussain, a driver and NYTWA member, announced that "the time has come to take on the city." New York is no easy city to live in, and it is certainly not endowed with a government that responds to the needs of its working people. In the late nineteenth century Boss Tweed made this undemocratic style of governance normal in Tammany Hall, as the New York machine used graft and violence to control the expanding city. A century later, Giuliani won the mayoralty, proceeded to reinvent Tammany Hall in the new City Hall building, and used his power to conduct a policy of domestic structural adjustment. He has "downsized" the municipal workforce, fought against tenant rights' and homeless organizations, thrown recipients off social welfare to the wolves of destitution, cracked down on unions, and given the police free reign to act viciously.

But Giuliani came to the city at the tail end of an enforced and planned recomposition of the urban landscape on behalf of the financial, insurance, and real estate (FIRE) sectors of the economy and of plutocratic families like the Rockefellers. With the death of manufacturing and of the port, working-class families lost union jobs and the city began to import immigrants to run restaurants and taxis and to keep the unoccupied buildings clean.[29] From 1980 to 1990 the top decile of income earners earned almost twenty-six times that earned by the bottom decile.[30] An overlay to the economic war against the working poor is the rise in police brutality. Giuliani's predecessor, David Dinkins, appointed the Mollen Commission to investigate the police, but they could not have been more thorough than Amnesty International, which found that the police targeted nonwhite residents of devastated neighborhoods.[31] The Mollen Commission recommended the creation of an independent monitor over the police, something Giuliani has refused to do. In "Giuliani time," the agents of power feel emboldened to act with impunity against the residents of the city. Resistance against Giuliani's neoliberal juggernaut has seemed futile. Only when acts of immense brutality occur (such as the brutalization of the Haitian Abner Louima and of the West African Amadou Diallo) do people feel emboldened to protest against the regime, though the unions have provided some holding operations against the worst excesses of City Hall. In this context, the taxi workers' strikes have been remarkable. Those who know labor politics in the city recognize that this has been perhaps the most significant event in the city's labor history in the past three decades.

That most of the taxi workers are immigrants has allowed the mayor to belittle them by coasting on the general anti-immigrant sentiment in the United States. From the start, the mayor's office threatened to call in the INS and the IRS. "When there is a strike or a demonstration," Giuliani said on 12 May, "it's largely for more wages. This is a strike and a demonstration for the purpose of being able to drive recklessly and have nothing done about it. This is a theater of the absurd." As is typical, Giuliani portrayed himself as a champion of the "concerned consumer" and the "responsible citizen" in opposition to the "irresponsible worker" and the "lawless immigrant." The taxi workers see his characterization as just another example of the systematic disrespect they face. "There has been a constant bashing of the taxi driver by the media and the politicians," said Bhairavi Desai of NYTWA, "until the public feels that the taxi driver is a bad person who can be punished and punished." Giuliani's seventeen new rules (including increases in fines, some up to $1,000, for rude behavior, smoking, and speeding) are "not so much pro-safety as anti-driver," said Javed Tariq. "It is easy to be anti-driver because people do not consider us human."

The taxi has become a sweatshop on wheels. The mayor's seventeen rules simply add to the burden of the drivers, who ply the streets for eighty-four hours per week on twelve-hour shifts, seven days a week. For each of these twelve-hour periods, the driver leases the taxi from a garage owner for about $100. This lease rate and the additional expense of gas prevents the drivers from making more than a rudimentary wage. Since they are seen

Taxi worker, New York City (1998). Courtesy of Amitava Kumar.

as "independent contractors," the drivers are not entitled to health benefits, vacation time, or retirement benefits. The drivers are kept in a vise by a triumvirate that enjoys the fruits of this $1.5 billion business: the garage owners, the brokers (who often provide the drivers with advances), and the Taxi and Limousine Commission (who not only regulates the industry for the city but also earns fabulous fees from sale to the garage owners of the "medallions" that give them the right to operate a taxi). The New York City police, long famous for its acts of harassment against the mainly immigrant drivers, assists this trinity. Beatings and routine citations for trivial infringements of traffic rules appear to be the norm in the drivers' lives. The strike's organizers did not have to produce resentment; they simply harnessed it.

In 1992 Vivek Renjan Bald's documentary *Taxivala/Autobiography* revealed the extent of the frustration and anger among the drivers. As Bald made his film, the drivers organized themselves into the Lease Drivers' Coalition (LDC), notably due to the efforts of Saleem Osman. The next year, the drivers conducted a major demonstration against police brutality. Since then, other skirmishes with the city have occupied the drivers, 800 of whom joined together to form the NYTWA in early 1998. With a handful of volunteers and no stable financial source, the NYTWA decided on the work stoppage on 3 May (after Giuliani published the rules in the rarely read city's legal journal on 27 April), and the next day flyers hit the streets. "We knew immediately we'd be successful," Mathew noted. "The outpouring was tremendous." Drivers took the flyer and made more copies with their own resources, sometimes adding their own notes and drawings to the posters. One driver was happy to declare that he had handed out 4,000 flyers in the week preceding the strike. The NYTWA also advertised the action by CB radio (in many languages), since it is used by about 4,000 taxis and is generally the main way drivers communicate with friends during their long shifts. Organizers stood at the locations where drivers changed shifts, handing out flyers and talking to the drivers. Cabbies buzzed with conversation about the strike at every stoplight.

On 13 May esprit de corps among the strikers was very high. City Hall, meanwhile, continued to be vindictive. Giuliani joked that perhaps the city would be better served with one "taxi-free day." This humor, however, was hollow, since the residents of the city felt the effects of the action. In his vindictive style, the Mayor vowed to destroy the taxi workers' initiative. He signed an executive order allowing vans and livery cars to encroach on the taxi industry. This was in retaliation both for the strike and for the planned 21 May demonstration by the taxi workers. "I don't negotiate with people who want to close the city down," the mayor said on 14 May, "never have, never will." The judiciary refused to endorse Giuliani's executive order, a small victory for NYTWA. The bigger victory was the 80 percent support for the second strike on 21 May as well as the sensational march of 400 taxi workers across Queensboro bridge that day. This time the owners of the taxis worked against the drivers (since many felt that a deal could be cut with the city). NYTWA reaffirmed the need for the drivers to hold fast against the administration. "We cannot back down," said Desai, "the stronger we get, the harder [the city and owners] will fight."[32]

We cannot back down. The fights are endless and our leftist morality must draw us consistently to the front lines, whether for taxi workers in New York, auto workers in Michigan and Mexico, or landless peasants in Peru and Bangladesh. Faced with the onslaught of neoliberal "realism," Guarani Indians in Brazil threatened suicide in 1994; farmers in Andhra Pradesh, India, did commit suicide in 1998. In the United States there are now more suicides than homicides, as people lose faith in themselves and in humanity's collective future. The "realism" that abounds does not empower people; rather, it ensures that they lose sovereignty over their own destinies, and it erodes the basis of fellowship. In struggle, we can re-create our bonds and we can fight, ceaselessly, for what we deem to be our rights and for what we envision, however clumsly, as our freedom, not just for ourselves, but for working people in general. The taxi workers show us how immigrants and their children can be radical within the belly of the beast. Theirs is a pedagogy of hope.

NOTES

Preface

1. W. E. B. Du Bois, *The Souls of Black Folk* (New York: Modern Library, 1996), 4.

2. Robin D. G. Kelley, *Yo Mama's Disfunktional!* (Boston: Beacon Press, 1997), 15–42.

3. W. E. B. Du Bois, *Pittsburgh Courier,* 30 May 1938, in *Newspaper Columns,* ed. Herbert Aptheker (White Plains, N.Y.: Kraus Thomas, 1986), 1: 79–80.

4. Walter Rodney, *The Groundings with My Brothers* (London: Bougle-l'Ouverture, 1969), 16.

5. George Lipsitz, *The Possessive Investment in Whiteness: How White People Profit from Identity Politics* (Philadelphia: Temple University Press, 1998).

6. Malini Johar Schueller, *U.S. Orientalisms: Race, Nation, and Gender in Literature, 1790–1890* (Ann Arbor: University of Michigan Press, 1998); and John Kuo Wei Tchen, *New York before Chinatown* (Baltimore: Johns Hopkins University Press, 1998).

7. On the idea of a racist polity, see Charles W. Mills, *The Racial Contract* (Ithaca, N.Y.: Cornell University Press, 1997), 16.

Of India

1. Valerie Flint, *The Imaginative Landscape of Christopher Columbus* (Princeton: Princeton University Press, 1992), 115.

2. There are about 10 million South Asians who live outside the territory of South Asia, with about 1.5 million each in Africa, West Asia, East Asia, Europe, the Americas, and the Pacific islands.

3. Statement made on 8 May 1996.

4. Barbara Crossette, "India Day Joins City's Ethnic Parade," *New York Times,* 17 August 1981, B3.

5. This discussion relies upon my "Anti-D'Souza: The Ends of Racism and the Asian American," *Amerasia Journal* 24, no. 1 (1998); quotation at 23.

6. *The Jerry Seinfeld Show* (NBC, episode 86, 1994/95).

7. "Whiz Kid," *Brown Alumni Magazine,* May/June 1998, 17.

8. Viji Sundaram, "'Americanization' of Immigrant Children Lowers GPA," *India West,* 11 March 1994, 39.

9. "Success Story of One Minority Group in US," *US News & World Report,* 26 December 1966.

10. Gary Okihiro, *Margins and Mainstreams: Asians in American History and Culture* (Seattle: University of Washington Press, 1994), ix.

11. Aziz Haniffa, "Helms, at Forum, Calls for Better Ties with India," *India Abroad,* 12 September 1997, 18.

12. Stanley Fish, *There's No Such Thing as Free Speech, and It's a Good Thing, Too* (New York: Oxford University Press, 1994), 90.

Of the Mysterious East

1. R. W. Emerson, 4 April 1820, in *Journals of Ralph Waldo Emerson, 1820–1872,* ed. E. W. Emerson and W. E. Forbes (Boston: Houghton and Mifflin, 1909), 1: 21–22.

2. Quoted in Carl T. Jackson, *The Oriental Religions and American Thought: Nineteenth Century Explorations* (Westport, Conn.: Greenwood, 1981), 31.

3. G. W. F. Hegel, *The Philosophy of History* (1830/31; reprint, New York: Dover, 1956), 105.

4. R. W. Emerson, 11 November 1823, in *Journals,* 1: 326–27.

5. R. W. Emerson, 27 October 1845, in *Journals,* 7: 123.

6. R. W. Emerson, *English Traits* (1856), in *The Collected Works of Ralph Waldo Emerson* (Cambridge: Harvard University Press, 1987), 5: 26.

7. We are again not far from Hegel, the highest exponent of German orientalism, who noted that "the English, or rather the East India Company, are the lords of the land; for it is the necessary fate of Asiatic Empires to be subjected to Europeans; and China will, some day or other, be obliged to submit to this fate" (Hegel, *The Philosophy of History*, 142–43).

8. R. W. Emerson, *Representative Men* (1850), in *The Collected Works*, 4:30.

9. H. D. Thoreau, *A Week on the Concord River and Merrimack* (1849), in *A Week, Walden, Maine Woods, Cape Cod* (New York: Library of America, 1985), 120.

10. Thoreau, in *A Week*, 114.

11. Joan Jensen, *Passage from India: Asian Indian Immigrants in North America* (New Haven: Yale University Press, 1988), 13.

12. James Duncan Phillips, *Salem and the Indies: The Story of the Great Commercial Era of the City* (Boston: Houghton Mifflin, 1947), 364, 369.

13. In 1717 Mather wrote to Yale that "there are those in these parts of the *western* India, who have had the satisfaction to know Something of what you have done and gain'd in the *Eastern*, and they take Delight in the Story" (quoted in Mukhtar Ali Isani, "Cotton Mather and the Orient," *New England Quarterly* 43 [March 1970], 47).

14. Quoted in Jackson, *The Oriental Religions*, p. 53.

15. Mary P. Ryan, *The Empire of the Mother: American Writing about Domesticity, 1830–1860* (New York: Harrington Park, 1985), chapter 1.

16. R. W. Emerson, 10 January 1847, in *Journals*, 7: 242.

17. Thoreau to Thomas Cholomondeley, 8 November 1855, in *The Correspondence of Henry David Thoreau*, ed. W. Harding and C. Bode (New York: New York University, 1958), 398.

18. P. J. Marshall, *Problems of Empire: Britain and India, 1757–1813* (London: Allen and Unwin, 1968), 17.

19. Voltaire, *The Philosophy of History* (London: Allcock, 1766), 101. Voltaire saw Christianity as already having been drawn into the dynamic of commercial society, with its various ethical concessions to

mercantilism. It seems at times that these thinkers turned to the "Eastern religions" in the hope of finding an adequate ethical base from which to critique their own world—before long, however, even these religions were swept into the centrifugal effect of capitalism, as I shall show in the section "Of Sly *Baba*s."

20. Thoreau, *A Week*, 114.

21. Thoreau, *Walden* (1854), in *A Week*, 326.

22. Thoreau, *Walden*, 327, 343–44.

23. Thoreau, *A Week*, 114.

24. Thoreau to H. G. O. Blake, 20 November 1849, in *The Correspondence*, 251.

25. Mark Twain, *Following the Equator: A Journey around the World* (Hartford, Conn.: American Publishing Company, 1899), 2: 19, 26.

26. C. L. R. James, *American Civilization* (Cambridge: Blackwell, 1993), 52.

27. Dorothy B. Jones, *The Portrayal of China and India on the American Screen, 1896–1955* (Cambridge: MIT Press, 1955), 52–53. The tradition continues in film, as for example in Steven Spielberg's 1984 *Indiana Jones and the Temple of Doom,* well reviewed by Moishe Postone and Elizabeth Traube in *Jump Cut,* no. 30 (March 1985).

Of the Oriental Menagerie

1. Roger Catlin, "Step Right Up and See the . . . um . . . Unusual Humans," *Hartford Courant Magazine,* 7 May 1998, 20–21.

2. *Detroit Journal* (14 February 1894), quoted in Marie Louise Burke, *Swami Vivekananda in America: New Discoveries* (Calcutta: Advaita Ashrama, 1966), 199.

3. "Poetry of the Orient," *The Nation* 1, no. 17 (26 October 1865): 535–36.

4. "The Heathen Mother," *Songs for the Little Ones at Home* (New York: American Tract Society, 1884), 243–44, and "Children in India," ibid., 245–46.

5. Isador Lowenthal, "The Revolt of the Sepoys," *Biblical Repository and Princeton Review* 30 (1858), quoted in Bernard Saul Stern, "American Views of India and Indians, 1857–1900," (Ph.D. diss., University of Pennsylvania, 1956), 44.

6. R. S. Minturn, *From New York to Delhi* (1859), quoted in Stern, "American Views," 87.

7. Stern, "American Views," 17.

8. The Brahmo Samaj (Society of Brahma) was founded by Raja Ram Mohan Roy (1772–1833) in 1828 in Calcutta as a monotheistic reform movement within Hinduism. Many claim that it drew its inspiration from Christianity, but it is more accurate to say that it remained wedged between the heritage of Brahmanism, the realities of colonial rule, and the arrogance of colonial Christianity; Suresh Sharma, "Raja Rammohan Roy: The Inaugurator of the Modern Age," *Indian Responses to Colonialism in the Nineteenth Century,* ed. Alok Bhalla and Sudhir Chandra (Delhi: Sterling, 1993).

9. Ishvar Chandra Vidyasagar (1820–91) was a remarkable innovator who attempted to steer Bengali social mores in the crucible of colonial rule, particularly in terms of the social problems posed by urbanism and capitalism; Sumit Sarkar, "Vidyasagar and Brahmanical Society," in *Writing Social History* (New Delhi: Oxford University Press, 1997).

10. Uma Chakravarti, *Rewriting History: The Life and Times of Pandita Ramabai* (New Delhi: Kali for Women, 1998).

11. Jotibhai Phule, *Collected Works* (Bombay: Government of Maharashtra, 1991), I: xxix.

12. A fine assessment of Katherine Mayo can be found in Mrinalini Sinha, "Reading *Mother India*: Empire, Nation, and the Female Voice," *Journal of Women's History* 6, no. 2 (Summer 1994).

13. Joguth Chunder Gangooly, *Life and Religion of the Hindoos: With a Sketch of My Life and Experience* (Boston: Crosby, Nichols, Lee, 1860), xxviii. To correct these tales, Gangooly wrote a short book for a "silver penny series," *Juthoo and His Sunday School, or Child Life in India, by a Native Brahmin* (Boston: Walker, Wise, 1861).

14. A very valuable excavation of the production of *sati* as an object of knowledge may be found in Lata Mani, "A Discourse on Sati," in "The Production of Colonial Discourse: Sati in Early Nineteenth Century Bengal" (M.A. thesis, University of California at Santa Cruz, 1983).

15. Marian Murray, *From Rome to Ringling Circus!* (New York: Appleton-Century-Crofts, 1956), 159.

16. Such as *The Thousand and One Nights, or The Arabian Nights'*

Entertainments (Boston: Crosby, Nichols, Lee, 1861); *The Arabian Nights' Entertainments,* trans. E. W. Lane with woodcuts by W. Harvey (Boston: Little, Brown, 1853); *The Arabian Nights' Entertainments,* arranged for the perusal of youthful readers by the Hon. Mrs. Sugden (New York: Routledge, 1863).

17. "Hindu Literature," *The Nation,* 26, no. 673 (23 May 1878): 344. Indeed, the narrative of the Arabian Nights is well explored in Vincente Minnelli's 1955 *Kismet.* Incidentally, in the film we also get a dance sequence that draws from classical South Asian themes to produce another oriental fantasy, this in the year of Bandung (1955) when Chuck Berry was producing music in solidarity with the meeting in Indonesia (see his song "Brown-Eyed Handsome Man"). On *Kismet,* see Adrienne McLean, "The Thousand Ways There Are to Move: Camp and Oriental Dance in the Hollywood Musicals of Jack Cole," in *Visions of the East: Orientalism in Film,* ed. M. Bernstein and G. Studlar (New Brunswick: Rutgers University Press, 1997).

18. Thomas Moore, *Lalla Rookh: An Oriental Romance* (New York: Leavitte and Allen, 1817).

19. Stern, "American Views," 84.

20. Paul Tabori, *Alexander Korda* (New York: Living Books, 1966), 194.

21. *Motion Picture News,* 19 June 1915, quoted in Dorothy B. Jones, *The Portrayal of China and India on the American Screen, 1896–1955* (Cambridge: MIT Press, 1955), 54.

22. Stern, "American Views," 21. Stern is in error as to the town and on some other details.

23. Bluford Adams, *E Pluribus Barnum: The Great Showman and the Making of U.S. Popular Culture* (Minneapolis: University of Minnesota Press, 1997), 175.

24. P. V. Bradford and H. Blume, *Ota Benga: The Pygmy in the Zoo* (New York: St. Martin's Press, 1992).

25. Meyda Yegenoglu, *Colonial Fantasies: Toward a Feminist Reading of Orientalism* (Cambridge: Cambridge University Press, 1998), 42–55.

26. *New York Herald,* 28 April 1874.

27. Angela Y. Davis, *Women, Race, and Class* (New York: Vintage, 1983), chapter 11.

28. Adams, *E Pluribus Barnum,* 186.

29. Quoted in Stern, "American Views," 219.

30. David Roediger, "Guineas, Wiggers, and the Dramas of Racialized Culture," *American Literary History* 7 (1995): 654.

31. David Burg, *Chicago's White City of 1893* (Lexington: University of Kentucky Press, 1976), 218.

32. Burg, *White City,* 115.

33. "The Reason Why the Colored American Is Not in the World's Columbian Exposition" (1893) in *Selected Works of Ida B. Wells,* edited by Harris Trudier (New York: Oxford University Press, 1991), 46–137.

34. Charles Fanning, *Finley Peter Dunne and Mr. Dooley: The Chicago Years* (Lexington: University of Kentucky Press, 1978).

35. Romain Rolland, *Prophets of the New India* (London: Cassell, 1930), 291.

36. Quoted in Burke, *Swami Vivekananda,* 160–61.

37. Quoted in ibid., 50.

38. Quoted in ibid., 135.

39. Quoted in ibid., 181.

40. Quoted in ibid., 182.

41. Quoted in ibid., 369.

42. Quoted in ibid., 412.

43. Paramahansa Yogananda, *Autobiography of a Yogi* (New York: Philosophical Library, 1952), 342. In his 1946 autobiography, Yogananda noted that "I had heard many stories about the materialistic Western atmosphere, one very different from the spiritual background of India, pervaded with the centuried aura of saints" (353) and "in the Orient, suffering [is] chiefly on the material plane; in the Occident, suffering [is] chiefly on the mental or the spiritual plane. The nations are in the painful grip of unbalanced civilizations. India, China and the other Eastern lands can greatly benefit from emulation of the practical grasp of affairs, the material efficiency, of Western nations like America. The Occidental peoples, on the other hand, require a deeper understanding of the spiritual basis of life, and particularly of scientific techniques that India anciently developed for man's conscious communion with God" (487).

44. Wendell Thomas, *Hinduism Invades America* (New York: Beacon Press, 1930), 218–21.

45. Ibid., 218.

46. Emily Brown, *Har Dayal* (Tucson: University of Arizona Press, 1975), 87, 117.

47. C. L. R. James, "Preliminary Notes on the Negro Question" (1939), in *CLR James on the "Negro Question"* (Jackson: University of Mississippi Press, 1996), 7.

48. Dizzy Gillespie with Al Fraser, *To Be or Not To BOP: Memoirs* (Garden City, N.Y.: Doubleday, 1979), 291–93.

49. Babs Gonzalez, *I Paid My Dues: Good Times . . . No Bread* (East Orange, N.J.: Expubiedence, 1967), 18–20.

50. Thomas, *Hinduism*, 219.

51. Jessie Redman Fauset, *Plum Bun: A Novel without a Moral* (1929; reprint, London: Pandora, 1985), 218.

52. *The Correspondence of W. E. B. Du Bois*, vol. 1, *Selections, 1877–1934*, ed. Herbert Aptheker (Amherst: University of Massachusetts Press, 1973), 386.

53. A wonderful account is available in Sudarshan Kapur, *Raising Up a Prophet: The African American Encounter with Gandhi* (Boston: Beacon, 1992).

54. Janice MacKinnon and Stephen MacKinnon, *Agnes Smedley: The Life and Times of an American Radical* (Berkeley and Los Angeles: University of California Press, 1988), 68; Peggy Lamson, *Roger Baldwin* (Boston: Houghton Mifflin, 1976), 144.

55. Hannah Josephson, *Jeannette Rankin: First Lady in Congress* (Indianapolis, Ind.: Bobbs-Merrill, 1974), 101, 173–77.

56. Quoted in Stern, "American Views," 219.

57. Michael Kalecki, "Political Aspect of Full Employment" (1943) in *Selected Essays on the Dynamics of the Capitalist Economy* (Cambridge: Cambridge University Press, 1971), 140–42.

58. *The Collected Works of Swami Vivekananda* (Calcutta: Advaita Ashrama, 1976), 2: 512.

59. Gareth Steadman Jones argues that U.S. imperialism is rooted in the foundation of the Republic in 1776 in his wide-ranging essay, "The Specificity of U.S. Imperialism," *New Left Review* 60 (March/April 1970).

60. *The Collected Works of Swami Vivekananda*, 1: 20.

61. Ibid., 5: 106, 233.

62. Ibid., 6: 381.

63. Marie Louise Burke (Sister Gargi), *Swami Trigunatita: His Life and Work* (San Francisco: Vedanta Society of Northern California, 1997), 192. This sadhu, it needs to be said, was also an occasional informer for the Canadian agent W. Hopkinson; Brown, *Har Dayal*, 132.

64. Swami Prakashananda, "Socialism as a Phase of Vedanta," *Voice of Freedom*, November 1911, 151.

65. Special report of State Bureau of Labor Statistics (6 January 1919), quoted in *California and the Oriental: Japanese, Chinese, and Hindus. Report of State Board of Control of California to Gov. Wm. D. Stephens* (Sacramento, 19 June 1920), 181.

66. Ibid., 101–2.

67. Quoted in Joan Jensen, *Passage from India: Asian Indian Immigrants in North America* (New Haven: Yale University Press, 1988), 92–93.

68. I. Muthanna, "East Indians in BC," *Rungh* 2, nos. 1, 2 (1993): 11.

69. Quoted in Jensen, *Passage from India*, 62.

70. Quoted in Rick Fields, *How the Swans Came to the Lake: A Narrative History of Buddhism in America* (Boulder, Colo.: Shambala, 1981), 124.

71. Hugh Johnson, *The Voyage of the Komagata Maru* (Delhi: Oxford University Press, 1978).

72. An early and amusing answer to Mayo can be found in Khalid Latif Gauba, *Uncle Sham* (New York: C. Kendall, 1929).

73. Brown, *Har Dayal*, 98.

Of Sly *Baba*s and Other Gurus

1. Deepak Chopra, *Seven Spiritual Laws of Success: A Practical Guide to the Fulfillment of Your Dreams* (San Rafael: Amber-Allen, 1995), 3.

2. Wendell Thomas, *Hinduism Invades America* (New York: Beacon Press, 1930), 136–37, and Harvey Cox, *Turning East: The Promise and Peril of the New Orientalism* (New York: Simon and Schuster, 1977), 18.

3. Paul Goodman, *Growing Up Absurd: Problems of Youth in an*

Organized Society (New York: Vintage, 1960), 123; for a far more nu-anced study, see Daniel Belgrad, *The Culture of Spontaneity: Improvisation and the Arts in Postwar America* (Chicago: University of Chicago Press, 1998), 167–68, 199–200.

4. Donald S. Lopez Jr., *Prisoners of Shangri-La: Tibetan Buddhism and the West* (Chicago: University of Chicago Press, 1998), 42.

5. William Bowen, "The Decade Ahead: Not So Bad If We Do Things Right," *Fortune,* 8 October 1979, 84.

6. R. J. Barnet and R. E. Muller, *Global Reach* (New York: Simon and Schuster, 1974), 17, and Lester Thurow, *Zero Sum Society: Distribution and the Possibilities for Economic Change* (New York: Basic Books, 1980), 45–46.

7. Harry Braverman, *Labor and Monopoly Capital* (New York: Monthly Review, 1974), 31–39.

8. Stuart Hall, "The Hippies: An American 'Moment'" (Birmingham, England: University of Birmingham Centre for Contemporary Cultural Studies, 1968), 8.

9. Cox, *Turning East,* 49, 33.

10. Shiva Naipaul, *Journey to Nowhere: A New World Tragedy* (New York: Simon and Schuster, 1981), 273, 187.

11. George Jackson, *Blood in My Eye* (Baltimore: Black Classics Press, 1990), 122.

12. Lopez, *Prisoners of Shangri-La,* 71.

13. Gita Mehta, *Karma Cola: Marketing the Mystic East* (New York: Simon and Schuster, 1979); John Lennon, *Instant Karma (We All Shine On)* (Apple 1003, released on 6 February 1970).

14. E. Franklin Frazier, "The Negro and Non-Resistance," *The Crisis* 27 (March 1924), and the editorial note in *The Crisis* 28 (June 1924).

15. In the Coltrane oeuvre, the following tracks bear a direct link to India: "Om" (played at the Village Vanguard Theater on 1, 2, 3, and 5 November 1961, recorded on 1 October 1965, released on *Om,* Impulse Records, A9140, and played live at Lincoln Center on 19 February 1966); and "Reverend King" (recorded on 2 February 1966 in San Francisco), a tune that begins with the band members chanting "Om Mani Padme Om" (*Cosmic Music,* Impulse Records, AS9148). On the complexity of Coltrane's spirituality, one might want to see his interview in Frank

Kofsky, *Black Nationalism and the Revolution in Music* (New York: Pathfinder, 1972), and Eric Nisenson, *Ascension: John Coltrane and His Quest* (New York: De Capo Press, 1995), 153, 167.

16. Quoted in Nisenson, *Ascension,* 185.

17. There is much work to be done on the linkages between blacks and Asians. Some of this will appear in Robin Kelley and Betsy Esch, "Black Like Mao," *Souls,* forthcoming; Jeff Chang, "The End of the Century: Ice Cube's Death Certificate" (in progress) and a project in "polycultural" history on which I am at work.

18. *New York Times,* 7 November 1998.

19. This history is drawn from Joseph Kett, *The Formation of the American Medical Profession* (New Haven: Yale University Press, 1968).

20. Deepak Chopra, "What Is the True Nature of Reality?" (transcript of a talk given at the Seattle Center, 18 May 1991).

21. M. K. Gandhi, *Hind Swaraj* (Ahmedabad: Navajivan, 1938), 53.

22. Catherine Hoffman, Dorothy Rice, and Hai-Yen Sung, "Persons with Chronic Conditions," *Journal of the American Medical Association* 276, no. 18 (13 November 1996): 1476.

23. Arnold S. Relman, "The New Medical-Industrial Complex," *New England Journal of Medicine* 303, no. 17 (23 October 1980): 963–70.

24. Martin Luther King Jr., "Showdown for Nonviolence," *Look,* 16 April 1968, in *A Testament of Hope,* ed. James M. Washington (New York: Harper, 1986), 71.

25. Gwen Kinkead, "Humana's Hard-Sell Hospitals," *Fortune,* 17 November 1980, 70.

26. Ivan Illich, *Medical Nemesis: The Expropriation of Health* (New York: Pantheon, 1976).

27. Paul Starr, *The Social Transformation of American Medicine* (New York: Basic Books, 1982), 336–37.

28. Deepak Chopra, *Ageless Body, Timeless Mind* (New York: Crown Books, 1993), 258.

29. Chopra, *Seven Spiritual Laws,* 10.

30. Chopra, *Ageless Body,* 258.

31. Paul Heelas, *The New Age Movement: The Celebration of Self and the Sacralization of Modernity* (Oxford: Blackwell, 1996), 2.

32. Chopra, *Ageless Body,* 258.

33. Ibid., 259.

34. Ibid.

35. Chopra, *Seven Spiritual Laws,* 64.

36. Chopra, *Ageless Body,* 258, and Deepak Chopra, *Journey into Healing* (New York: Avenal/Random House, 1995).

37. Chopra, *Ageless Body,* 259.

38. Ibid., 258.

39. Chopra, *Seven Spiritual Laws,* 58.

40. *W. E. B. Du Bois Speaks,* ed. Philip Foner (New York: Pathfinder, 1970), 130–31.

41. Richard Goldstein, *Reporting the Counterculture* (Boston: Unwin, 1989), 87. We have Allen Ginsberg, jotting in his journal: "But the great Hunger of the Undeveloped Nations . . . But how ever recreate India? Bang Bang Bang continues the bronze gong of Kali downstairs. Well its flowing fast enough & oddly conditioned but my eyelids are heavy from 4 AM Ganja and I need an excuse to sleep" (*Indian Journals,* 193).

42. Susan George, *How the Other Half Dies* (Totowa, N.J.: Rowman and Allenheld, 1983), 181.

43. Goldstein, *Reporting the Counterculture,* 87–88.

44. Chopra, *Seven Spiritual Laws,* 35–36.

45. Vijay Prashad, "Mother Teresa: Mirror of Bourgeois Guilt," *Economic and Political Weekly* 32, nos. 44, 45 (8 November 1997).

46. Deepak Chopra's foreword to Gautama Chopra, *Child of the Dawn: A Magical Journey of Awakening* (San Rafael, Calif.: Amber-Allen, 1996), xi–xii.

47. New Age orientalism returns to India to make its mark among an alienated middle class. For some details, see Vimala Thakar, *Himalayan Pearls* (Ahmedabad: Vimal Prakashan Trust, 1989); Vishal Mangalwadi, *In Search of Self* (London: Hodder and Stoughton, 1992); two articles in *India Today* (Parveen Chopra, "The Gurus for the '90s," *India Today,* 31 July 1993, 50–56; Prakash M. Swamy, "Hotline to Solace," *India Today,* 15 August 1993, 66); and the publication of *Life Positive* in New Delhi (a magazine of the New Age). Chopra's books sell fast in the metropolitan areas, and the products of the beautician and alternative healer Shahnaz Hussein offer some examples of the use of exotic indulgences to heal alienation. An analysis of this will need to be conducted elsewhere.

48. "The business of America is business, and that includes the religion business. The greatest irony of the neo-Oriental religious movements is that in their effort to present an alternative to the Western way of life most have succeeded in adding only one more line of spiritual products to the American religious marketplace. They have become a part of the 'consumer culture' that they set out to call in question" (Cox, *Turning East*, 129–30).

49. Quoted in Lawrence Grafstein, "Messianic Capitalism," *The New Republic*, 20 February 1984, 14–16.

50. See Carter, *Charisma*, for a discussion of the antidemocratic, even authoritarian, structure of life in Rajneeshpuram.

51. Glenn Rupert, "Employing the New Age: Training Seminars," quoted in Heelas, *The New Age Movement*, 127.

52. Ronald Inden, *Imagining India* (Oxford: Blackwell, 1990), 123–24.

53. Quoted in Grafstein, "Messianic Capitalism," 16; and see Gerald Swanson and Robert Oates, *Enlightened Management: Building High Performance People* (Fairfield: Maharishi International University, 1989).

54. "Hindu economics," a doctrine of the Hindu Right both in India and the United States, offers a similar line of thought; Meera Pandya, "Ethical Economics," *Hinduism Today*, March 1998.

55. Chopra, *Ageless Body*, 259.

56. Chopra, *Seven Spiritual Laws*, 2.

57. Deepak Chopra and friends (Madonna, Demi Moore, Debra Winger, Goldie Hawn, Rosa Parks, Blythe Danner, Martin Sheen, and others), *A Gift of Love* (1998, Deepak Chopra); "Mystical Mélange," *New York Times*, 5 November 1998.

58. Deepak Chopra, *Creating Affluence: Wealth Consciousness in the Field of All Possibilities* (Novato, Calif.: New World Library, 1993), 7.

59. Quoted in Sanaya Roman, *Creating Money* (Tiburon, Calif.: H. J. Kramer, 1988), p. 18.

60. Chopra, *Creating Affluence*, 56.

61. Peter Baida, *Poor Richard's Legacy: American Business Values from Benjamin Franklin to Donald Trump* (New York: William Morrow, 1990); Jeffrey Williams, *Manipulation on Trial: Economic Analysis and the Hunt Silver Case* (Cambridge: Cambridge University Press, 1995);

and Michael Binstein and Charles Bowden, *Trust Me: Charles Keating and the Missing Billions* (New York: Random House, 1993).

62. Chopra, *Creating Affluence*, 41.

63. Charles Wilber and Kenneth Jameson, *Beyond Reagonomics: A Further Inquiry into the Poverty of Economics* (Notre Dame, Ind.: University of Notre Dame Press, 1990).

64. Chopra was one of many headliners (via satellite) at the Ayurveda conference organized by Bharat Vidya Bhawan in New York City from 31 October to 1 November 1998.

65. Deepak Chopra, *Perfect Health: Maharishi Ayurveda, the Mind-Body Program for Total Well-Being* (New York: Crown Books, 1990).

66. I strongly recommend that the reader look at Agnivesa's text. It offers detailed instructions to physicians for the treatment of particular illnesses, such as abdominal diseases, internal hemorrhage, leprosy, fever, epilepsy, and many others. Along with these clinical suggestions, the text instructs physicians in the character of the illnesses, offers insights for the life of patients, and tells us of the material conditions of healing.

67. Kumkum Roy, "Unravelling the *Kamasutra*," *Indian Journal of Gender Studies* 3, no. 2 (1996).

68. Agnivesa (annotated by Caraka and redacted by Drdhabala), "Sutrasthana," in *Caraka-Samhita*, ed. and trans. P. V. Sharma (Varanasi: Chaukhamba Orientalia, 1981), 15: 18.

69. Ibid., 15: 19–21.

70. Agnivesa, "Vimanasthanam," in *Caraka-Samhita*, 8: 92.

71. Deepak Chopra, *Perfect Weight: The Complete Mind-Body Program for Achieving and Maintaining Your Ideal Weight* (New York: Crown Books, 1996), *Restful Sleep: The Complete Mind-Body Program for Overcoming Insomnia* (New York: Crown Books, 1994), and *Overcoming Intestinal Disorders* (Avenal, Calif.: Random House, 1995).

72. It is deceitful to critique these "alternative" techniques from the standpoint of an indefensible allopathy. In 1997 Americans spent $27 billion dollars on alternative therapies. Even the AMA opened an office on "alternative" medicine in 1996, and some funds have now been used to conduct clinical studies on its arts. "Alternative" medicine seems to be better equipped to deal with degenerative diseases (cancer or heart disease), whereas allopathy seems better at the treatment of trauma. There

needs to be more research on these matters, but preliminary results on them have appeared in *Journal of the American Medical Association* 280, no. 18 (11 November 1998); and for some discussion of its reception, see Denise Grady, "To Aid Doctors, AMA Journal Devotes Entire Issue to Alternative Medicine," *New York Times,* 11 November 1998, A23.

73. This was also the problem with the absorption of Zen Buddhism into the United States. As Goodman noted, Zen "was the flower of an intensely loyal feudal system that fed, protected and honored its masters, and to which the Zen masters in turn had fealty." In the United States, "Zen without farmers and servants is an airy business" (Goodman, *Growing Up Absurd,* 113).

74. Agnivesa, "Sutrasthana," 8: 22.

75. Ibid., 5: 104; 30: 24.

76. Laurie Goodstein, "Hare Krishna Movement Details Past Abuse at Its Boarding Schools," *New York Times,* 9 October 1998, A1, A6.

77. "Veda Lost?" *New York Times Magazine,* 22 February 1998, 15.

Of the Origin of Desis and Some Principles of State Selection

1. *India Abroad,* 10 November 1995.

2. John Bregger and Steven Haugen, "BLS Introduces New Range of Alternative Unemployment Measures," *Monthly Labor Review* 118, no. 10 (October 1995).

3. Saskia Sassen, *The Mobility of Labor and Capital: A Study of International Investment and Labor Flow* (Cambridge: Cambridge University Press, 1988), chapter 2.

4. "Coolie Labor in the South," *Nation* 1, no. 9 (31 August 1865).

5. Lucie Cheng and Edna Bonacich, eds., *Labor Immigration under Capitalism: Asian Workers in the U.S. before World War II* (Berkeley and Los Angeles: University of California Press, 1984); Peter Kwong, *Forbidden Workers: Illegal Chinese Immigrants and American Labor* (New York: New Press, 1997), 161–83.

6. Hugh Tinker, *A New System of Slavery: The Export of Indian Labour Overseas, 1830–1920* (London: Oxford University Press, 1974).

7. Vishnu Padayachee and Robert Morrell, "Indian Merchants and Dukawallahs in the Natal Economy, c. 1875–1914," *Journal of Southern African Studies* 17, no. 1 (March 1991).

8. Ronald Takaki, *Strangers from a Different Shore* (New York: Little, Brown, 1989), chapter 8; Karen I. Leonard, *Ethnic Choices: California's Punjabi Mexicans* (Philadelphia: Temple University Press, 1992). There is a torrent of research soon to be published that will enhance Takaki's useful summary.

9. Karen Leonard, "The Pakhar Singh Murder Case," *Amerasia Journal* 11, no. 1 (Spring/Summer 1984).

10. Harry Schwartz, "Battle for Science Lead: An Analysis of Differences between U.S. and Soviet Strategy on Research," *New York Times*, 4 November 1957, 9.

11. Sheldon Ungar, "Moral Panics, the Military-Industrial Complex, and the Arms Race," *Sociological Quarterly* 31, no. 2 (1990): 174–77.

12. Paul Goodman, *Growing Up Absurd: Problems of Youth in an Organized Society* (New York: Vintage, 1960), 14.

13. Hearings on HR 7700 to amend the Immigration and Nationality Act, Part 1, Serial no. 13, before House Subcommittee No. 1 of the Committee on the Judiciary, 88th Cong., 2nd sess.

14. Ibid.

15. John F. Kennedy, *A Nation of Immigrants* (New York: Harper and Row, 1964).

16. Bill Ong Hing, *Making and Remaking Asian America through Immigration Policy, 1850–1900* (Stanford, Calif.: Stanford University Press, 1993), 38–41, 101–5.

17. Philip Leonard-Spark and Parmatma Saran, "The Indian Immigrant in America: A Demographic Profile," in *The New Ethnics: Asian Indians in the United States,* ed. Parmatma Saran and Edwin Eames (New York: Praeger, 1980); John Liu, "The Contours of Asian Professional, Technical, and Kindred Work Immigration, 1965–1988," *Sociological Perspectives* 35, no. 4 (1992).

18. Joseph Needham, *Science in Traditional China: A Comparative Perspective* (Cambridge: Harvard University Press, 1981).

19. Debiprasad Chattopadhyaya, *Science and Society in Ancient India* (Amsterdam: Grüner, 1978), 3–19; Zaheer Baber, *The Science of Empire: Scientific Knowledge, Civilization, and Colonial Rule in India* (Albany: SUNY Press, 1996).

20. Jawaharlal Nehru, "Science in the Service of the Community"

(3 January 1947), in *Selected Works of Jawaharlal Nehru,* ed. S. Gopal (New Delhi: Oxford University Press, 1984), 2nd series, 1: 377.

21. L. S. Chandrakant, *Technical Education in India Today* (Delhi: Ministry of Scientific Research and Cultural Affairs, 1963), 3; A. Rahman, "Financing of Scientific and Technological Research in India," in *The Role of Science and Technology in Economic Development* (Paris: UNESCO, 1970), 203.

22. Mark Stricherz, "Bill of Wrath," *The Nation,* 11 May 1998, 7.

23. Ray Rist, *Guestworkers in Germany* (New York: Praeger, 1978).

24. Fred Halliday, "Migration and the Labor Force in the Oil Producing States of the Middle East," *Development and Change* 8, no. 3 (July 1977); Myron Weiner, "International Migration and Development: Indians in the Persian Gulf," *Population and Development Review* 8 (March 1982); J. S. Addleton, *Undermining the Centre: The Gulf Migration and Pakistan* (Karanchi: Oxford University Press, 1992); F. Eelens, T. Schampers, and J. D. Speckmann, *Labour Migration to the Middle-East: From Sri Lanka to the Gulf* (London: K. Paul, 1992).

25. Sassen, *The Mobility of Labor and Capital,* 48.

26. Clive Harris, "Post-War Migration and the Industrial Reserve Army," in *Inside Babylon: The Caribbean Diaspora in Britain,* ed. Winston James and Clive Harris (London: Verso, 1993); Ron Ramadin, *The Making of the Black Working Class in Britain* (Aldershot, England: Gower, 1987), 187–204.

27. A. Sivanandan, *A Different Hunger* (London: Pluto, 1982), 7–8; Ramadin, *The Making of the Black Working Class,* 226–31.

28. Retirement itself is a very modern concept, and even more modern is the reconstruction of "community" in which the elderly retire to an old-age home rather than to the front stoop; William Graebner, *A History of Retirement* (New Haven: Yale University Press, 1980), 139–49.

29. Suvarna Thaker, "The Quality of Life of Asian Indian Women in the Motel Industry," *South Asia Bulletin* 2, no. 1 (Spring 1982): 68–73.

30. Jyotsna Vaid, "Seeking a Voice: South Asian Women's Groups in North America," in *Making Waves: An Anthology of Writings by and about Asian American Women,* ed. Asian Women United of California (Boston: Beacon, 1989), 396–97; Lavina Melwani, "Bonded in America," *India Today,* 31 January 1995.

31. Marcelle Williams, "Ladies on the Line: Punjabi Cannery Workers in Central California," in *Making Waves,* 150–51.

32. Conversation with Biju Mathew, New York Taxi Workers' Alliance (NYTWA). There is now a large literature that shows how those who travel as temporary workers learn the lay of the land, accumulate social capital, and then mobilize such skills to travel elsewhere, such as Europe or North America; Douglas Massey and Zai Liang, "The Long-Term Consequences of a Temporary Worker Program: The U.S. Bracero Experience," *Population Research and Policy Review* 8 (1989); James Coleman, "Social Capital in the Creation of Human Capital," *American Journal of Sociology* 94, supplement (1988); David Reimers, *Still the Golden Door* (New York: Columbia University Press, 1985), 96.

33. Quoted in "America's Diverse Immigrants," *San Francisco Examiner,* 23 September 1993.

34. Aziz Haniffa, "Key Republican Reopens Debate on Legal Immigration," *India Abroad,* 1 May 1998.

35. Quoted in Thomas Muller, *Immigrants and the American City* (New York: New York University Press, 1993), 277.

36. For some discussion of this problem, see my "Contract Labor: The Latest Stage of Illiberal Capitalism," *Monthly Review* 46, no. 5 (October 1994): 8.

37. Spencer Abraham, quoted in Aziz Haniffa, "Bills Aim to Boost Visas for Computer Professionals," *India Abroad,* 13 March 1998, 40; Aziz Haniffa, "High-Tech Firms Oppose Immigration Cut," *India Abroad,* 22 September 1995, 44; "Congress H-1Bs Up, Farm Workers," *Migration News* 5, no. 10 (October 1998).

38. U.S. Department of Labor, *Foreign Labor Certification Programs: The System Is Broken and Needs To Be Fixed,* report no. 06-96-002-03-321 (1996); General Accounting Office, *Immigration and the Labor Market: Nonimmigrant Alien Workers in the United States,* GAO/PEMD-92-17 (28 April 1992).

39. "Four Accused of Smuggling Immigrants from India," *New York Times,* 29 July 1998, B6; Matthew Strozier, "Four Accused of Smuggling Immigrants from India," *India Abroad,* 7 August 1998; "Transcontinental Traffic," *India Today,* 19 October 1998, 20e.

40. David E. Rosenbaum, "U.S. Breaks a Huge Alien-Smuggling Ring," *New York Times,* 21 November 1998, A11; Somini Sengupta, "Scope of Smuggling Ring Stuns an Enclave," *New York Times,* 23 November 1998, B5.

41. Quoted in Tunku Varadarajan, "The Spoilers," *New York Times Magazine,* 19 April 1998, 96.

Of a *Girmit* Consciousness

1. Loretta Ross, *White Supremacy in the 1990s* (Somerville, Mass.: Political Research Associates, 1995), and *They Don't All Wear Sheets* (Atlanta, Ga.: Center for Democratic Renewal, 1987), 17; Umberto Eco, "Eternal Fascism," *Utne Reader,* November/December 1995, 57.

2. For a sense of the commonness of white privilege, see Eric Foner, "Hiring Quotas for White Males Only," *Nation,* 26 June 1995; Stephanie Wildman, with Margalynne Armstrong, Adrienne D. Davis, and Trina Grillo, *Privilege Revealed: How Invisible Preference Undermines America* (New York: New York University Press, 1996).

3. Martin Luther King Jr., "Testament of Hope," *Playboy* 16 (January 1969), in *A Testament of Hope,* ed. James M. Washington (New York: Harper, 1986), 316.

4. Aziz Haniffa, "GOP May Shift Stand on Legal Aliens," *India Abroad,* 20 January 1995, 32; Aziz Haniffa, "Committee Unveils Sweeping Reforms," *India Abroad,* 30 June 1995, 42.

5. Aziz Haniffa, "Modified Immigration Bill Signed by Clinton," *India Abroad,* 11 October 1996, 42.

6. Michel W. Potts, "Welfare Bill Hits Legal Aliens," *India West,* 9 August 1996, A1.

7. Steven A. Holmes, "Anti-Immigrant Mood Moves Asians to Organizing," *New York Times,* 3 January 1996, A11.

8. Maxine Fisher, *The Indians of New York City* (New Delhi: Heritage, 1980), 48.

9. *The Indian American,* April 1993, 21.

10. *The Indian American,* July 1993, 34–35.

11. Michel Marriott, "In Jersey City, Indians Protest Violence," *New York Times,* 12 October 1987, B2.

12. National Asian Pacific American Legal Consortium, *Audit of Violence against Asian Pacific Americans* (Washington, D.C.: NAPALC, 1996), 17.

13. As reported to me by Anjana Samant.

14. Michael W. Potts, "Seven Arrested in Alleged Racial Attack on Indians," *India Abroad*, 28 August 1998.

15. Somini Sengupta and Vivian S. Toy, "United Ethnically, and by an Assault," *New York Times*, 7 October 1998, B1; also *Trinidad Express*, 12 October 1998.

16. Associated Press, 7 May 1998.

17. Glass Ceiling Commission, *Good for Business: Making Full Use of the Nation's Human Capital* (Washington, D.C.: GPO, 1995).

18. Aziz Haniffa, "Fears of Managed Care at AAPI Regional Parley," *India Abroad*, 14 April 1995, 42.

19. Fisher, *Indians of New York City*, 18–20.

20. Quoted in G. G. Manrique and C. G. Manrique, "Immigrant Faculty and American Higher Education," *Proteus*, Fall 1994, 31–34.

21. Aziz Haniffa, "Thirty-five Percent Increase in Hate Incidents Is Reported," *India Abroad*, 11 August 1995, 40.

22. Aziz Haniffa, "Hate Crime Seen Up Slightly, but More Violent," *India Abroad*, 23 August 1996, 42.

23. A dossier on the taxi workers' struggle needs to be created. For events prior to their strike of 13 May 1998, see Michel W. Potts, "NY Asian Cabbies Protest Arrest of Fellow Driver," *India West*, 10 June 1994, 1, 44; Lavina Melwani, "Taxiwallas of New York: Facing Growing Anti-Immigrant Sentiment," *India West*, 8 March 1996, B1, B20; Lynn Hudson, "Two Indian Women among Arrested Protesters," *India Abroad*, 5 May 1995; Lynn Hudson, "Cabbie Gets a Break in Police Assault Case," *India Abroad*, 21 July 1995, 38; Lynn Hudson, "Film Eyes Discrimination against Taxi Drivers," *India Abroad*, 8 September 1995; Anannya Bhattacharjee, "Yellow Cabs, Brown People," *SAMAR*, no. 2 (Summer 1993); S. Shankar, "Ambassadors of Goodwill: An Interview with Saleem Osman of Lease Drivers' Coalition," *SAMAR*, no. 3 (Summer 1994); "Focus on Cabbies: CAAAV Takes on Systematic Violence," *The CAAAV Voice* 7, no. 1 (Spring 1995): 1, 4–5; Vivek Renjan Bald's wonderful documentary *Taxi-vala/Auto-biography* (1995); Biju Mathew,

"Peelay Paiyon ki Nayi Ummeed, or Reshaping Immigrant Identity Politics," *Sanskriti* 6, no. 1 (25 December 1995); Bhairavi Desai, "Struggle of the Taxi Driver," *Sangat Review,* December 1997.

24. Nahar Alam, "Domestic Workers Do Their Homework," *SAMAR,* no. 8 (Summer/Fall 1997); Athima Chansanchai, "Maid in the USA," *Village Voice,* 7 October 1997, 49–50.

25. Jamiluddin Ali, *Tamasha Mere Aage: Safarnama* (Lahore: Shaikh Ghulam Ali, 1985), 380.

26. Sadhu Binning, "Chameleons," *No More Watno Dur* (Toronto: TSAR, 1994), 43.

27. Quoted in *India Today,* 4 August 1997.

28. Ien Ang, *Watching Dallas: Soap Operas and the Melodramatic Imagination* (London: Meuthen, 1983), 2.

29. As told to me by Rithwick Rajagopal.

30. Phiroze Vasunia and Vijay Prashad, "The Strange Career of Aryan Man," manuscript, 1998.

31. Bharati Mukherjee, "An Invisible Woman," *Saturday Night,* March 1981, 38.

32. *David Duke* [Homepage of David Duke] [Online]. Available: www.duke.org/eindia.htm.

33. Dinesh D'Souza, *The End of Racism: Principles for a Multiracial Society* (New York: Free Press, 1995), 30–31.

34. Shanti Sadiq Ali, *The African Dispersal in the Deccan: From Medieval to Modern Times* (New Delhi: Orient Longman, 1996).

35. Walter Rodney, *A History of the Guyanese Working People, 1881–1905* (Baltimore: Johns Hopkins University Press, 1981), 179.

36. Quoted in ibid., 188.

37. Quoted in Ronald Inden, *Imagining India* (Oxford: Blackwell, 1990), 63.

38. Brian K. Smith, *Classifying the Universe: The Ancient Varna System and the Origins of Caste* (New York: Oxford University Press, 1994).

39. Rashmi Luthra, "Matchmaking in the Classifieds of the Immigrant Indian Press," in *Making Waves: An Anthology of Writings by and about Asian American Women,* ed. Asian Women United of California (Boston: Beacon, 1989), 337–44.

40. Irawati Karve, *Hindu Society: An Interpretation* (Poona: Desh-mukh, 1968), 132.

41. A. S. Altekar's useful synopsis of the *Dharmashatric* literature notes that "wealth, beauty, health, intelligence and good family were the main considerations in the selection of the bride and bridegroom. Natu-rally opinion was not unanimous about the relative importance to be at-tached to each of these factors, and we find different advocates claiming superiority for each of them" (*The Position of Women in Hindu Civi-lization* [Delhi: Motilal Banarsidass, 1959], 72–73).

42. This relationship to skin color is similar to that which occurs with-in the U.S. black community, but inflected, no doubt, by the prejudices of white supremacy. On this, see bell hooks, *Black Looks: Race and Represen-tation* (Boston: South End Press, 1990); M. Wilson, K. Russell, and R. Hall, *The Color Complex: The Politics of Skin Color among African Americans* (New York: Harcourt, Brace, and Javanovich, 1992); Kathe Sandler, au-thor and producer, *A Question of Color* (PBS, 15 February 1994).

43. Peter Robb, ed., *The Concept of Race in South Asia* (New Delhi: Oxford University Press, 1998).

44. "Other racial minorities are often not potential allies so much as portents of blackness and so to be kept at a distance" (Arvind Rajagopal, "Better Than Blacks? Or, Hum Kaale Hain to Kya Hua," *SAMAR*, no. 5 [Summer 1995]: 5).

45. Sucheta Mazumdar, "Race and Racism: South Asians in the United States," in *Frontiers of Asian American Studies,* ed. G. Nomora (Pullman: University of Washington Press, 1989), 35.

46. Quoted in my "Crafting Solidarities," in *A Part, Yet Apart: South Asians in Asian America,* ed. Lavina Shankar and Rajini Srikant (Philadelphia: Temple University Press, 1998). For more on this theme, see A. Sivanandan, *A Different Hunger* (London: Pluto, 1982); Paul Gilroy, *Small Acts* (London: Serpent's Tail, 1993), 49–62.

47. Quoted in Dilip Hiro, *Black British/White British* (New York: Monthly Review Press, 1973), 110.

48. Paul Foot, *The Rise of Enoch Powell* (Harmondsworth, England: Penguin, 1969), 38; Ron Ramdin, *The Making of the Black Working Class in Britain* (Aldershot, England: Gower, 1987), 498–99.

49. J. Enoch Powell, *Freedom and Reality,* ed. John Wood (Kings-

wood, England: PaperFronts, 1969), 305. For an overview, see Tom Nairn, "Enoch Powell: The New Right," *New Left Review*, no. 61 (May/June 1970).

50. J. M. Nazareth, *Brown Man, Black Country: A Peep into Kenya's Freedom Struggle* (New Delhi: Tidings, 1981); Dana Seidenberg, "The Asians and Uhuru: The Role of a Minority Community in Kenyan Politics, 1939–1963" (Ph.D. diss., Syracuse University, 1979).

51. David Martin, *Idi Amin* (London: Faber and Faber, 1974), 165. I recommend Jagjit Singh's wonderful play, *Sweet Scum of Freedom*, in *African Theatre: Eight Prize-Winning Plays for Radio*, ed. Gwyneth Henderson (London: Heinemann, 1973).

52. I strongly recommend Mahmood Mamdani's *From Citizen to Refugee* (London: Frances Pinter, 1973) for a firsthand analytical account of the crisis.

53. U.S. Census 1990, Database no. C90STF3C1, various tables on household income, individual income, and mortgages on homes and vehicles—all by race; also, various studies on wealth in the United States by race, such as Dimitri Papadimitriou, ed., *Aspects of Distribution of Wealth and Income* (New York: St. Martin's Press, 1994).

54. Robert E. Park, in 1922, offered only part of my interpretation of nostalgia, as a reaction to strangeness: "Loneliness and an unfamiliar environment turn the wanderer's thoughts and affections back upon his native land. The strangeness of the new surroundings emphasize his kinship with those he has left" (*The Immigrant Press and Its Control* [Westport, Conn.: Greenwood, 1970], 49). My interpretation is that nostalgia is a substitute for protest.

55. Quoted in Fisher, *Indians of New York City*, 110.

56. The Rama parallel (drawing from the *Ramayana*) is used, for different purposes, to good effect in Vijay Mishra, ed., *Rama's Banishment* (Auckland: Heinemann, 1979), notably 139–43.

57. Fisher, *Indians of New York City*, 17.

58. Lata Mani, "Gender, Class, and Cultural Conflict: Indu Krishnan's *Knowing Her Place*," in *Our Feet Walk the Sky*, ed. Women of South Asian Descent Collective (San Francisco: Aunt Lute, 1993), 34–35; and Amrit Wilson, *Finding a Voice: Asian Women in Britain* (London: Virago, 1984), chapters 2, 3.

59. Priya Agarwal, *Passage from India: Post-1965 Indian Immigrants and Their Children* (Palos Verdes, Calif.: Yuvati, 1991), 52–53; Sayantani Dasgupta and Shamita Das Dasgupta, "Sex, Lies, and Women's Lives: An Intergenerational Dialogue," in *A Patchwork Shawl: Chronicles of South Asian Women in America* (New Brunswick, N.J.: Rutgers University Press, 1998).

60. Yashoda Gowda and Elisabeth Armstrong, "Establishing a Women's Support Group: Yashoda Gowda Interviewed by Elisabeth Armstrong," *SAMAR*, no. 3 (Summer 1994): 23; Jyotsna Vaid, "Seeking a Voice: South Asian Women's Groups in North America," in *Making Waves*, ed. Asian Women United of California (Boston: Beacon, 1989), 398–405; Bandana Purkayashta, Shyamala Raman, and Kshiteeja Bhide, "Empowering Women: SNEHA's Multifacted Activism," in *Dragon Ladies*, ed. Sonia Shah (Boston: South End Press, 1997); Satya P. Krishnan, Malahat Baig-Amin, Louisa Gilbert, Nabila El-Bassel, and Anne Waters, "Lifting the Veil of Secrecy," in *A Patchwork Shawl*; Pragna Patel, "Two Struggles: Challenging Male Violence and the Police," in *The Boys in Blue: Women's Challenge to the Police*, ed. C. Dunhill (London: Virago, 1989); *Sakhi for South Asian Women* [Homepage of Sakhi], [Online], available: www.sakhi.com and *Manavi: An Organization for South Asian Women* [Homepage of Manavi], [Online], available: www.research.att.com/~bala/manavi/.

61. *India West*, 19 April 1996. The Dasguptas offer a stimulating theory that domestic violence in the United States among desis may have to do with men being "emasculated" by racism; Sayantani Dasgupta and Shamita Das Dasgupta, "Women in Exile: Gender Relations in the Asian Indian Community in the US," in *Contours of the Heart*, ed. Sunaina Maira and Rajini Srikant (New York: Asian American Writers Workshop, 1996), 391–92.

62. Manju Sheth, "Asian Indian Americans," in *Asian Americans*, ed. Pyong Gap Min (London: Sage, 1995), 176.

63. Georg Simmel, "The Stranger," in *The Sociology of Georg Simmel* (Glencoe, Ill.: Free Press, 1950), 403.

64. Gary Okihiro, *Margins and Mainstreams: Asians in American History and Culture* (Seattle: University of Washington Press), 141–47.

Of Authentic Cultural Lives

1. Quoted in Thomas Muller, *Immigrants and the American City* (New York: New York University Press, 1993), 221.

2. Thomas Jefferson to James Monroe, 24 November 1801, in *The Writings of Thomas Jefferson* (Washington, D.C.: Thomas Jefferson Memorial Association, 1903), 10: 296.

3. Alfred Crosby, *Ecological Imperialism* (Cambridge: Cambridge University Press, 1986), 300.

4. Robert E. Park and H. A. Miller, *Old World Traits Transplanted* (New York: Arno Press, 1969), 280.

5. For a debate on McConigley's candidacy, see the exchange between Asha Knott (Los Angeles Republican Party) and myself in Vijay Prashad, "Does McConigley Deserve Support?" *India West,* 23 August 1996, A5; and Asha Knott, "McConigley Did Deserve Support," *India West,* 6 September 1996, A5.

6. Dinesh D'Souza, "Multiculturalism 101: Great Books of the Non-Western World," *Policy Review,* no. 56 (Spring 1991): 22.

7. Heritage is sometimes seen as marketable, especially in the field of niche marketing; Sivaram Srikandath, "Ethnicity and Cultural Identity in the Diasporas and Opportunities for Niche Media Marketing: An Audience Analysis of the Jains of North America" (Ph.D. diss., Ohio University, 1993).

8. Jalal Al-I Ahmad, *Occidentosis* (Berkeley, Calif.: Mizan, 1984), 34.

9. Terence Turner, "Anthropology and Multiculturalism: What Is Anthropology That Multiculturalists Should Be Mindful of It?" *Cultural Anthropology* 8, no. 4 (1993): 426; Slavoj Zizek, "Multiculturalism, or The Cultural Logic of Multinational Capitalism," *New Left Review,* no. 225 (1997): 44; A. Gordon and C. Newfield, eds., *Mapping Multiculturalism* (Minneapolis: University of Minnesota Press, 1996). *Hijab,* which literally means "boundary," refers to a headscarf; felafel is a West Asian snack food.

10. June Jordan, *Technical Difficulties* (London: Virago, 1992), 165.

11. Gita Sahgal, "Secular Spaces: The Experience of Asian Women Organizing," in *Refusing Holy Orders: Women and Fundamentalism in Britain,* ed. Gita Sahgal and Nira Yuval-Davis (London: Virago, 1992), 192.

12. M. K. Gandhi, "'Ganga-Swarup' Basanti Devi," *Navajivan,* 28 June 1925, in *The Collected Works of Mahatma Ghandi* (Ahmedabad: Navajivan Trust, 1968), 27:308.

13. This is a tenuous allowance, since places of religious worship continue to be vandalized, as were the temple in Queens, New York (see Paul Grimes, "Immigrants from India Find Problems in America," *New York Times,* 2 August 1977, 31, 49), the Jain temple in Pittsburgh, Pennsylvania, in February 1983, and the Yuba City, California, mosque in September 1994. On mosques in the suburbs, see Kathleen Moore, *Al-Muqhtaribun* (Albany: SUNY Press, 1995), chapter 6.

14. Raymond B. Williams, *Religions of Immigrants from India and Pakistan: New Threads in the American Tapestry* (Cambridge: Cambridge University Press, 1988), 226. A gurudwara is a Sikh shrine.

15. For information on South Asian places of worship and community centers, I recommend the CD-ROM by Diana Eck and the Pluralism Project at Harvard University, *On Common Ground: World Religions in America* [CD-ROM] (Available: Columbia University Press [1997]).

16. Trish Willingham, "Worshippers Draw Near: New Prayer Space at Hindu Temple," *Hartford Courant,* 7 June 1998, C1.

17. Or indeed to both desis and white Hindus, who oftentimes see the temple as merely a spiritual space and fail to recognize that it is also an ethnic space; Nurit Zaidman-Dvir, "When the Deities Are Asleep: Processes of Change in the Hare Krishna Temple" (Ph.D. diss., Temple University, 1994).

18. For some sense of these spaces, see Madhulika Khandelwal, "Indian Immigrants in Queens, NYC: Patterns of Spatial Concentration and Distribution, 1965–1990," in *Nation and Migration,* ed. Peter van der Veer (Philadelphia: University of Pennsylvania Press, 1995).

19. Arthur Helweg and Usha Helweg, *An Immigrant Success Story: East Indians in America* (Philadelphia: University of Pennsylvania Press, 1990), 127.

20. Susan Slyomovics, "New York City's Muslim World Day Parade," in *Nation and Migration,* 160.

21. Sunita Sunder Mukhi, "'Underneath My Blouse Beats My Indian Heart': Sexuality, Nationalism, and Indian Womanhood," in *A Patchwork Shawl: Chronicles of South Asian Women in America* (New

Brunswick, N.J.: Rutgers University Press, 1998), and "Performing Indianness in New York City" (Ph.D. diss., New York University, 1997).

22. James Baldwin, "Negroes Are Anti-Semitic Because They're Anti-White," in *Black Anti-Semitism and Jewish Racism,* ed. Nat Hentoff (New York: Schocken, 1969), 11.

23. The appropriate text in this war is Mary Lefkowitz, *Not out of Africa: How Afrocentrism Became an Excuse to Teach Myth as History* (New York: Basic Books, 1996).

24. Biju Mathew, *Byte Size Nationalism: The Saffron Dollar and Murder as Foreign Exchange* (forthcoming), 17.

25. Jayshree Sengupta, "NRIs Need To Be Patient with India's Ways," *India Abroad,* 13 October 1995, 2; "Non-Resident Indians Lukewarm toward Deposit Schemes," *India Abroad,* 5 June 1998; Charanjit Chanana, "Active Role of Overseas Indians Seen," *India Abroad,* 3 July 1998, 4; Vyuptakesh Sharan, "Foreign Investments in India: Role of Non-Resident Indians," *Economia Internazionale* 46 (1993).

26. Quoted in Ayub Syed, ed., *The Swaraj Paul Factor* (Bombay: Palakmati Printers, 1983), 2; V. Balasubramanian, *Indians Abroad: The NRI Syndrome* (Bombay: Business Book, 1987), 43; India West, 6 October 1995.

27. A useful list of such organizations can be found at *India Charity* (1996–1998—copyright). [Homepage of India Charity], [Online], available: www.indiacharitynet.com.

28. "A Bid to Build a New Bridge with Parents," *India Abroad,* 27 December 1996, 43.

29. G. S. Shukla, "A Parent's Response," *India Abroad,* 7 March 1997.

30. Sunaina Maira, "Chaste Identities, Ethnic Yearnings: Second Generation Indian Americans in New York City" (Ph.D. diss., Harvard University, 1998), 165, 195.

31. R. Radhakrishnan, *Diasporic Mediations* (Minneapolis: University of Minnesota Press, 1996), 210–11.

32. Nayan Shah, "Sexuality, Identity, and the Uses of History," in *A Lotus of Another Color,* ed. Rakesh Ratti (Boston: Alyson, 1993), 119; Ram Gokul, "Understanding Our Gay and Lesbian Children," *Trikone,* July 1997, 8.

33. O. P. Malik, "Up in Smoke: A Look at Drug Use among the Next Generation," *Masala,* April 1995, 11; Amar Dhillon, "Gangsta', Gangsta'," *Hum* 1, no. 2 (Summer 1994).

34. Ashley Dunn, "As the World and Soap Operas Turn: Blondes, Brain Tumors, and Buckets of Tears on Hindi TV," *New York Times,* 26 September 1995, B1, B4.

35. "The Decision of a Lifetime: How Children Feel about Marriage," *Avaaj,* Spring 1988, 14.

36. Apache Indian, "Arranged Marriage," *No Reservations,* Music India, 514: 112–14 (1993), analyzed briefly by Nina Asher, "Don Raja: Britain's Multicultural Music Phenomenon," *SAMAR,* no. 2 (Summer 1993): 47.

37. Asra Q. Nomani, " To Wed, Some Fans of Rock and Pizza Revert to Tradition," *Wall Street Journal,* 14 April 1998.

38. *Chicago Tribune,* 23 June 1998.

39. Yvonne Presten, "Bhutto's Choice," *Ms. Magazine* 16, no. 9 (March 1988): 44.

40. Radha Kumar, *The History of Doing* (London: Verso, 1994).

41. Nilda Rimonte, "A Question of Culture: Cultural Approval of Violence against Women in Pacific-Asian Community and the Cultural Defense," *Stanford Law Review* 43, no. 6 (July 1991): 1311–26; Christine Ho, "An Analysis of Domestic Violence in Asian American Communities: A Multicultural Approach to Counseling," in *Diversity and Complexity in Feminist Theory,* ed. L. S. Brown and M. P. Root (New York: Haworth Press, 1990); *In Visible Terms: Domestic Violence in the Asian Indian Context. A Handbook for Intervention* (New Jersey: Manavi, 1995).

42. Vindu Goel, "Two Identities, One Person," *Avaaj,* Spring 1988, 19.

43. Orvar Löfgren, "The Nationalization of Culture," *Ethnologia Europaea* 19, no. 2 (1989): 7.

44. Ved Vatuk and Sylvia Vatuk, "Protest Songs of East Indians on the West Coast, U.S.A.," in *Thieves in My House* (Varanasi: Viswavidyalaya Prakashan, 1969), 75.

45. Malini Sood, "Expatriate Nationalism and Ethnic Radicalism: The Ghadar Party in North America, 1910–1920" (Ph.D. diss., SUNY, 1995).

46. *Ghadar,* 1 November 1913.

47. Quoted in Sohan Singh Josh, *Baba Sohan Singh Bhakna* (New Delhi: Peoples' Publishing House, 1970), 12.

48. Kartar Dhillon, "The Parrot's Beak," in *Making Waves: An Anthology of Writings by and about Asian American Women,* ed. Asian Women United of California (Boston: Beacon, 1989), 217.

49. Letter from Kartar Dhillon, 20 November 1995; see also Kartar Dhillon, "Bud Dhillon," *The Ghadarite* 1, no. 1 (1998).

50. Vatuk and Vatuk, "Protest Songs," 76.

51. South Asian American students around the country are nevertheless poised to resurrect Gandhi through an event pioneered by University of Michigan students entitled Gandhi Day of Service. (Its first year was 1997, but in 1998 about 400 students participated, mainly, but not exclusively, South Asian American). On this day (in early October), students across the country will do community service and challenge each other to make this experience commonplace in their daily lives.

52. One rendition of the acronym runs American-Born Confused Desi Emigrated From Gujarat House In Jersey Kids Learning Medicine Now Owning Property Quite Reasonable Salary Two Uncles Visiting White Xenophobia Yet Zestful!

53. Sunaina Maira, "Conflicting Ideals for Men, Women," *India Abroad,* 15 March 1996, 50.

54. W. E. B. Du Bois, *The Souls of Black Folk* (New York: Modern Library, 1996), 6.

Of Yankee Hindutva

1. I am drawing liberally from Biju Mathew and Vijay Prashad, "The Saffron Dollar: Pehle Paisa, Phir Bhagwan," *Himal* 9, no. 7 (September 1996), and "The Protean Forms of Yankee Hindutva," *Ethnic and Racial Studies,* forthcoming (Spring 2000).

2. Aijaz Ahmad, "On the Ruins of Ayodhya: Communalist Offensive and Recovery of the Secular," in *Lineages of the Present* (New Delhi: Tulika, 1996), 271.

3. This is hinted at in Samuel P. Huntington, *The Clash of Civilizations and the Remaking of the World Order* (New York: Simon and Schuster, 1996), and it is made explicit by Arvind Ghosh (a research

fellow at the Freeman Center for Strategic Studies, a Zionist think tank based in Houston, Texas) in "Jew-Hindu Relations," *Macabean,* September 1997.

4. Purnima Bose, "The Global Context of Communalism: The Case of Salman Rushdie," *SAMAR,* no. 2 (Summer 1993).

5. *India Abroad,* 29 May 1998.

6. Yash Pal Lakra, "Let Us Call Ourselves 'American Hindus,'" *Hinduism Today,* October 1997.

7. I am drawing from my "Tracing a Lineage of Conservatism," *SAMAR,* no. 9 (Winter/Spring 1998), and quoting from the letter from Taraknath Das to Lala Lajpat Rai, from Geneva, Switzerland, dated 11 January 1926, All-India Congress Committee Papers, file no. 512, Nehru Memorial Museum and Library, New Delhi.

8. Kelvin Singh, *Bloodstained Tombs: The Muharram Massacre, 1884* (London: Macmillan Caribbean, 1988), and the forthcoming work by Prabhu Prasad Mohapatra.

9. For example, Singaravelou, *Les Indiens de la Caraibe,* vol. 3 (Paris: L'Harmattan, 1987).

10. "Youth: Searching for Roots," *Hinduism Today,* October 1997.

11. This recipe quality to cultural literacy is also evident in such articles as Sumit Arya, "Marathi Wedding Album," *Masala,* January 1995; V. G. Julie Rajan, "A Tamil Wedding Album," *Masala,* July/August 1995; and in Celia W. Dugger, "In India, an Arranged Marriage of Two Worlds," *New York Times,* 20 July 1998, A1, B6–B7, and Lois Smith Brady, "Kalyani Mohan and Nikhil Shah," *New York Times,* 16 August 1998, 7.

12. "Profile of Vishwa Hindu Parishad of America," *The Hindu Universe* (1997–98 copyright) [Homepage of Global Hindu Electronic Network], [Online], available: www.hindunet.org.

13. Alliance for a Secular and Democratic South Asia, *Vivekananda's Message and Social Justice* (Boston: ASDSA, 1993).

14. On Bofors and the alleged role of the Hindujas, see Chitra Subramaniam, *Bofors: The Story Behind the News* (New Delhi: Viking, 1993).

15. VHP, *Memorandum of Association, Rules, and Regulations* (1966; amended on 5 September 1983), 18.

16. Uma Bharati, Bharatiya Janata Party, member of the Indian Parliament, quoted in India West, 15 November 1996.

17. Vijay Prashad, "Packaging Tradition into Official Customs," *SAMAR*, no. 3 (Summer 1994): 28.

18. H. V. Seshadri, *Hindus Abroad: The Dilemma, Dollar or Dharma?* (Delhi: Suruchi Prakashan, 1990).

19. On the latter, one might keep in mind the words of Muktananda Saraswati, a VHP member, who wrote that "by giving inheritance rights to women the unity of society gets broken," and those of Mridula Sinha, president of the BJP's Mahila Morcha (Women's Front), who noted that "we in the BJP are opposed to women's liberation because it is against men. It is led by a handful of intellectual women in the cities who have no understanding of common people's ideology and aspirations. We tell women [in domestic violence circumstances] to be more adjusting, because they will have nowhere to go if they leave their husbands" (quoted in Niraj Pant, "Look Ma! The *Sangh Giroh*'s gone progressive! [And Newt's a Revolutionary!]," *Sanskriti* 6, no. 1 [25 December 1995]: 9). There are, incidentally, about 5 million activists of the All-India Democratic Womens' Association, which is associated with the Communist Party of India–Marxist.

20. This is the tenor of the interviews reported by Priya Agarwal, *Passage from India: Post-1965 Indian Immigrants and Their Children* (Palos Verdes, Calif.: Yuvati, 1991), and by Sunaina Maira in "Chaste Identities, Ethnic Yearnings: Second Generation Indian Americans in New York City" (Ph.D. diss., Harvard University, 1998).

21. *India West,* 17 November 1995.

22. In 1993 a group of Sikh professionals set up a camp for Sikh youth in Chambersburg, Pennsylvania designed to consolidate Sikh identity. It is named the Lohgarh Retreat, after the fort Lohgarh, from which Guru Hargobind in the 1600s "waged battles against the Mughal forces" and from which Guru Gobind Singh defended the Sikhs "against the armies of the Mughal Empire and the Hindu Hill Kingdoms." Now, in the United States, the battle is "against the armies of ignorance and hatred, and the lure of assimiliation." The camp's rhetoric responds to parents' fear of assimilation, but it also promotes a religious exclusivity that does not bode well for such an ecumenical tradition as Sikhism; see *MaBoli Systems* (1995 copyright) [Homepage of MaBoli Systems, Inc.], [Online], available: www.maboli.com/seva/lohgarh/index.html; and Laurie

Goodstein, "At Camps, Young U.S. Sikhs Cling to Heritage," *New York Times,* 18 July 1998, A1, A7.

23. Vijay Prashad, "Generations of Culture," *Little India* 8, no. 1 (January 1998): 46.

24. C. M. Naim, "Ambiguities of Heritage," *Toronto Review* 14, no. 1 (Summer 1995): 3–4.

25. Ibid., 4.

26. Quoted in Lavina Melwani, "Towards Stronger Women," *Femina,* 15 September 1996.

27. For more on this, see Rustom Bharucha, "The Shifting Sites of Secularism: Cultural Politics and Activism in India Today," *Economic and Political Weekly* 33, no. 4 (24–30 January 1998): 167.

28. N. Ram, "'Global Vision 2000' Indeed!" *Frontline,* 10 September 1993, 15. I am relying upon several articles in that issue of *Frontline* (Krishna Kumar, "Behind the VHP of America," *Frontline,* 10 September 1993, 10–12; Arvind Rajagopal, "An Unholy Nexus: Expatriate Anxiety and Hindu Extremism," *Frontline,* 10 September 1993, 12–14; Uma Ramesh, "The Global Grip: Many Tentacles of Hindutva," *Frontline,* 10 September 1993, 14–16; N. Ram, "'Global Vision 2000' Indeed!"); Shashi Tharoor's intervention in the *Washington Post* ("Growing Up Extreme: On the Peculiarly Vicious Fanaticism of Expatriates," *Washington Post,* 25 July 1993, C5), and *India: From Midnight to Millennium* (New York: Harper, 1997), 139–58; two unpublished papers by Lise McKean; "Ten Thousand Rally in Washington DC to Honor Vivekananda," *Hinduism Today* 15, no. 10 (October 1993); Peter Steinfels, "Religions Endorse Peaceful Paths," *New York Times,* 5 September 1993; and my own memory of the event.

29. Arvind Rajagopal, "An Unholy Nexus: Expatriate Anxiety and Hindu Extremism," *Frontline,* 10 September 1993, 13.

30. E-mail sent to Sangeeta Kamat from a young man (29 May 1996) in response to her critique of HSC published on the Internet on 27 April 1996.

31. Suresh Grover, "The Malady Back Home Hurts the Diaspora Too," *Communalism Combat,* November 1996, 20–21.

32. Much of what follows draws from my "Diwali and Decolonization," *Toronto Review* 15, no. 2 (Winter 1997): 30–33.

33. *The Hindu Universe* (1997–98 copyright) [Homepage of Global Hindu Electronic Network], [Online], available: www.hindunet.org/festivals/deevali.html.

34. J. C. Jha, "The Indian Heritage in Trinidad," in *Calcutta to Caroni: The East Indians of Trinidad,* ed. J. LaGuerre (St. Augustine, Trinidad: University of West Indies, 1985), 7.

35. Grover, "The Malady," 21.

Of Antiblack Racism

1. For Jews, see David C. Gross, *Pride of Our People: The Stories of One Hundred Outstanding Jewish Men and Women* (Garden City, N.Y.: Doubleday, 1979), and for those of African ancestry, see Langston Hughes, *Famous American Negroes* (New York: Dodd, Mead, 1954).

2. For me this fascination extended all the way to Engelbert Humperdinck, the Madras-born Raja of Romance, who took the name of a nineteenth-century opera composer and rejected his Indian past entirely. Nonetheless, I find it hard to get too excited about "Release Me" (1967).

3. *India West,* 5 July 1996.

4. Lewis Gordon, *Bad Faith and Anti-Black Racism* (Atlantic Highlands, N.J.: Humanities Press, 1995), 95.

5. E. M. Forster, *A Passage to India* (London: Arnold, 1924), 78; Mrs. James Elliot, *A Guide to Indian Household Management* (London: Ward Locke, 1926), 43.

6. Elizabeth Hay, *Sambo Sahib: The Story of Little Black Sambo and Helen Bannerman* (New York: Barnes and Noble, 1981), 28–29. This is contradicted by Phyllis Yuill, *Little Black Sambo: A Closer Look. A History of Little Black Sambo and Its Popularity in the United States* (New York: Racism and Sexism Resource Guide for Educators, 1976).

7. These are summarized in J. R. Barrett and D. Roediger, "In-between Peoples: Race, Nationality, and the 'New Immigrant' Working Class," *Journal of American Ethnic History* 16, no. 3 (Spring 1997).

8. G. W. F. Hegel, *The Philosophy of History* (1830–1831; reprint, New York: Dover, 1956), 81, 99.

9. James Walsh, "The Perils of Success: Asians Have Become Exemplary Immigrants, But at a Price," *Time,* special issue, Fall 1993, 55.

10. For a concise introduction, see Thomas C. Patterson, *Inventing Western Civilization* (New York: Monthly Review Press, 1997).

11. Theodore Allen, *The Invention of the White Race,* vol. 1, *Racial Oppression and Social Control* (London: Verso, 1994), and *The Invention of the White Race,* vol. 2, *The Origin of Racial Oppression in Anglo-America* (London: Verso, 1997).

12. W. E. B. Du Bois, *Black Reconstruction in America, 1860–1880* (New York: Athenaeum, 1992), 17.

13. Jacques Rancière, *The Nights of Labor* (Philadelphia: Temple University Press, 1989), 349–416; Paul Buhle, *Marxism in the United States* (London: Verso, 1991), 19–57.

14. Mike Davis, *Prisoners of the American Dream* (London: Verso, 1986), 28–29.

15. Du Bois, *Black Reconstruction,* 18.

16. Philip Foner, *Organized Labor and the Black Worker, 1619–1973* (New York: Praeger, 1974).

17. Toni Morrison, "On the Backs of Blacks," *Time,* special issue, Fall 1993, 57.

18. Doug Henwood, "Race and Money," *Left Business Observer,* no. 69 (September 1995).

19. Dinesh D'Souza, *The End of Racism: Principles for a Multiracial Society* (New York: Free Press, 1995), 252, and "Myth of the Racist Cabbie," *New Republic,* 9 October 1995. D'Souza is disingenuous in his use of sources. It is true that the Bureau of Labor Statistics noted that driving a cab is one of the most dangerous jobs in the United States, but it does not especially indict blacks as perpetrators of the crimes. Conversation with those associated with the New York Taxi Workers' Alliance makes it clear that the perpetrators do not follow a distinct profile.

20. On "innocence," see Thomas Ross, "White Innocence, Black Abstraction," *William and Mary Law Review* 1 (1990); and for details of structural racism, see Victor Perlo, *Economics of Racism, vol. 2, The Roots of Inequality, USA* (New York: International Publishers, 1996).

21. Martin Luther King Jr., "Where Do We Go from Here?" in *A Testament of Hope,* ed. James M. Washington (New York: Harper, 1986), 246.

22. Karl Marx, "On the Jewish Question," in *Early Writings* (New York: Vintage, 1975), 219.

23. Martin Luther King Jr., "Negroes Are Not Moving Too Fast," *Saturday Evening Post* 237 (7 November 1964), in *A Testament of Hope,* 176–77.

24. For Gingrich and Wilson, see Emil Guillermo, "White Asian America," *Asiaweek,* 28 July 1995; the chancellor's position was expressed in, among others, Chancellor Tien, "A View from Berkeley," *Time,* 31 March 1996; a general essay on Asian support for Proposition 209 is Lucie Hwang, "A House Divided: Asian Americans and Affirmative Action," *Third Force* 4, no. 5 (November/December 1996); a particularly unfortunate and racist "satire" was penned by D'Souza's protégé, Kishan Kumar Putta, "The Dot on My Head: An Affirmative Action Satire," *Tana Patrika,* November 1995.

25. Hortense J. Spillers, "Mama's Baby, Papa's Maybe: An American Grammar Book," *diacritics,* Summer 1987, offers some stimulating ways to unpack this logic.

26. Quoted in Stephen Steinberg, "The Liberal Retreat from Race during the Post–Civil Rights Era," in *The House That Race Built,* ed. Wahneema Lubiano (New York: Vintage, 1998), 22.

27. Jan Lin, *Reconstructing Chinatown: Ethnic Enclave, Global Change* (Minneapolis: University of Minnesota Press, 1998).

28. Irving Kristol, "The Negro Today Is Like the Immigrant Yesterday," *New York Times Magazine,* 11 September 1966, 124.

29. Ibid., 138.

30. Prior to 1990, immigrant women had no rights independent of their husbands who sponsored their immigration. Fearful of deportation, women did not report domestic violence. Divorce, in this case, was deportation. The Battered Spouse Waiver allows women to petition the courts for a review of their visa status independent of their husbands in case of domestic violence. June Unjoo Yang, "The Domestic Front," *A Magazine,* special women's issue, 1994; and Constance Hays, "Fighting Spousal Abuse in Immigrant Families," *New York Times,* 6 December 1993. This situation is well known in Britain, for which see Southall Black Sisters (SBS), *Domestic Violence and Asian Women* (Southall, England: SBS, 1993), chapter 3 on immigrant laws and violence against

migrant women (the chapter draws from SBS's submission to the Home Affairs Select Committee on Domestic Violence, 11 November 1992).

31. United Nations Development Program, *Human Development Report* (Washington, D.C.: UNDP, 1992), 57.

32. Francis Fukuyama, *Trust: The Social Virtues and the Creation of Prosperity* (New York: Free Press, 1995).

33. Stuart Hall, "The Whites of Their Eyes," in *Silver Linings,* ed. G. Bridges and R. Blunt (London: Lawrence and Wishart, 1981), 36–37.

34. As D'Souza does, *The End of Racism,* 486.

35. Arvind Rajagopal, "Better Than Blacks? Or, Hum Kaale Hain to Kya Hua," *SAMAR,* no. 5 (Summer 1995): 6.

36. U.S. Census Bureau, *Census of Population: The Foreign-Born Population in the United States* (Washington, D.C.: U.S. Census Bureau, 1993), 1990 CP-3-1, item 159-G; and "African Immigrants Best Educated in the U.S.," *Contra Costa Times,* 23 September 1993.

37. "Black Like Me," *The Economist,* 11 May 1996.

38. Langston Hughes, *Afro-American* (Baltimore, 20 February 1943), in *The Collected Poems of Langston Hughes,* ed. Arnold Rampersad (New York: Vintage, 1994), 578.

39. Faiz Ahmed Faiz, "A-jao Afriqa" (1956), in *Pratinidhi Kavitayen* (Delhi: Rajkamal, 1984), 113–14: A-jaao, main-ne sun-li tere dhol ki tarang, / A-jaao, mast ho-gai mere lahu ki taal / A-jaao, Afriqa. / A-jaao, main-ne dhul se maatha uthaa-liya, / A-jaao, main-ne chheel-di aankhon se gham ki chhaal, / A-jaao, main-ne dard se bazu chhura-liya, / A-jaao, main-ne noch-diya beksi kaa jaal, / A-jaao, Afriqa. / Panje mein hathkari ki kari ban-gai hai gurz / Gardan ka tauq torke dhali hai main-ne dhaal / A-jaao, Afriqa. / Jalte hain har kachaar mein bhaalon ke mirg-nyn, / Dushman lahu se raat ki kaalikh hui hai laal / A-jaao, Afriqa. / Dharti dharak-rahi hai mere saath, Afriqa, / Darya thirak-raha hai to ban de-raha hai taal. / Main Afriqa hun, dhaar-liya main-ne tera roop, / Main tu hun, meri chaal hai teri babbar ki chaal / A-jaao, Afriqa. Aao babbar ki chaal / A-jaao, Afriqa.

40. Sudarshan Kapur, *Raising Up a Prophet: The African American Encounter with Gandhi* (Boston: Beacon, 1992), 22.

41. Tony Martin, *The Pan-African Connection: From Slavery to Garvey and Beyond* (Dover: Majority Press, 1983), 81.

42. Leonard A. Gordon, "Bridging India and America: The Art and Politics of Kumar Goshal," *Amerasia Journal* 15, no. 2 (1989); Penny Von Eschen, *Race against Empire: Black Americans and Anticolonialism, 1937–57* (Ithaca, N.Y.: Cornell University Press, 1997).

43. *The Crisis* 18 (June 1919), in *The Seventh Son: The Thought and Writings of W. E. B. Du Bois,* ed. Julius Lester (New York: Random House, 1971), 2: 299–300.

44. Arnold Rampersad, "Du Bois' Passage to India: Dark Princess," in *W. E. B. Du Bois on Race and Culture,* ed. B. Bell, E. Groshalz, and J. Stewart (London: Routledge, 1996).

45. W. E. B. Du Bois, *Dark Princess* (Jackson: University of Mississippi Press, 1995), 16.

46. Ibid., 308.

47. W. T. Lhamon, *Deliberate Speed: The Origins of a Cultural Style in the American 1950s* (Washington, D.C.: Smithsonian Institution Press, 1990), 81. Incidentally, on Bandung, one should read Richard Wright's little-known report in which he noted, perceptively, that "I began to sense a deep and organic relation here in Bandung between race and religion, *two of the most powerful and irrational forces in human nature.* Sukarno was not evoking these twin demons; he was not trying to create them; he was trying to organize them. . . . The reality of race and religion was there, swollen, sensitive, turbulent" (*The Color Curtain: A Report on the Bandung Conference* [Cleveland, Ohio: World Publishing Company, 1956], 140).

48. Carl Rowan offered this memory of his 1954 trip to India: "Welcome, Rowan, to a lecture assignment where you'll face hundreds of questions over the weeks about white people in America murdering a black fourteen year old named Emmett Till because he allegedly whistled at a white man. . . . I was not a State Department lackey. I simply went from Darjeeling to Patna to Cuttack to Madras, saying good things about my country because I believed that the society that had given me a break was in the process of taking great strides towards racial justice" (Carl T. Rowan, *Breaking Barriers: A Memoir* [Boston: Little, Brown, 1991], 123–24).

49. Martin Luther King Jr., "My Trip to the Land of Gandhi," *Ebony,* July 1959, in *Testament of Hope,* 24.

50. Quoted in Marie Louise Burke, *Swami Vivekananda in America: New Discoveries* (Calcutta: Advaita Ashrama, 1966), 393.

51. *The Crisis* 36, July 1929, in *The Correspondence of W. E. B. Du Bois,* ed. Herbert Aptheker (Amherst: University of Massachusetts, 1973), 1: 402–3.

52. Jawaharlal Nehru, *The Discovery of India* (New Delhi: Oxford University Press, 1989), 250–51; Vijay Prashad, "Comrade Robeson," *Social Scientist,* nos. 290–91 (July/August 1997).

53. There is an ongoing linkage made between Dalits and blacks. I am currently working on an essay on this connection, one that stretches from the Black/Dalit Panthers to the recent scholars who work on the Afro-Dravidian thesis; Vijay Prashad, "Afro-Dalits of the Earth, Unite!" *Journal of African Studies,* forthcoming (December 1999).

54. Du Bois, *Dark Princess,* 300.

55. D'Souza, *The End of Racism,* 286.

56. Gordon, *Bad Faith,* 9.

57. Ibid., 5.

58. Ibid., 94.

59. Ibid., 47.

60. Lewis Gordon, *Fanon and the Crisis of European Man* (London: Routledge, 1995), 22.

61. Aditi Mehta and Harini Reddy, "Class, Culture, and Consciousness: The Socioeconomics of Indian-American Identity," *Diversity and Distinction* 3, no. 2 (Winter 1998); this article can be accessed online at http://www.hcs.harvard.edu/~dnd/issues/302/classculture.html.

62. For an introduction, see George Lipsitz, *Dangerous Crossroads: Popular Music, Postmodernism, and the Poetics of Place* (London: Verso, 1994), 119–34.

63. There are similar themes in Canada, for which see Jacqueline Warwick, "Can Anyone Dance to This Music? Bhangra and Toronto's South Asian Youth" (M.A. thesis, York University, 1996).

64. Sam Prestianni, "Into the Gap," *Daily Californian,* 19 May 1995; Derk Richardson, "Do It Yourself," *San Francisco Bay Guardian,* 24 May 1995.

65. Sanjay Sharma, "Noisy Asians or 'Asian Noise'?" in *Dis-*

Orienting Rhythms: The Politics of the New Asian Dance Music, ed. Sanjay Sharma, John Hutnyk, and Ashwani Sharma (London: Zed, 1996).

66. Paul Gilroy, "Between Afro-centrism and Euro-centrism: Youth Culture and the Problem of Hybridity," *Young* 1, no. 2 (1993).

67. *India Abroad,* 24 February 1995; and a flyer circulated by the students entitled "It *Was* Racism."

68. Somini Sengupta, "To Be Young, Indian, and Hip," *New York Times,* 30 June 1996, 11.

69. Sunaina Maira, "Chaste Identities, Ethnic Yearnings: Second Generation Indian Americans in New York City" (Ph.D. diss., Harvard University, 1998), 283–87.

70. Sandhya Shukla, "India Abroad: Transnational Ethnic Cultures in the United States and Britain, 1947–97" (Ph.D. diss., Yale University, 1997); and on the development of an Indo-Caribbean identity, see Sean Lokaisingh-Meighoo, "Dialectics of Diaspora and Home: Indentureship, Migration, and Indo-Caribbean Identity" (M.A. thesis, York University, 1997).

71. Amar Dhillon, "Gangsta', Gangsta'," *Hum* 1, no. 2 (Summer 1994): 16.

72. Tuku Mukherjee, "The Journey Back," in *Multi-Racist Britain,* ed. P. Cohen and Harwant Bains (London: Macmillan, 1988), 223.

73. Harwant S. Bains, "Southall Youth: An Old-Fashioned Story," in *Multi-Racist Britain,* 237.

74. The Jat are a peasant community of northern India.

75. Pragna Patel, "Southall Boys," in *Against the Grain: A Celebration of Survival and Struggle,* ed. Southall Black Sisters (Southall, England: SBS, 1990), 46.

Of Solidarity and Other Desires

1. *Ghadar,* 14 July 1914.

2. Sohan Singh Josh, *Hindustan Ghadar Party* (New Delhi: People's Publishing House, 1977), 170–72.

3. Among other works, see Maureen Swan, "The 1913 Natal Indian Strike," *Journal of Southern African Studies* 10 (April 1984); Brij V. Lal, "Kunti's Cry: Indentured Women on Fiji Plantations," *Indian*

Economic and Social History Review 22 (1985); Basdeo Mangru, "The Rose Hall Sugar Workers' Strike of 1913: The Beginning of the End of Indian Indentureship," *Indenture and Abolition* (Toronto: TSAR, 1993); and my summary essay, "Coolie Purana: The 1913–1916 Rebellion against Indenture in the Indian Diaspora" (manuscript).

4. Santosh Seeram, "Practicing Tolerance: Homophobia and Isolation in the South Asian community," *Hum*, no. 1 (Summer 1994): 11–12.

5. In 1975 Prime Minister Indira Gandhi installed a political dictatorship as she suspended civil liberties and suppressed the political opposition. Sustained struggle overthrew her regime in 1977 and a new, more democratic group took power.

6. "New Priorities for Rejuvenated ISA," *The Bridge* 5, no. 1 (24 January 1975): 1–3. Documents such as this can be found in the Sharat G. Lin Collection, held at the Bancroft Library, University of California, Berkeley; the Hoover Library, Stanford; and the University of Wisconsin, Madison.

7. "Indian Students Association and Political Action," *The Bridge* 5, no. 3 (23 December 1975): 9–10.

8. Campaign against Racism and Fascism, *Southall: Birth of a Black Community* (London: CARF, 1982), 54.

9. A. Sivanandan, *Communities of Resistance* (London: Verso, 1990), 32–39.

10. Rinku Sen, Sandip Roy, Dipti Ghosh, Jayanth Eranki, and Raka Ray, "Talking Strategy in San Francisco," *SAMAR*, no. 8 (Summer/Fall 1997): 12; Sivanandan, *Communities of Resistance,* 43–44.

11. Etienne Balibar, "Class Racism," in *Race, Nation, Class,* ed. Etienne Balibar and Immanuel Wallerstein (London: Verso, 1991), 213.

12. Norberto Bobbio, *Left and Right: The Significance of a Political Distinction* (Cambridge: Polity, 1996), 69–75. Some of the intricacies of Bobbio's argument are clarified in a useful debate with Perry Anderson in *New Left Review,* no. 231 (September/October 1998): 73–93.

13. Etienne Balibar, *La Crainte des masses: Politique et philosophie avant et après Marx* (Paris: Galilée, 1996), 421–22.

14. Michael Omi and Howard Winart, *Racial Formation in the United States: From the 1960s to the 1990s* (New York: Routledge, 1994), 57.

15. Francis Calpatura and Kim Fellner, *Square Pegs Find Their*

Groove: Reshaping the Organizing Circle (Oakland, Calif.: Center for Third World Organizing, 1996), 10.

16. George Friday, "Ideology on the Table," *The Ark: Membership Newsletter of the National Organizer's Alliance*, no. 7 (July 1996): 18.

17. Quoted in Gary Delgardo, *Beyond the Politics of Place: New Directions in Community Organizing in the 1990s* (Oakland, Calif.: Applied Research Center, 1997), 54.

18. Quoted in Hoon Lee, "Building Class Solidarity across Racial Lines: Korean-American Workers in Los Angeles," in *Beyond Identity Politics: Emerging Social Justice Movements in Communities of Color*, ed. John Anner (Boston: South End Press, 1996), 59.

19. Anuradha G. Advani, "The Development of a South Asian American Labor Organization: An Examination of Identity-Based Organizing," *Positions 5*, no. 2 (1997): 596.

20. Quoted in John Anner, "Having the Tools at Hand: Building Successful Multicultural Social Justice Organizations," in *Beyond Identity Politics*, 159.

21. Robin D. G. Kelley, *Yo Mama's Disfunktional!* (Boston: Beacon Press, 1997), 150.

22. Interview with Biju Mathew, May 1998.

23. Quoted in Joseph North, "Taxi Strike," *New Masses*, 3 April 1934, in *New Masses: An Anthology of the Rebel Thirties*, ed. Joseph North (New York: International Publishers, 1969), 167–68.

24. Gihan Perera, "Heading out to Deeper Waters," *The Ark: Membership Newsletter of the National Organizers Alliance*, no. 7 (July 1996): 3.

25. Fred Hampton, *You've Got to Make a Commitment!* (Chicago: Black Panther Party, 1969), 10.

26. Alberto Melucci, *Nomads of the Present* (Philadelphia: Temple University Press, 1989), 60; the special issue of *Social Research 52*, no. 4 (1985).

27. Stuart Hall, *The Hard Road to Renewal* (London: Verso, 1988), 281.

28. Elisabeth Armstrong's ongoing work on the U.S. feminist movement is making some of this clear, notably the distinctions between "organization," "struggle," and "movement."

29. Robert Fitch, *The Assassination of New York* (London: Verso, 1993).

30. Courtesy of Doug Henwood (1 November 1994), based on data in Michael Stegman, *Housing and Vacancy Report: New York City, 1991* (New York: Department of Housing Preservation and Development, 1993).

31. Amnesty International, "Police Brutality and Excessive Force in the New York Police Department," June 1996; A1 index no. AMR 51/36/96.

32. NYTWA now has a newsletter *(Shift-Change: The Voice of the NYC Taxicab Driver. Long Live the Spirit of May 13th)* that can be obtained by calling them at (212) 627-5248.

INDEX

Vijay Prashad is assistant professor of international studies at Trinity College, Hartford, Connecticut. He is the author of *Untouchable Freedom: A Social History of a Dalit Community,* and he has coedited a special issue of *Amerasia Journal* entitled *Satyagraha in America: The Political Culture of South Asian Americans.* He writes regularly for magazines such as *Frontline* (India), *ColorLines* (United States), *Z Magazine* (United States), and *Himal* (Nepal). He is on the editorial board of *Left History* (Canada), *Amerasia Journal* (United States), and *SAMAR: South Asian Magazine of Action and Reflection* (United States), as well as on the board of the Center for Third World Organizing (CTWO), Oakland, California.

Read about tourism in Charlestown Trunk
Read about past glory in "Provalry"
Read about criminalization of Latino
"Movement" relegation to aesthetic

"has one dimension as the text
on a menu"

What is the nature of this tourism?

- reductivist
- ancient past / static
- escape
- turn Black experience into my festive
- leisure
- in the "New World"
- escape
- entertainment
& relaxation

to portray   for short story
the Mexican - American   lit teachers
in this nostalgic   students, + grants
light is to   must credit story
render an or   students
image
of him or her   stereotyping
that is stuck
in the past, static,
convenient (is cuz it denies —
(& because it offers

Mixed culture

Read about kitsch and performing
culture in ~~God of Small Things~~ Audiotopia

Exile

- "Mother" country. Tradition
Feminize & desire?
p130

p141
for final
147-8

too easy to
bigotry w
bigotry